HARRY GUEST · A PUZZLING HARVEST

Also by Harry Guest

HARRY GUEST

A Puzzling Harvest

Collected Poems 1955–2000

Anvil Press Poetry

Published in 2002
by Anvil Press Poetry Ltd
Neptune House 70 Royal Hill London SE10 8RF
www.anvilpresspoetry.com

This book is published with financial assistance
from The Arts Council of England

Designed and set in Monotype Ehrhardt by Anvil
Printed and bound in England
by Cromwell Press, Trowbridge, Wiltshire

ISBN 0 85646 354 X

A catalogue record for this book
is available from the British Library

CONTENTS

The Cutting-Room (1970)

A House Against the Night (1976)

Lost and Found (1983)

HISTORY / PREHISTORY

Coming to Terms (1994)

So Far (1998)

I   *loci*

Versions (1999)

Uncollected Poems

PREFACE

GAZING BACK at the successive fields, a poet at seventy may wonder once again at the discrepancy between dry seeds stuck in bare earth and swaying rectangles of ripe barley – between the first words scrawled on the back of an envelope and the eventual flattery of the printed page.

The initial reaction must be a bewildered thanksgiving to events and people, to books and music and pictures, to marvels seen around the world. An afterthought would be a hope that other inspirations will continue to glimmer just beyond the reach of the pen. The creative process resembles a baffling search, one that is urged on by a presumptuous wish to transform each quest into more than a mere record – the contrast between reality, which is the aim of journalism, and truth, which is the motive for art.

A splendid Jewish proverb claims that nothing makes God laugh so much as the sight of a human being making plans. Nevertheless, coming so gratefully to terms with all I have been given by my wife and children, by so many friends in so many countries (and especially, here, by Peter Jay who has published my work for nearly four decades), I dare to dream that poems I attempt still to write may not only please other readers but go on surprising me.

H.G.
October 6th, 2002

Arrangements
(1968)

to my wife

A TWILIGHT MAN

The black flakes on the quiet wind
    drift through the rib–cage:
Charred reductions of evidence –
    letters, dossiers,
Photographs. The bonfire
    crackles to silence.
Smell of dew supersedes
    the acridity
In back of the heat.
    A wry peace now. Embers
Creep, write enigmatically, twist,
    fade. No messages.
Scraps float, soon lost in the
    thicker air contours abandon.
A skeletal hand disturbs
    the site, prods, stains the
Bone. Faces, afternoons on
    sofas, decisions, success, now
Ash. The head tilts towards the
    stars of slower change
Whose light prickles the empty eye-
    sockets and, dropping into the black
Skull, vanishes, unretained.
    Water beads coldly on
Spine, jaw, poised knuckle,
    and the darkness settles
Substantiate since the last red
    point has gone leaving only
Meaningless wafers for the night to
    obliterate, disperse.

AT SHOREHAM

for Lynn

Nightfall and my hands awake.
A white bird wings upriver,
    Greets the water and
Glides to silence where the
    Scars of sunset heal.

I turn to you, loins bared.
                    Your hair
Floats, blonde on linen.
                    The beat of darkness
Shifts the curtain.
                    Your nakedness
Expects my hands which give you me,
My love, the quiver of my need.

Discovery of your body takes mine out to sea,
Past the safe harbour-bar: last
Reflections of crimson die out,
Diminishing in the glassy walls that rise,
Succeed each other, pass: and the final wave I meet
Brings oblivion, the depth of you.

I lie, cradled, heavy, midsea.
The singing in my ears falls to quiet –
Only the rustle your liquid hand
Makes on my hair.

                Our skins, slowly,
Become familiar. Landfall. We alight,
Moist from the salt, and the one lamp –
Coming nearer to re-create us as a pair –
Dries us to rest.

            The tide recedes.
                        A last wind
Touches the water as your smile lifts.
In my dark breathing you are there. The knowledge of you
Undoes a solitude called sleep.

The river holds the sleeping bird
Nightlong; a section of moon
Flicks at the water, whose profundity
Is tidal, no longer dangerous.
                                    Lost time
Passes. The east greys. I stir
To a fresh entity. There is
A swan behind your eyelids when you wake.

ABOUT BAUDELAIRE

for Eiji Yamazaki

1

The dark nerve of sin lay like lightning
on the pavements. Paris was flawed.
The heels of prostitutes tapped open the frost
and a passer-by who existed
and then didn't exist
noticed the world and its reliance upon hell
as circles of gaslight hurried past him.

2

Certainty, colour, in her room. Although
her loins prove as elusive as the sky
and in his arms she twists into a corpse;
all mortality; vapour.

Each time foreknowledge is no help. He knocks,
eager to hold her, keep the void at bay.
The carpet's smooth between the fire and bed.
Time, the old pain, damnation – lost here:
a lift to peace . . . There was
one raging night that squeezed the stars to brightness . . .

The city calls, a fog
drifts around the heart, his reaching hand
discerning worms behind the wall.

3

To rape the air, the dark air of night,
burying an ice-like orgasm in clouds –
thrown backwards on the globe, splayed there,
moist legs apart and her frail perfume
lingering in the nostril. Sunrise.

4

       Too late: the schooner's left
buoyant for the golden islands.
His feet echo in the morning;
the docks are empty; a scrap of paper
is blown across the silence and a clock chimes.

5

Sunset immobile lifts the Seine to it:
the past, seen obstinately through the glare,
summons an allegory
and the observer on the fragile bridge between air and air
shivers in the sudden gust
from the wing of imbecility
and the hour-hand of regret starts moving.

6

Now the rain won't stop falling,
the iron hand tightens slowly on the heart.
Now rhetoric's over and the coffin's made
and knowledge of earth replaces mind.

7

But,
in the lunatic's cell,
where whiteness negates the thirst for innocence
and trees stretch their aspiration on pale air,
the fly of consciousness still goes on
drumming against the hard invisibility
until,
beaten by time,

which so insidiously lames the breath,
he gives up and, wondering, drops into
the three-dimensional cobweb that is God.

SEQUENCE

Two old paederasts sitting together
At the Café du Terminus over a hand of cards.

The boy who serves them knows their tastes and grins.
They reprove him for his slowness, unsmiling;
Grey profiles with downcast eyes.

Monsieur Duplessis was a schoolmaster. Daily
He used to expound – Ronsard, the alexandrine, Taine –
Gesturing with his glasses from his chair.
He would with over-conscious symbolism read
The part of Cyrano to some blond unknowing boy's
Roxane.
        Subtler, his friend Monsieur Couzillon
Strolls after office-hours most circumspectly –
Though he has a slight limp – and lights a casual Gitane
Near the plane trees by whose dusty shade
A bronze-legged urchin absorbed in his game
Momentarily becomes his Antinous.

Photographs of Greek sculpture adorn their rooms;
And reproductions of Michelangelo;
Gide, Genet, Peyrefitte on the shelves with
Certain translations from the English.

There has never been a breath of scandal about either.

Monsieur Duplessis is still a virgin.
One day in his thirties Monsieur Couzillon fell:
It was in Marseille and the August day was hot.

Monsieur l'abbé, himself a womaniser, joins them;
His church, Notre-Dame de la Charité.

They talk together as the young on scooters pass,
As trains arrive and stop, as sunset comes and as

A mule draws a cart up the narrow hill
To the cemetery.

VILLANELLE

for Peter Jay

Veering towards midday we soon lose speed.
Conviction fails in movements we've rehearsed.
The concentration's lacking, not the need.

The lies we tell can never supersede
A conscious doubt which aggravates our thirst.
Veering towards midday we soon lose speed.

Distracted while experiments proceed,
The charms all crack, the glass containers burst.
The concentration's lacking, not the need.

Somehow it's two o'clock and then we're freed –
The afternoons of failure are the worst.
Veering towards midday we soon lose speed.

The gold sun waits. – When nothing would impede
Our progress to the moment, we're immersed.
The concentration's lacking, not the need.

A newer Icarus might yet succeed
Who has a sense of knowing what goes first.
Veering towards midday we soon lose speed.
The concentration's lacking, not the need.

MATSUSHIMA

(The Pine Islands)

These islands   gathering images
dry slowly from the night
                 Words
comb the pine-trees free of snow
        Saffron limestone
lurching up from the sea-floor,
quivers dripping in the telescope,
        recedes into stillness

Cameras click and conversation
misses me. Before we move on
as tourists (there being
a choice of views from the peninsula)
        our awkward,
isolating minuet
mazes the snow.
         Death hitherto
was others'
        Metal doors eventually
slamming to on it, the
volubility's boxed up,
driven downhill, leaving
the light to merge into one wet slope
the black footprints
        recalled in prayer
or literature.
        (Now
nothing resembling
smashed windscreens, atomic fire

        (Shown the end, 'the
shadow-line traversed': theoretic
security was, the armour,
merciful complacency,
wrenched from me and a shove in the back
had me stumbling in the seismic desert
. . . hailstones   . . . drifting
gases   . . . chasms
) never

reaching the gate to see my wife
smiling in the shadow on the
window of our dark orange-tree
        comfort of books and music
laughter and whisky and bed

        These islands mount the sky

Surrounded by no-one I love,
        a tour a
        microcosm, the horizon
        deceptive,
transfixed as never before
on no future)

                'enisl'd'

                my private mouth goes over
                the dark memory of your body

A semi-colon of death
inside my glance
lends   the islands, my presence,
        that grey salt-beaten temple,
        untrodden snow, shift of conifers
        from colourlessness back to green,
        scud of a gull across the sunlight,
            all these, the grace,
        a break in them like finality

                Shops face the water. I buy
                a wind-bell, some pottery,
                a necklace

                wanting that sailor
                lounging in indigo
                against the melting quay
                uninterested stance, bulge
                in the tight jeans

and not forgetting what I'm not thinking of
        the poems cut in rock,

theories of Japanese wives,
the postcards and the ghastly dolls,
the Zen priests' caves

                   Credible an unborn breeze
                   in mid-Pacific then; green tea,
                   poured, steams near the paperbacks
                   and the vase of carnations; or
                   next year's neon
                   trickling into the cone of shadow
                   between her breasts

We separate
             till lunch
fuses gossip and impressions
          eroded
shape beyond shape
trapped in black plastic,
joining anonymous groups
to be ignored in albums

Fear in my chest, I'm dying quicker now
        memories   illicit
                    sanctioned desires
crowd
        The pamphlet shows
two views from each peninsula
        and disbelief
as an acrid coil of mist
strangles the eyeball
                    remains

The islands   along the bay
        horde distance
as growing light assembles
the scooped stone and contorted pine

             Fake, fake correlatives
          islands accrue
          nothing, solving

sunrise and the flesh gains
nothing,
the fear, Ransome's fear,
stays a lump of pain

the shutting-off of the pulse
my mother knew
    at her Christmas cards

breath halted
my father knew
    'phoning from the darkness

the   gasp, the
squeezed lung, the
heart's irregularity, night
rammed down your throat
I shall know

my wife,
my daughter,

you, you

engulfed, dropped, enearthed

    Indifferent, grown hard and ill,
This place we're emptying jostles me

from the tour, what,
emblem, we visited,
my spattered eyes, the gone past,
to, glimpsed, the notes

    fragments, which, slopes
bar of shadow   only half–
remembered   a boat
cancelled by islands
    maybe
            blurred
tree-trunks from the car-window

desultory, haunted

    are left with, littered,
a complex of terror,
cravings and souvenirs

Kugahara, 1967

ALPS

Peaks and clouds.
Orgasm under the rain.
Sadness coming down from the hills.
A sketch of words indicating
silence. Thrust of rock behind mist;
no narrative; the simple
reduction of it all to
clarity, blurred. Perforce.
A mood.

The quiet
emphasised by the rain,
the torrent; the scum's pattern
comprehensible,
subjective. Bad words.
Words that never
define, catch. The need
for disintoxication, the rugged
light of bygone summers
reachable.

A limb,
human,
bronzed by intangible pasts,
present in the mind's tristesse
as the rain goes on filling
another empty afternoon.

PORTRAIT FROM MEMORY

He's always eager to a visitor,
Holding the overcoat almost lovingly
That's been where he cannot afford to go,
Not now at any rate, not since they've known
His asthma will not let him work at all
And that his wife can keep her mother and
Himself only in bare necessities.

His fingertips burned brightly once, but now
Leave not even a charred vestige on the paper.
He bends to fill a saucer full of milk
Hearing the cries of 'Author!' as he bows;
Brushing his still receding hair he'll pause
As one short sunset phrase is still vouchsafed him;
And in the darkness by his sleeping wife
Shapes still emerge – But nothing lasts. He loves
To talk about the library books he's reading,
Non-fiction mostly. What's it all about?
These great philosophies – and Yoga now –
There must be some clear pattern somewhere. Something
An ordinary man might understand.

His day is circumscribed by bicycle-trips,
The basket full of books and groceries,
Walks through the fields on sunny afternoons,
A half of mild at six in the public bar,
Occasionally a Third Programme play.

He dreams of London sometimes as he stands
Drumming his fingers on the windowsill,
Although eventually there obtrudes
Between his eyes and what they're focused on
His actual reflection in the pane,
The sunken cheeks, the sense of something missing,
A gap, a change of gear, a moment lost, –

And face to face with his remembered talent
He shaves and feeds the cats and washes up.

THE SUMMERS OF NOWHERE

Capture the linked hands over a rock
    the shadow eats. Sunfall.
Obsession with camera-angles
    and the diminishing
spill of light behind your blurred profile.

Our forced lips and the night's white blossoms
    echo the lost splash your
bronze arm made – once – water gone, the tide
    swept out and in again,
seasons rubbed on permanent markings.

The dent in the sea, your head's pressure
    under my eye, longing –
the tears on your unchanged expression,
    forever where? An ache
to be naked again in some brown

slanting afternoon. A walk then. Through
    rising avenues of
flowering trees to the ruin in that
    overgrown garden and
the long sea-look over the railings.

My glance near the grain of skin, I brush
    off frequent petals: no
stain – not even light's which greyer days wash
    over. Evening now, our
descent from colour and the need for

warmth shivering over you. My kiss with
    its taste of the moment
ago, the breeze already dying
    which caught every other
word shouted through your laugh from the waves.

AWAKE

Seabird noises
like atmospherics
scratch the darkness.

Low tide.

The mirror
hanging somewhere between two days
introduces absence.
Looking-glasses never
reflect the dead.

I lie inside the night
noting my own disintegration –
a twinge, an ache,
a heaviness.

A sudden wind
moves the moon:
the gulls' fuss gone inaudible
starts again.

A limbo of days lost
stretches either side of the bed:
containing
poems I do not want to write,
the violence, the terror, bereavement.

On the main road
under the glare of sodium
a frequent lorry
makes the flat tremble.

My eyes weep
for safety and music and eternity
as the estuary behind the window
flows on towards morning.

MONTAGE

I swing round the corner, still alone.
There's no-one now at the saluting-base,
and the pavements here in the centre
are all deserted.
                I wrote once
'Very drunk I raped you and the rain outside
fell on to roses.'
                    The morning lies empty
to another sky, half the street indigo,
half dusty yellow. After so long.

The lamp made your skin glow, at last
naked underneath my kisses. Our year started.

The regime's altered, that I know. A breeze
takes the gulls across the blue gap
between the gutted block of the Royal Hotel
and the bomb-scarred Post Office over which
a new flag strains its colours.

                    In my arms
you were always elsewhere: an absent mouth
soured my embrace. Enigma
of your possession. Once, a tarnished exile
in a borrowed room over a café,
I lay with you on the rumpled bed,
and talked about Axel Heyst, the paperback
tossed on the one table by the cheap wine,
the tooth-mug stained a hard, irregular maroon,
and the cigarette-packets in an alien script.

Months of preparation, briefing, prayers even.
For this. The patient advance by night,
over cold ploughed fields, through the uninterested
villages. Gained confidence. Pre-dawn
in the rain: watches fixed for the attack.
Vengeance on a capital which had for so long
refused to recognise an opposition,
let alone the third party. One green flare;
quick penetration; clubbing

the indifferent sentries; concrete pyramids
across the road; contact with saboteurs;
brief fighting in the squares and the usual
anticlimax. Shirt-sleeved with a bottle
by the shattered fountain. Garlands
assorting oddly with the dirty khaki.
You miles away.

            Some bunting
blows across my path, its rustle and the wind
surround the echo as I tread
the locale of victory, unarmed. There's
the overturned streetcar we used as cover,
the piles of rubble where a ministry was.
Pitted walls here and there still flap
with bygone posters. 'CAUSE FOR ALARM'
'TERRORISTS' '23rd' 'WANTED' 'FORMATION'

When, satisfied, I got off that first time,
pulled up my trousers in the quiet, you'd
already re-arranged the past, contrived
to crown the moment with your privacy.
(So long ago now – noise of the rain – heavy
sense of the summer flowers through
the tang of liquor, perplexed desire, smell
of our rough nakedness and your bruised lips.)
Nowhere to stay, no legal papers yet,
I had to leave you for the tricky streets
at dawn, the danger, no address.
I'd done what I could in service of myself
though you could always champion me
up over roses, violence, still later
the dog's bark in the clogged yard, trickle all night
from the rusty cistern.
               I can remember
divers codes, the grimy lantern in the farmhouse,
Colonel Hand's eye-patch, the dash for the railway-yards.

You'd skein the triumph out of me and even to-day
it stirs uneasily at my temples . . . The odd
moonlight over the curfewed town,
your boredom with my body, our ambitions
altering in subversive pamphlets with their
conflicting rumours of achievement.

And then you yielded to me, all straining gone soft,
your pupils huge, liquid.
                                    Reaching the far end of the street
I glance back at the desolation, at
the torn streamers of victory, the empty stands –
frameworks for a memory of cheering.
I move on, turn the other corner.
They are all there as I had expected,
wearing different uniforms, waiting for me,
rifles levelled.

TOWARDS A PINDARIC ODE

> *'All follow sev'ral games, and each his own'*
> VIRGIL'S ECLOGUE II, TR. DRYDEN

I

I want to get you in perspective
And at a distance try analysis.

Cold I sit, striving to understand,
But the easy rhythms of your life can't tell me
What motivates my past or present or
How futile is my want.
                            I go on wondering
(Because one's never poised enough on irony)
And would like, my love, to speak more honestly,
But adulthood, you know, binds me to lies.

Lost. Lost like this. I live, as you might say,
Hopelessly complicated by desire,
For I crave truth if nothing else.

II

Butch you sit, listening to jazz.
The disc spins. You smile, tracing lines
Of a casual way of life I cannot share.

Has anyone had the privilege of knowing
What makes up the issue of your poems?
Who's reached into what evening with you?

You're writing secrets. I shall never know
If recognition of you is forbidden me;
No questions seem to tangle your existence.

I stare, embarrassed, at your beauty.
You have an athlete's power of choice.
You're tough and self-contained, your candour merciless.

You go on carefree playing out your blues.
My feelings are such I'm bound to remain
In beautiful conjecture. You're remote.

My wish to emulate your freedom is
Something resembling despair – and flattery
Means my appraisal has a certain pathos.

III

Butch you sit, listening to jazz.
        I want to get you in perspective.
The disc spins. You smile, tracing lines,
        And at a distance try analysis
Of a casual way of life I cannot share.

Has anyone had the privilege of knowing?
        Cold I sit, striving to understand
What makes up the issue of your poems;
        But the easy rhythms of your life can't tell me
Who's reached into what evening with you.

You're writing secrets I shall never know.
        What motivates my past or present, or
If recognition of you is forbidden me,
        How futile is my want, I go on wondering.
No questions seem to tangle your existence.

I stare, embarrassed at your beauty,
        Because one's never poised enough on irony:
You have an athlete's power of choice

And would like my love to speak more honestly –
You're tough and self-contained, your candour merciless.

You go on carefree playing out your blues,
    But adulthood, you know, binds me to lies.
My feelings are such I'm bound to remain
    Lost, lost like this. I live, as you might say,
In beautiful conjecture. You're remote.

My wish to emulate your freedom is
    Hopelessly complicated by desire.
Something resembling despair and flattery
    (For I crave truth) if nothing else
Means my appraisal has a certain pathos.

CINEMA

after Michelangelo Antonioni

The un-hurt from the near past, the
absence of your suddenness, the
non-touch of your darkened hands. In
the void memories replace, an
unravelling occurs that spools
sex back on to conscience where it
should not be. Retreat. Uncolour.

The non-feel of your soft weight, a
need that blows the swift kiss to the
long violence, un-journey no
longer taken without movement
from the one place. Un-thrust: dry air
flowing where the gift was once wet.
Non-being that's cancelled when two

return down the slow avenue
whom the spreading light reveals. Sky
sullen, threatening a noiseless
storm. Parting with promises meant
through forced lips as the mind can't yet

bridge the space between the last hard
moment and the next when love falls.

And not the pain brought by letter.
And not the separation, hands
unclenching over a bed stained
with honesty. Adieu. Mouth twists
an evening mirror. Absence cools
the sheet where dreams empty out a
kiss: the new fall of the bright rain.

Never again both feel defined:
losing together as their tongues
work, the clouds break. A single maze
of footsteps prints the drenched earth. Cold
and conscious of his skin only.
The wry thought of the other warmth
and the night cry and the sole thrill.

And silence in the negative
landscape. Grey flowers. The thirsty hand
seizes air. A window full of
lost tones proves the pain of the blond
fall, rustle of skin and skin. From
irresolute nights is now the
waking to a monochrome world.

SONNET

An answer poses further questions once
    the words release their ambiguity,
        and transfixed birds which spiralled down to die
flash from the pyre to weave another dance.

The pause between refusal and consent's
    the only stasis we can ever try –
        where nothing's stated no-one dare rely
on differing exposures of the sense.

If acquiescences contain denial,
     a random check discovers early that
         attainment equals unsuccess. The cry
of triumph sours into a baffled smile,
     the land goes strange and in the acid light
         a darker phoenix soars up mockingly.

THE PAINTER . . .

The painter,
light dimming,
quits the studio

Leaving noon
to flare at seven,
blossom, vase, sky

Washing the sunlight
from his hands
he enters evening

A caress of colour
inside time
has caught time

Stopped the scissors
closing on the dial.
Separated from midday

by no lie of brightness
the rhetorical flowers
are hammered to the canvas

state themselves.
A match spurts up
and the door closes

Shadows encroach
ink the painting over
while the man

following the tip
of his cigarette
goes down the now dark street

STATEMENT

Mallarmé said the poem is
A brush of arrows round a void,
And meant to indicate the ways
An idea leaps and freezes, points
To what can never quite be said
And dies fixed in a sterile trance:

To show the colour of a flower
In total darkness, or to kiss
A mouth that is no longer there –
Words speeding to a vacuum.
There must be something there than this;
More than an intellectual game.

All I know is the poem's you
At five o'clock in the morning when
By the grey light my dreams all go,
The images of conquest fade
And darkness drains from the garden in
An access of disclosure made

With splendour and indifference.
Lonely by the window, sour my tongue,
Our last night gone, our final chance,
As light comes cruelly I recall
The silence of our love-making
And take an orange from the bowl.

Last night we heard some Brahms and tried
To come to some agreement as
The whisky bottle emptied. Dead
Your eyes while I longed to explain
The reason for my going was
Inevitable as the pain

I felt at it. You seemed to be
Uncaring as my words ran on
Probably more to justify
My action to myself. At last
I had to concede, your lips on mine,
We lived already in the past.

This empty dawn, this senselessness,
This mood apparently so unstable,
Means orange-pips lying on the grass
While in cold ecstasy beneath
My window roses burn immobile,
Their very structure one of death.

So in pyjamas I descend,
Crossing the sunlit gravel to
The dew-wet flower-beds that send
Great heavy blossoms up and pick
A still night-smelling rose which through
The peaceful house I bring you back.

You're now awake and watching me.
I go and place it in a vase,
Sit by you, take your hand. We see
A different flower. No contact's made.
Once more our tragedy because
This rose absents you from my side.

UNKNOWN QUANTITY

Your voice affects my adult spine

Opaqueness from your eyes explains
the drenching reveries I've had

Glance and then both hands turned from mine
head poised on naked shoulders feigns
incomprehension of a deed
you've done the acquiescing to

Starburnt with hope your mouth enjoins
looking my best though greying I
flirt swiftly with your nudity
as fragrance rising from your loins
proves unknown grass is lit with dew

PRIVATE VIEW

for Trevor Goodman, painter

I

Scratched bronze bent to make an angle
Kneebone to pelvis: the regal torso stripped
To metal spine and shoulder-blades with curved,
Unjointed arms: unseeing eyes from a helmet watching
Patient no unexpected distance.

II

I stand, faintly uneasy, with a sherry-glass.
Charcoal suits and stiff dresses with roses on them –
Glances and laughter cat's-cradling across the room –
A pattern having no relationship at all
With what is exhibited upon the wall.

III

'Shape's only colour. Light on colour. I
Am nothing but the faculty of sight.
Interpretation happens through the eye.
Now dissect that square of river in terms of light –
Split up this folded slab of snow to rose
And old lilac – slightly chocolate-box (yet with
A freshness no nearer novelty than truth) –
So your shadows lose those sooty qualities.

I am a man for whom the external world exists.'

IV

A green bird
Hardly a foot long by six inches broad
Rests though in flight on marble –
The artist's convention its own paradox.

Not just a bird,
'Bird' – the clumsy concept starting in the mind of God
Before man got on to names: vigorous,
The divine blueprint for thrush and vulture

Recalled. I put out a guilty finger
(Eyes slide sideways for the attendant)
To touch a tremor of life before we fell –
Poised and sexless, utterly self-contained.

Someone I know grins at me; my answering grimace
Misses her quickly re-averted face.

Confused I turn unhealthily to the canvases,
Not forgetting what I'd said that day in class
About Flaubert.
                        Who is on life's side?
                                    Exact Klee tones these,
A thought of winter written on the wall.
And there, an uncombed landscape, suranné charm,
Audrey Mildmay singing Susanna. And that portrait,
A face reduced to lozenges of colour.
Here a rough surface and paint in dark scabs.

None of these gives that great unknotting
In the stomach. Not like that jade-tense bird.
What can a poet do at an art-exhibition –
Or anywhere –
Except phrase about what he sees,
Bernard in *The Waves*?
Exactly.

A tall bronze jug
Sends a blurred shadow down
Into the mahogany;
Roses cloud each end of the metal stick;
Five petals hang in the darkness
And glow before they shrivel.

If I could catch his eye, we'd bolt for a pub
And over Guinness alternate the old crude gags
With laments for oh the brevity of beauty,
The change within a year of the expression on flesh,
The slender moving to the coarse,
Metamorphosis of the delicate.

Hyacinths if picked might have had
A briefer though more dedicated glory:
Beneath the press of ordinary days,
After the rain,
Virgin their firmness withers and turns brown.

Perhaps a cynical attempt
To justify containing in a vase
(A shape of glass cut with a loving care)
A bloom that I was envious of.
The cost is moral, not aesthetic.

This is one of the things we could discuss –
Our rôles with those we love –
The parts we play as artists.
The artificial vocabulary creeps in.

Mark you, if I were talking to whom he is talking to
I shouldn't want to come out drinking with me either.

V

Circle round with sculptor's eyes
Fix the image inside space
Standing there with dark gold head
Give your colours to my hand

No dispassion as I choose
Porcelain tones for breast and face
Committed to a form that's made
I want to stand you in my mind

Can I say your complexion is a red flower on wood?
Your body a blade hovering in twilight,
One last slant of light catching the metal?
You're strung between two rectangles of sunset.

VI

Inside the reverie I've claimed
No conversation can be heard
Beneath the silence of the bright cascade
The distant figures lie dark and unstirred

Bracken-free the mountains framed
By so vast a solitude
I observe with anguish the lovers aren't afraid
But guiltless cling magnificently nude

VII

The distance from this overcrowded room
To the terror of those moors where strangers alone
Are safe since uncommitted is
The segment on my watch between
This jealous moment and my privacy.

The walls have fallen away. Voices rise
To an hysterical and meaningless pitch.
Beyond the pictures, on fire, hanging in the void,
The razed city sweeps up to the darker tor.

On this divan as in *L'Âge d'or* I could
With you my latest foreign lover rest,
Ignore the scandal of the gathering
And concentrate for one brief passionate epoch
On the forbidden C from waist to knee.

VIII

However gay the pen or paintbrush
The momentary profile stays indifferent
Or, worse, is simply not aware.

Barbaric dreams are temporary.
The civilised rooms come back again.
All – nighttime, suffocation, landscapes – pass.

Once in the street even the pictures leave
Shape by shape the retina they've pressed.

My soul, as they say, has its secret.

IX

The image at the speed of light
Traverses air and eyeball, hits
The brain to splay and dissipate
And fade.
              Hard body to hard body. Scalp
On fire: cold blond, my sort of love,
A restricted flame. My hand's forbidden to ignite.

Externalise in colour. Freeze the muscle.
Now has turned into then and cheats.

The agony to see them walking
In a garden of other flowers.
                        You,
Blond, like a throw of gulls, casually
Perfect. Gone. Mine no longer although of course
Mine never.
On a windburnt cliff which the sea licked
A seabird, white, cut out on the blue,
Hung in the screaming air a hand away.

Immense and dangerous as that dizzy fall
Is the gap between my finger-ends and you.

Paint that. Depict that postage-stamp of sky
Which separates us as significant.
Get into empty space a sense of dynamite,
So nothing contains a spark to set the brain on fire.

Another glass? The wine trembles.
I sip and peer. After all, this is a Private View.
To shake the mind into a new awareness.

A window opens on to an unexciting orchard.
The trees flare. Apples burst and catherine wheels
Twirl and dazzle along the spars of trees.

When does the pen hit the paper?
Can recollection hit it off?
Must poems lag behind experience?

The king grins from his envelope of metal.

I look across the room again
And my throat contracts.
Whole translucent years of peace
Span the interval before I swallow.
Watching your brushed blond hair go dull
My fingers wither from the nail.
    Between your leg and my appalling hand,
A tactile section of room, stiff as dried oil paint,
Separates my stillborn sunrise –
A charred landscape and level white light –
From your impossible midday.

A few birds of prey go into the fresh sky.

Noon.
And see the dream for what it's worth;
Love-making in absentia.

A shaft of sunlight
Illuminates your cold head of hair.

It's only a picture.

This blue tree bending with a harsh light in its branches
Becomes a mast, we're off, rooted to the linoleum,
To an Eldorado. No escape.
No frivolity. Release into awareness.
Equate the Alltag here not with this room,
But with absence of significance.

And always the anguish. These huddled objects,
Light dropped on them from above,
Suggest unease. A ripple runs through the saucepan –
A lack of security drifts about these onions –
Angst at the sink.
And an infinite distance always there
Between the quiet hand and the mad self
That churns inside the jigsaw of toothed bone:
Between the surely not ambiguous canvas
And the blurred eye.

I sit at the table and the light leaves the coast.
At Broadstairs I write about rain over Nafplion.
Dressed and alone apart from the buzz of the electric fire
I start to analyse a Saturday of love.
Am I on life's side?
There has to be a time-lag but
Poetry must not be a substitute:
Not reportage but not escape.
Better perhaps to leave experience alone,
Remember the moment has its uses and
Never attempt the serio-comic business
Of trying to cohere on paper, do
A cold unhappy vaudeville turn
For an unseen few.
Humour is after all what we're outside of.
Once you start fearing what you're doing's funny,
There's an end to involvement, there's
The doppelgänger's face
In winter passionately dark
Beyond the pane.
And perhaps the gas oven.
Or, if not that, bitterness in the lung
And a scream of fury in answer to
All music, however personal.

Desire lifts up in absence
And the pen's unscrewed.
The nag, the phallic loneliness, once you're gone.
Sterility and regret are the only muse
Plus an anger at what we call injustice.
Injustice of choice, injustice of orgasm,
Injustice of the letter that doesn't arrive
When meaningless envelopes go on littering the hall,
Injustice of the one stabbing letter that does arrive,
Injustice when a request of twilight
Is answered by the electric light switch,
Injustice of marriage, injustice of false teeth,
Injustice of the knock on the door that interrupts,
Injustice of the poem no-one wants to read,
Injustice of this crowd that keeps me from you,
Injustice of a different reaction,
Injustice of the often far too slow
Realisation what is love, injustice
That being born you have to die
And being human you have to feel desire
More times than the year and your own face allow.

                    X

No slick reply.

                    XI

With Mike and Joan who don't really take me seriously,
I walked one evening along the Arno.
A cab came at us so that a street-lamp
Made the road underneath it shine.
The horse for a second was suspended
And its weightless legs stroked the bright tarmac.

The concert at the Salle Pleyel was nearly over.
We craned from our balcony to see the last movement.
The pianist's hands (it was K.488, I think)
Brushed the keys as lightly as floating hair.

Under the bridge at Canterbury
The water delicately combed the weeds.

XII

The white bird trapped in its misshapen cage
Of spine and ribs sings and the king's mask
Conceals some sort of answer.
You have to force to some extent the medium,
Especially nowadays.

The river flows past the piano and,
Hanging from the stars that burned above Florence,
The illuminated hooves of a black stallion
Play Mozart for an ear six years have drowned.

XIII

A world of summer finished tragically.
A painting goes out of fashion. Flowers fall.
There was a dispute over the succession.
Daybreak tracks the marvellous enigma
Down the labyrinth of the embrace.
Violence destroyed the harvest.
Years and sidelong glances fray the edge of childhood.
We stand on a careening sphere and shift ourselves.
Half–chewed corpses lay among October.

And then King Saturn went.
But the Golden Age has left a glint of innocence
In every eye. How else can I explain this stone–green bird?
The Impressionist wish to short–circuit artifice
And simply be an eye but what an eye?
Or Klee? Or rococo music?

With all this fleck of innocence in my iris
You I know will go from this gathering
Alone, leaving him to squeeze your complexion
On to his palette and leaving me
A fragrant space where your profile sang.

Unjust. But there are lilacs.
No answer but a complement.
Cher Marcel.

Accept as far as you can, then stand appalled.
The sound of laughter on the Lungarno Acciaioli
Illustrates the magic and the bathos.
Besides, true explanation's late.
The tones that make up any nervous landscape
Need time to crystallise.

Time to observe
The discrepancy between the flash and the printed page,
Between the swirling words and the opaque smile,
Between the hum of conversation and the pictures,
Between my hungry skin and the retreating footsteps,
Between the bored audience and the pain-touched stage,
Between that drunken evening and his finished painting,
Between the singing loins and the love-poem,
Even between the meteor inside the skull
And the opening mouth.

He puts a fence of colour up
Through which we try to understand
What it was he saw that moved him.
And even graffiti on a square of canvas
(Which might be myopia in the viewer)
Are able to contribute something.

XIV

Enthroned on sleet-thrashed uplands, the impassive guard
Wears a slit-eyed helmet for protection;
There on the last frontier of civilisation,
There on the bleak rocks between knowledge and certain death.

And we drinking wine alone with our confusion
Send our senses out groping for some sort of order.
One profile will disturb concentration and yet
Out fall the roses.

The silent witness in the bronze mask
Sits in the moment between exposure and secrecy.

Depict from love
Even when the appeal goes out in silence
And blossoms litter the table

Causing no eyebrow to lift while the heart cries.
Depict from love, and the metal king,
Rigid in merciless judgement over the gathering,
Will accept the vision and the awkward birth –
A still life which with all its faults
No-one else composed.

Felsted, 1960–Cornwall, 1961

A CREED FOR OUR TIME

I can live without religion,
said the man, as he washed the Triumph,
churchbells annoying the grey distance

The wine's in the fridge, our garden's looking nice.
The house is being paid for, so's the wife,
knuckling her hair back as she roasts the lamb

I can live without adultery,
said the man, eyeing the secretaries
as they tap past eager for engagement-rings

Christ, don't you know that
sacrifices are sometimes called for,
said the man to his employees

I can live without death,
said the man in his deckchair,
watching his trinity of kids affirm the sunlight

I can live without love,
said the widower on his deathbed,
lying in the crowded antiseptic darkness

PRETERITE

to the memory of my mother and father

The cat has lost its entity and is,
in the half-rooms of the past, a presence not
a definition. My love for it. A source
of movement. Weight on my absent lap
and fur glimpsed in the dark orchard.

Fewer trees now.

Anecdotes. The gone years offer
abbreviated narrative, the interims
mislaid. Permanently.
                        From being
partially predictable, the dead achieve
an absolute parenthesis for their actions.

What was a home becomes a house again,
an individual accretion
losing sense at the owner's death.
The coherence goes, as belongings
dwindle into objects.
A drawer full of fossils,
an unfinished embroidery in a sewing-bag,
a diary for 1913.

Toying unnervingly with recollections
we theorise where we had never asked:
ascribe to events and souvenirs
a pattern often meaningless,
the one code that could decipher them
being destroyed.
Key in the water,
the glossary missing.

Names, labels, strut about the past,
obedient as our conversations send them
down grey photographed streets and into
the incomplete gardens.
                        Their substance
being made up only of results,

a conjured memory,
we circumscribe their deeds with laughter,
tenderness, wonder – yet,
before they reach the fact we're aiming for,
there is some gap they don't exist in, a blur
in the foregone outlines.
                          Walking to
the lost hydrangeas, they vanish
ghostlike on the lawn. A hiatus
in the story, unaccounted for, remains
their secret and the way they have attained
a certain triumph of identity.

AN INVITATION TO TEA

Never rehearse the lines of love
Nor practise tenderness before a glass:
    Alone, you're bound to organise
    Without that element of farce
    Which will upset the pattern of
    Your pre-arranged solemnities.

    To calculate in solitude,
    Arrange the absent flowers and see
    The glance that never will exist,
Precipitates a secret misery.
    Impromptu gestures will preclude
    The anti-hero's being kissed.

You'd tried the lilt of an appealing phrase,
    Nonchalant to conceal its charm; –
    Somehow the words are garbled or
    The throat gets tightened in alarm.
    A blankness in the other's gaze
    Destroys what you'd been planning for.

The comic flaw is, you assume
The right responses to each act –
In your hand puppet-strings to twitch:
The head will turn with perfect tact,
The lips will be apart in time,
The tender play performed without a hitch.

In fact, the arm shrinks from the touch,
Your dialogue is ludicrous,
The telephone-bell interrupts, a cup
Is spilt, transmitting nervousness.
The mood you've brought about is such
Your diffident captive will escape.

Apparently a foreign face
Stares at you from the other chair,
Still beautiful, though stripped of all
Compassion. Now it seems too far
To move from helplessness to your disgrace,
You'd rather failure than the fall.

Advised from no experience,
Alone and unamused and poor,
Abandoned by the pre-supposed,
How often left staring at the door,
Which, calm, in blond indifference,
The marvellous body has just closed.

A BAR IN LERICI

The sea starts its immense cooling.
We stop for a moment on our journey back.
Reflecting on what's done, the days contract.

Television flickers over the smart décor
On to a few cold square feet of pavement
Catching the ankles of infrequent passers-by.

In the unnatural marine light
A fern of coral might issue from the sleeve
Twisting a stem manufactured to hold up
This triangle of Martini. (The desire
To bridge becomes inevitably plastic.)

For a time we sit and inattentive watch
A dubbed version of *Journey into Fear*.
You turning glance idly across the brain-dark gulf
To Porto Venere. We talk of love,
Balanced as always between the recollection –
The afternoon spent across the bay in sunlight –
And anticipation of the stars
Tending to disappoint.
                              Darkness
After being born should be familiar
And natural as the scenery of the Milky Way.

A human tremor that we feel
When summer goes or night has fallen
Makes us take to antral refuges away
From honesty. We attitudinise
And call our actions communication.
Images of lucidity in the skull even
Protect such artificiality.
                              Beneath
The deceptively void autumnal sky,
Between the past and present horns of the bay
Defiant with lighthouses, the sea gates close.

FERRYBOAT

We left the early harbour hung in white.
(Or was it evening, a wintry sun
Falling through smoke?) Anyway,
There was a deck, the hiss of ropes
Through salt wind. We knew,
The feel of the quay eventually
Not swaying underneath us,
There would be a parting. We drank,
Smoked, talked. Sliding into the distance
Withdrew my past. And a future
Edged into the sea towards us.
(It would be dark, oily lights
Queueing into the calmer water.
Or the port hazy underneath
A different afternoon.
The light anyhow changed
Dramatically or more subtly.)
I remember . . . what? Your profile,
The confession you made concerning
An event of summer so long before
It seemed to make no difference.
We had begun. Our hands had joined
On the nearer shore, pledged
Something. The water
Rocked us over the gulf, the boat moving
Inexorably. Halfway. I ask you
To hold fast that renaissance bed,
The kiss in the museum
Snatched when the attendant
Moved to other colours for a moment,
Me lying beside you as the night
Pushed us forward to the morning train.
(Boats were perhaps waiting
Bright under vertical sunlight.)
We move up on to the deck,
The bow, two silhouettes
Preparing for the jutting future.
A defiance. Our mouths meet, stay.
You perhaps no less eager than I
To hold the present tense as still

As movement can be. (Though
Always valid when my untouched mouth
Opens to darkness these winter solitudes.)
You understood the reason why
We cling together dangerously, the bitter air
Forcing our endearments backwards,
From us. You understand. There's time
For so few kisses between shore and shore.

SAMUEL BECKETT 1961

for Michael Bakewell

A crocus flashes from the darkness. Trapped
in the mud spread-eagled the hero conjures
up yesterdays. Without too much screaming. That's
the way things are. What consolation? Simply

the occasional gag – though the grinding humour's fading –
an illusory blaze of grace from time to time;
each agonising vision always then.
A white gate somewhere – a tramp without his trousers –

remember – a boat moored where the water shines.
Hang on to detail. Peer. That saves the moment.
Get out the tin-opener. Feel. Count the marbles.
Mortality is all we've got. The gag

in the darkness or the crocus. Nothing else.
Nowhere to get to. That's the way things are.

LINES

Losing myself in you, I discover
a different darkness, and I bend
awkwardly to you in the curtained room,
sunset happening outside somewhere:
brief screen of dwindling rage behind bare trees.
Our legs involve themselves. Bartók
on the pick-up, muffled conversation
from next door. Your hands, clumsily,
meet at my nape; we shift and balance; then
you sit back and our kiss occurs
at an angle sculptured from the twilight.
A tension. Black. Made up of spars.
Maintaining mass through strain.
My mind says I want you, seeing you blindingly
poised over an empty future. You fear
failure, I departure. Your departure.

Your eyes are closed and the inadequate lamp
must give a redness to my absence.
Unless my shadow dominates. Slack,
line of arm curved from form to form,
balanced between resistance and desire.
Our tongues desperate. Their silence
active. Searching for peace.
A stasis. The sun dies. The empty evening
gives the curtains colour. The string quartet
involves the room netting us in time.
Yet part of me remains our symbol, a
semi-abstract figure. Equilibrium
by asymmetry. We make an object,
but only temporarily in space.
My mind goes down the concave
flow of your body and in the uncomplex
necessity of our embrace we discover
nothing. Nothing but itself which is its own
anguish. Our image making triumph
badged with red. The lamp impinges,
makes us entities, carving instability
from the shadow.
                    We have to move. The room
rocks as you get up and I cross to the door.

The pick-up hums. In your eyes
the admission each time something valid happens.
A newer consciousness both of our pattern
(a kiss for sunset) and our uncertainty.
For ever has no meaning. I leave
to the toneless evening gone dark.

RETURN

If we don't belong here
    (which seems probable noting the neglect
    the unswept leaves and the grimy panes)
what made us suddenly leave the neutral tea-room
where we had arranged to meet again

The bus went by half-remembered landmarks
– The Saracen's Head by the roundabout
– the churchyard re-aligning its gravestones
through the flickering palings
– the monkey-puzzle tree at that blind corner

It's now a one-way street
We had to go past the new No Entry sign
Men in sweaters hosing their cars,
children playing hopscotch, the odd mother
kneeling with a trug beside her on the lawn
regarded us curiously

How long had it been

Weeds have made the path uneven
There are sweet-papers in a corner of the porch,
a crushed cigarette-packet and a broken milk-bottle
The key is still on my ring
    (was it your glance that set me reaching for it)
and strangely shiny considering
the time it has been unused

Why are we here
standing on this threshold
looking along this empty hall
from which the uncarpeted stairs
lead up to our past

Leaving the front door ajar
we walk unwelcome in this house
listing the etiolated wallpaper,
the rusty taps, the blankness where furniture was,
the smell of the cold

And at the stop once more
making counterfeit conversation
our eyes stray furtively on the look-out
for a bus to take us back to the centre
The time before, whenever it was,
should have been the last time
The return has not proved a success

RUMANIAN STREET-SCENE

Cool interludes of boys and trees and distance.
The sun through fragmentary water fingers
The skin and the web is drawn tight on the blanched
Framework. Inside,
Obsessively, the patter
Of leaves under a fountain, young laughter. Slant eyes,
Greener than foliage, condemn
The walkers on the dry piazzas . . .
Click of their black shoes on the measured stones.

An arid language issues sparingly
Orders, accounts, from inhibited lips.
                                    Not the
Caress of dialect accompanying
Proffered lottery-tickets or blue flowers . . .

A pass by; shrug; elegant entry to
The white afternoon seats behind potted shrubs.

LOVER

You who cannot utter
        a sexual no,
who churn to spray and back
        creaming to my
wharves force the tide early,
        again; salt curves
of gale air smooth as your
        limbs have then drop
to temporary peace
        the weight of which
you encourage from all
        anticyclones
veering the weather–chart
        to negative;
when sombre arrows of
        the riding wind
wheel slowly, pivot, gain
        velocity
tightening the orbit
        and up to one
cumulus height at the
        null centre poise,
splash, diffuse; the twisting
        corridors of
space empty strength; your mouth
        is now the wet
traces of violence,
        rain out of taut
air falls thrice, your loving
        gone tangible;
you whose hand on my tongue
        has its note of
success, whom I lie with,
        sweat, quiver, use,
whose sexuality
        passes my heart,

exist: come into time
        from the typed page;
be the only one I've
        always had who
wants it more than I do.

ELEGY FOR JEAN COCTEAU

You played your death with cigarette-smoke
And centaurs carried you away.
                                A whiff of jazz,
The dry wind brought its own irreverence.
Now you're with Orpheus and the Chevaliers.

You're right, the mirror traps us all: death's oval mask
Steams the reflection over from the other side.
Now we can't see you any more. We call you dead
The way we called you hypnotised by death.

A poet has to die to rise as verse, you said.
All life you gave us nightbursts of your pain,
(Midnight made lucid) since you showed us
The flowers of your cinema had roots in blood.

Perhaps your Eurydice was death: perhaps
The grave's your new adventure and you've gone
To astonish silence with a forward look.

FORM

A garden sunk from expectation
  suffers the clouds to edge the sky
    away. There ebbs from the metal limb
    the egg-blue light that gave it line.
    No song or footfall. In the leaved
      seclusion nothing's asked or known,
        deciphering the whole. Surmise
      along the lawn is all: to have
      accepted so far means no hope
      in the coming cumulus for some
      event to give away the order.

      The birdcry, then the lift of light,
        as time grants one heart-rending flash
      revealing the significance
      of that mysterious statuette
        lost, gone, against the thunderstorm,
      before the dazzled brain is left
        to grope unaided through the burned
        expanse of garden for the truth
        that singed the iris, stopped the breath,
        and forced the knee on to the ground.

      The pattern's disappeared, the rift
    is sewn and, in the dark, the form
    escapes; enchantment having set
  an abstract puzzle, all the chance
of flesh discovers will be ash.

    Fire is as sterile as it's bright –
    the glory that transformed the border
    ignited painted whorls of bloom,
    licked round eager to char the shape
    that, isolated, perfect, gave
    the chaos of the peonies
    their only sense. Remote, alone,
  perhaps, the fullness unperceived
  through indolence or awe, divine
or if not sensual, will the dim
thrill of a lyric augury
remain intact from revelation.

AN AUTUMN RECORD

September–November, 1966

1   *Parting*

Parting
like my tongue ripped out
slowly

Tears
for what didn't have to be,
bad temper, hours wasted

and for what had to be,
the waiting-rooms, bureaucrats,
the trivia

The distance stretches
taut between us

A summer gone
from our shared lives,
a kiss severed
by needs not ours

The plane
lifts into the blue
and your beauty
as the land dwindles
makes wonderfully
no wry comment

2   *Birth*

The first cry of a baby
shakes the stratosphere
making nonsense of
telegrams, reaction

I did not belong
to the ceremony of midwives
pondering here
the desérts of casualness

Wet, blood–covered,
a strange identity
hidden across airlines

Love of
seasons ago
made tangible

3   *Journey with Natalie*

You bear our baby through the night

My unknown fathering in the upper air
one-sided meeting to look forward to

An empty diary in your arms
for wants and learning to be scrawled,
love daubed, despair become familiar

If we can't shield her from the dark,
ward off decay, the demons, grief,
let's give her clichés that we can, persuade
that much of it is flowers and gold

I lent you to her birth, abandoned my
identity, posed as a shadow here
and now you lift towards me still
whole lands away but with another kiss
your mouth become parentheses to time

Soon knowledge of you will out-cancel pain
your tongue will tell me of your absence and
a quality of us maintained in her
will squeeze the unfamiliar months
to one blank line that we have come across
and launch us past embraces to the dawn

4 *Haneda Airport, Tokyo*

Ten past eight

Luggage, scurry,
anticipation
Sepulchral announcements
in Japanese and American
refer to the globe casually
as visitors throng,
expectant,
nervous,
Thai International, Copenhagen,
Rangoon, Alaska,
BOAC

I hang about
waiting for your smile,
your blonde hair, your
fragrance

My private hands
require your beauty
Without you
there is no eloquence

The clock
shifts slowly
You force your way
past the stars
towards me

The tropics narrow

Unbearably long
since our last kiss
dry
frantic
through tears
at London

Half an hour to go

Rationally
it is impossible
we won't fight again
be difficult,
intolerant
Better that
than the ache of apart

Another beer
light up again
think of you
so wise
behind your loveliness

Forgive my depression
awkwardness of meeting
this the last letter
I ever want to write you

Stay close now
and let us love each other
in bed in a foreign land,
at table,
laughing

I stare
glumly at the past
full of loss, of emptiness,
with radiance
at the weeks ahead
all filled with you

LINES FOR A BYGONE COUNTESS

or

'September already – how ever
shall we get through the winter here?'

The summer's over; brown and scarlet tonguing
already across the slope of trees. A bowl
of cold roses stands on the piano. Longing
is five months old and dry and tired. Cool
the ground and dark the torrent. Only are
berries still definite, primary, among
a composition whose strength and colours pour
downwards, away. On the hill wan leaves now cling.

Listen to late September in the still
blurred air: occasional bugles run one more
branch yellow and some pale-turned petals fall.
Otherwise nothing has the will to stir.
Sap has a verbal meaning in the autumn –
the lift of spring and lateral delight
of summer come to this: a falling rhythm,
sad melodies along the angled light.

Subtly beneath the mist the landscape gives
up hope. The damp keys pressed cause the bouquet
to tremble; each slow successive chord revives
a pattern of circles that go out to die
from the player to the watched, making a pool
spread to the limit of the sound. Where, held
between the dew-touched dahlias in one thrill
of memory, the sunlight lingers cold.

THE DUSTS

*(In Zen parlance, sight, sound,
smell, taste, touch and thought
'defile the pure mind'. The
world which we perceive like
this is 'the realm of the six
dusts'.)*

I see you and a blur occurs
which I call love. The held you
vanishes. Lightly I interpret
gestures, smiles. You are
to me each absence
what I've never seen.

The flute
adds emptiness
to emptiness. And wet
chrysanthemums in autumn
touch the air.

A haze called
perception concealing
what?
      Golden
nothingness: jade-ash:
the mere
skeleton of the gods.

Radiance is where
sense is, you are.
Paucity of detour, of
withdrawal, the
recoiling from law.

Scattering the abstract
with questions like a blind man's
index. The nerves taut
as a finch pierces mist.
Bewilderment of
apples —
scarlet, tart —
in a curtained room.

Or the praise of
twilight circling the kiss.

Wine nor the grain of teak,
the silk you have
describing your skin,
sesame-seeds nor all
the magic of nakedness . . . Let's
think about that

THE ENIGMA OF THE DAY

Carnations
exploding from the vase
stop spattered in mid-air

Nor will my anonymity
detect one sweating night
tremors of beauty through the globe

Your used eyes
glutted with nakedness
forget our afternoons

Rags of shadow in the photograph
ignore the rain
the shut sky

Statues simpler than time
and gleaned truths
crumble to oblivion

Walking into the mirror
the grey-haired stranger
whose touch chills colour

And into the hanging darkness
an invitation

with no flowers

Tones going
absence of swallows
storm-green fires

FANCY BOY

Groomed for the evening, smile in trim, he sits
in drag at one of Tokyo's gayer bars –
the flirt, the surgeon, the unwoundable.
Professionally sweet, he's there to give
out of the safety of his twenty years
a cool brief comfort to the clientele.
Buy him a beer and get a kiss and watch
the cigarette-smoke sparkle to his laughter:
his beauty, like a rose in ice, explains
desire is distance and the jagged peril
in reaching for a heart with ungloved hands.
No room for amateurs on this terrain:
he has a job to do and does it well –
cold eyes look deep as colder hands assess
the pulsebeat of a lonely middle-age.
Always affectionate and never bored,
the sexy priest hears on; friend for an hour,
he so contrives it that you both keep up
the same ambivalent intensity.
Only existing here, he doffs a life
at closing-time, wipes off the make-up and
strolls out to greet his anonymity –
an unknown bed, a chosen orgasm,
from having been the servant, now the boss.
Abandoning no heart-break, commonsense
his legacy, he knows the fragile cure
depends on intimacy that depends
on ignorance, the probe must go so far,
the lancet single-edged. He keeps the role
of non-participant for those first few

eccentric hours of evening, and, when freed,
he reaches down involvement once again,
dares, means it, fumbles, wants, and, vulnerable,
strips himself bare to the electric light.

AUTOBIOGRAPHY

My mother dropped me dead on to
this planet some three decades back.
Hanged in her cord I fell into
a Welsh October. The midwife
unstrangled me. Acquainted with
death at this tender age, I was
bequeathed a double-jointed thumb,
myopia and half a lion
to go on my little finger.

We moved to suburban London:
Cheam. I wondered how glass could burn
when the Crystal Palace scorched the sky
behind the poplars. We displayed
a cardboard crown for George VI.
When Russia invaded Finland
my sister came in weeping. Then,
in the Morris 14, going
over Banstead Downs, I couldn't see
the barrage-balloons and was given
thick glasses. However I could
spell Czechoslovakia backwards.

A season of wheeling Spitfires:
we stood on the front steps and watched
smoke-trails that wrote death in the air.
From the school cellar we could hear
ack-ack fire. My cousin who smiles now
from the tennis-net in a blurred
photograph was killed at Dunkirk.
But Father joined the A.R.P.

I sang 'We'll hang out the washing
on the Siegfried Line'.

                    So Mother
took me to Aunt Gwen's house in New
England. Plumes of water spurted
from the illuminated bombs
in Liverpool harbour. Our ship,
the Scythia, dropped depth-charges.
I used a men's urinal for
the first time, and was the only
child on board who wasn't sea-sick.
After the London black-out we
marvelled at skyscrapers of light.
I stayed up till one o'clock at
the World's Fair with the Trylon and
Perisphere. And then the colours
of that Connecticut fall which have
spoiled me for all other autumns.

Superman, cream of wheat and snow
sliding heavily off the roof.
Fudge-ripple at the drugstore, Red
Skelton in a Harlem picture-
house. Two stitches in my lip when
disobedient to the teacher
but urged on by blonde Alice, I
fell bloodily on to the ice.
We stood round the Stars and Stripes on
certain days to sing 'My Country
'Tis of Thee'. I, patriotic
in those days, mouthed 'God Save the King'
as he then was: Elizabeth
was in uniform, changing tyres.

The funny papers each Sunday;
Fibber McGee and Molly on
the radio. The lake in June
and at a picnic throwing dry
ice. Poison ivy, a baseball-
bat, Niagara Falls and me in
knee-pants. Mother and I, twisted
against the winter, went uptown
to find Tarzan movies after

which I swung from flowered creepers
on Fifty-Fourth Street, where I was
to return two decades later
for my honeymoon.
                    I won The
Lakeville Poetry Contest For
Juveniles, being then one. Mother
taught me Chopin Nocturnes in the
cool light of my aunt's drawing-room
with its blue glance at the Berkshires.

We got back to Cheam just a month
before the V-Ones. One night there was
a loud putt-putting, then silence,
inexplicably. Father yelled
'Down on the floor everybody' –
I rolled on to the cold dusty
linoleum: waited, breathless, for
a bang to blow up the Century
Cinema. Re-opened three years
later it is probably now
a Bingo Palace. After school
we used to hang about and ask
strangers to take us in when there
were A films on, usually
Gainsborough Pictures.

                    'Cycling to
The Sugar Bowl, editing a
hand-written magazine, ping-pong,
Biggles, wrestling with Derek;
when we played at Neil's house, we had
to bring slippers as his mother
was particular.

                Peace and we
danced in the streets at Petworth, all
so thrilled about the atomic bomb.

Lying with Jane in a summer
garden under the sparkling hose,
we would discuss Dornford Yates; then,
leaving the laburnums glowing
as the sun went down over Ewell,

we'd take a new needle out of
the shiny bowl and, winding up
the gramophone, listen to songs
from *Bless the Bride*. And Jane kept dried
tarantulas in the garage.

To Malvern one damp autumn; there,
under the gold hills, I was taught
to construct French proses, masturbate,
play squash, conform and disobey
in correct proportions and to drink
British sherry gossiping with
friends. I read Racine, Grillparzer,
and Dorothy L. Sayers; played
Debussy's Preludes badly and
wrote sonnets to a dark, sexy
boy.
     Dick Barton at six forty-
five, the theme-tune hurried back to
through the fog from the Aeneid.
Dear Wilfrid Noyce, once *Minna von
Barnhelm* was coped with, showed us how
to abseil on the quarry. Sweets
were rationed, every week new jars
of sugar, butter, issued us.

The old man soon abandoned his
life's work of wresting taxes from
unwilling citizens and bought
a small cold house at Kingsgate where
he gardened, Mother stayed in bed
till half past ten and ginger wine,
and they both went to bridge five days
a week at different clubs. For me,
the holidays meant bicycling
to the Cameo or Plaza –
Madonna of the Seven Moons
or *Tawny Pipit*. Omelettes of
dried eggs and Monday Night At Eight.
Walking to Cliftonville and a
day in Canterbury looking through
second-hand books of poetry.

And then I talked three years away
wandering round Cambridge, where for
the last time all the cares I had
were of my own making; where I
learned something of Montaigne and Kleist,
heard Bartók, Jelly Roll, Bechet,
and marvelled at Pauls Klee and Nash.

Arguing from ignorance with
friends about Buñuel; falling
very drunk into the snow; on
the narrow college bed making
such satisfactory love with him
or her as the late suns dropped to
silence behind invisible
clock-towers; Parmée on Rimbaud;
tea in punts; Peter Hall's *Saint's Day*;
sandwiches at The Mill for lunch;
the viscous smell of the Cam. And
the chestnut-spikes in front of King's
alone announcing time.

          To France:
a double year – at the Sorbonne
writing a thesis which I still
find incomprehensible on
Mallarmé – and teaching all of
thirteen hours a week in a pale
yellow school on the outskirts of
a wood. So a vocation was
found for me in front of blackboards
discussing Molière, the c
cedilla and Algeria.

One Christmas week my mother died
and the crematorium on a
cold day destroyed her gaiety,
endless capacity for love,
her gameness, trimness, the way she
looked at flowers and read her Crime Clubs,
ash-tray and peppermints to hand.
She disliked solemnity and
found it hard to believe people

want to be unjust – her horror
when she saw the ladies' rooms in
Maryland were segregated.

Resources dwindle year by year,
and each commercial minute we're
encouraged stridently to waste
as much as we can manage and
despoil the rest: convert forests
to print detergent-vouchers, choke
a stream with chemicals and grind
whole hills away.
               This hard sense of
bitter concern at the mouthings
of the American Right. Fear
at inscrutable troop-movements
in Tibet. And no solution
save somewhat threadbare faith in man.

My wife was born in Saint Louis
on my seventh birthday, so we
have an astrologically
incestuous union. In her head
thirteenth-century kings still stalk
and plot. She loves red wine, hot baths,
the Beatles, Conrad, Fellini.
Marriage means drinks at six; falling
around at Dick Van Dyke; our cats
(one orange and one black-and-gold);
chili con carne; The King's Head;
Lynn blonde beside me mirrored in
the blue bedroom; sometimes waging
imaginary battles with
the landlord or the income-tax.
And travelling and seeing films
à deux; planning; carrying her
suitcase in Budapest and all
the long discovery of love.
If I can't help eyeing profiles
in the street, and if a swung thigh
gives daily rise to forbidden
dreams. No harm. Not hate.
               Enraged at
breakfast sometimes reading praise for

(say) Iris Murdoch, or any
Tory's trite pleas for selfishness.

Appalled at inhumanity
and greed – so long as they are not
our own – we stagger on, and vote,
and offer propaganda at
cross-purposes. For odd ideals.
Better, though, where possible, than
trigger-happy privilege, the
flash of cameras at the airport,
the boredom of the conference.

Perhaps my being hanged at birth
has given me this guilt I feel
in banks or on the telephone –
and, outcast, a healthy distaste
for stockbrokers and generals –
although easy targets, easy
like my untried pacifism.

Aware of what is going on,
but helpless when it comes to cures;
bemused by penicillin and
pop art, we're furtively alarmed
by terms we glibly use – 'fall-out',
'teach-in' and 'escalate'. Despite
optimism (or a certain
duodenal laziness) I
blink out short-sightedly at things,
and find myself condemned to watch
the encroaching winter with unease.

Shoreham-by-Sea, 1965

The Cutting-Room
(1970)

For Michael and Joan

DECEMBER IN KAGOSHIMA

for Lynn

The maples linger autumn on.
                              We buy
cold postcards and sit alone together
in out-of-season cafés.
                              Time here
in a paralysis. No wind. Lushness
fleeces the sheer rock behind the daimyô's palace
whose impeccable screens glance over smooth waves
to the volcano.
                              Boecklin tones.
The citron feathers of bamboo
prophesy sunset. The mountain smokes
to a bare sky. Palm-trees.
The shrivelled leaves on the banana
jag to clean earth.
                              We move through silence,
and under the threatening cold
need nothing but our love,
the triumph of these late year days
retaining foliage.
                              Stroll hand in hand,
noting the distant forms of cooled lava,
the tangled groves, the grey-spaced shrine,
as imperceptibly the empty air
thickens and the island smudges over.

The ground here's paper-thin,
stretched upon vertigo, the hot veins of the crust:
an earthquake danger underlines
a made security.

The daytime moon is curtained and the landscape narrows.
A blend of colours forgotten in the north
robs it of melancholy, the blood-clots of the maples
halting winter's advance.
                              On the slope,
heading for the bar in our hotel,
we turn and watch the ferries crossing,
hear the blare of their horns in mid-channel.

The sea steams.
              I hold you close.
The first snow flurries and we stand
a momentary shape in hectic whiteness
before, apart again,
hiss of the flakes in our differing hair,
                   we make for warmth.

MYTHS

          Behind her
and the other
delicate companions

     a yellow sunrise
redolent perhaps of spring

          Stepping lightly
on white ankles; blue-robed;
in such slender hands
starred orbs borne

          Approaching ever
for innocence, veined breasts
globed with milk

            The object-bringers

          hawk-
headed, thighed with
plumage, gold
manacles about the arm

     greaves stained by red earth

at a half-run,
fleeing, aiming

Light of
sacrifice behind them
Stench of
coiled smoke leaning on a sky

altars reeking

rivulets of blood, feathers,
vertebrae, smashed by the adzes
on to rough stone

The past-bringers

Through the
drifting bonfire's uncertainty,
tall, bronze-loined

Weary with lust, gentle-lipped,
dew on a thunderous cloud beyond them

Praise and
phallic loveliness

The honey-bringers

illiterate, foul-
mouthed, the hordes shamble, wielding
ripped books, brandishing
sub-machine-guns

(echoing, the crash of
celadon, ormolu,
lacquer frames)

chanting

the end of history, making for a
final hermitage where one
alone on the peninsula
illuminates last pages

(short saga in their wake
of sackings, torture)

Eyes empty of love,
hands hating creation

The future-bringers

Cold air stretched above the tarn
Under a taut noon
the water quivers

Wind-sung grass laid smooth,
hare-bells shaking

The leering god
wraiths into nothingness, his presence
a faint smear inside the wind

Long, slow approach
from monochromed horizon

No escape now

First
ants; and structure;
discernible; then detail

Those big, daubed, waist-length masks,
assegais poised,
bracelets of human hair, chains
of teeth above the knee

The end-bringers

ALLEGORIES

The work it took defining us . . .

Your carved helmet, spray of its plume
frozen prophetically on gold;
defence; scabbard; emblazoned shield
hoarding sunlight; doffed uniform
neutrally now the colour of
certain azaleas too cast
aside, you, Adam–naked, flex,
loyal conflict done, the struggle still
to come.

      Scarred water stretched across
your glance of morning from the east.
Flags in no breeze decking the pale
beach–head of the half–land. Horses plunged
in spray. The sands of noon. Foretold
rectangle of churned violence
where we close, cupped palms on sunburn,
tonguing for brine like glitter tossed
from hooves, shape blurred to quench with shape,
the enemy pushed back – old doubt,
a hand retained a fear away,
eyes flickering.
            Initial stage.

Sweat lingers on the darkness. Some
brilliance of metal in the
thrown pile of clothes lets the day go
and we diminish to no form,
to namelessness. Both watches tick
from nowhere. Furniture melts. And
kisses now bring no–one to a
blind Narcissus.

      Another graph
of ascent transcribed from floor to floor
has pierced the walls of sunset turned
you–colour. The roses of the
afternoon burning on male skin
dye me by touch to this drowning,

this liquid hour.

         The ocean now
puts out the journey seam by seam –
the white-long wake left by our craft
vanquished by nightfall and the slow
stitch of the imperceptible.

All traces of our triumph gone
as, merciless, the curtained room
tilts into twilight and the blue
inexorable failure of
time. Now the tendrils edge like shade
on to achievement, two ruined
branches strewing the clock-face with
toneless blossoms. Our relief once
more equips the past. I can hear
ironic shoots of death rasping
their foliage against my spine.

The work it took . . . Restrictions and
inherited agreements all
ripped up, selflessness forgotten.
A dual transformation to
citizens of nakedness, with
shreds of old, yellowed documents
staining the court.

         Existence at
that freedom only, loosed from the
tyranny of a second-hand
identity. Become ourselves.
As athletes pitted to the one
problem: pulse; rage; muscle; even pain,
commingled. The hard in-focus
of each other. The thirst.
               Controlled.
Life narrowed down to nothing but
absorption in a separate strength
plied in a non-existent world.

The last proximity of force,
your body flaring black against
my eye, and the moment hurtling

to explosion – rainfall – autumn
crashing around our solitude.
The room unfolding's cancelled to
a newer, sprawled equation as
angles of time clamp us to this
wet, dishevelled landscape reached though
such circumlocutions of flesh.

You. Touched for, ah, found,
                          suspended
in some corner of the evening,
firm, sculptured with, held, holding, worked,
lost.
      Exhausted by abstractions
we leave an unwritten treaty
nowhere. Curve of enquiry like
smoke, or water curing its seethe,
absorbed in starlessness. 'Where was
I then could you have been.'

                  Former
assumptions start putting on the
old dissimilarities as
colours by sudden lamplight stress
inaccurate memories. The map
tracing our route henceforth proclaims
attention and the dark lasso
around the violent moment
shrivels to soot. To absence. Air.

The effort made . . . To no avail.
The room that was no longer has
the same bed, view to the sunset,
smell of you.

           We're turned back to the
same dawn, the same reconnaissance
ahead, the slope of need, décor
progressively abandoned, clasp,
and the objects re-assembling
again.

          Return to perspective,
you, looped like a comet in the

non–hours.

>Approaching blaze, the work,
mixture of allegories, heat of
your mouth, the sinews of pride, brief
reduction of the dusk to our
joint spilling, clarity achieved.

October, 1967

DAUGHTER

to Tasha, 1967

Television over, your mother ill,
I enter the breathing darkness of your room.
For the moment the danger of winter,
of fall–out, ambulance and poisoned lung,
remains outside these thin walls.
I spill cruel light around you, dragging
your six months' consciousness away
from the security of no dreams.

You shift, protesting, frog-like, as I
haul you from your cot, wedge you in my left arm
and give you, grunting, the lukewarm bottle.
I watch you. Slurp. The down of your eyebrows
hints at a blonde mist in the shadow.

The wireless plays. Moist, tiny fingers
bat away at me, the blanket, night.
Chords I once groped for you perhaps will find.
My hands have grown so old now yours are there.
Sonatas, summers of exams, ahead for you,
funny half–entity, as the sirens wail
and a Japanese darkness you may never know
hovers beyond the window.
>What goes on
the other side of those opaque blue eyes?

Under the dentist's future drug will you
recall these mad Oriental evenings?
                                    Baby.
Ours. Dependent for so brief a time. Daily
coming to private terms with a personal
reality.
          Something of your mother. A bit of me.
A certain flow from mediaeval Wales,
Germany, Rheims, Lincoln's America,
trickles thinly into you, although
you issue, Vaughan-like, another whence
and are yourself.
                    To change you now,
beware of pins, make sure you're dry, cream you
for the long stationary trip to breakfast.

You clamber about the cot a moment,
collapse and suck your fingers. I tiptoe out.

I see you and I worry — so
fragile, unprotected, as I pour
myself a drink downstairs, imagine
your wedding which I'll have to pay for,
willingly, or you in navy-blue
attending dutifully my funeral.
The inventory. Where did they get *that*?
What taste they had in those days! Who'll buy it now?
The combing through my papers, decade-old
receipts, letters from lost faces, lines
for mercifully unwritten poems,
secrets perhaps in diaries to shock —
poor Mother, you'll say, we'll burn the lot:
just this insurance-policy and these few
photographs — the *clothes* they wore; but
Mother was lovely and Father had some hair.

We store up treats for death, file away
embarrassment for forty years
hence. The infant I feed now
and giggle with may well despise me, all
relationship gone acrid. So
good-night the unformed years to come,
remember me, a wondering father all

too ill-equipped, that streamlined moment when
the crematorium curtains judder to
and I am chucked into the final fire,
a problem, a forgettable time past:
then drive away with that yet faceless son-in-law
to tea and talk about our grandchild's future
as hour by hour my presence smokes away.

NOCTURNE

for Lynn

The room gives dark
on to a pea-green sky

Jazzed-up Bach on the stereo;
pregnant, you're now in bed; the city
writes distant neon on the night

Black cyclamens in a circular vase,
our cheap bronze horse
prances arrogant in the uncertainty

Rending cacophony
notices a jet
departing for Europe

A magazine discarded on the floor
displays perfect torsos

I feel the shadow of desire
since leaves cut out on artificial air
such promises of spring;
the orange-blossom, sombre magnolia,
record travelling to silence and
technicolour portraits

Eleven o'clock stirrings
of early April

sift the open drawing-room of tobacco-smoke
as cats yowl
in black–dimensional gardens

The day's wind drops,
the local line's last train
hoots on its way to rest

Upstairs our daughter sleeps,
dirty bears and rabbits littered round her,
already not remembering
to-morrow's dreams

                    And,
thrashing uncomfortably behind your skin,
a new creation is assertive

TO LYNN, JULY

Twice not alone as now
eight months beyond
the hour sperm quit me on
in her unborn the shape
stirs. Her then pierced to my
joy, oval pierced by my
black arrow, cell on cell
webbing history, a
figured crawl from slime
on the way to angels.
Her awareness week by week
spiralling in towards absorption,
the world's alleys gently
one by one sealed off
as the horizon enters
the tips of her hands,
touches her navel, lowered
eyelid. Her presence not
gone from me yet
distracted, sketched gestures

of breakfast, magazine-
reading, attentive ear
to my broadcasts. Gaze
past me, past now, but focused on
the new love in her womb,
circling round me, out from
back to her, brushing my shoulders
with pollen, star-ash, dust
from a butterfly's wing returning:
by-produced gifts to my
blank maleness,
assuring warmth
with casual tolerance,
confirming though
I cannot understand.

PHASES

I

Swans are dark this midnight.
One star only finds the water.
Smell the colour of roses.

II

The river skulks
under the footbridge
surface stained by currents.

A grey church.
One field on the downs
Martian with poppies.

We walk to a certain bed
for the last time
knowing soon
the geography of this place
will be just words.

III

Not to trust it
when begonias conceal pistols
and the white kings process

        Gold crowds chanting
knife raised for the fake sacrifice
blue smoke twisting into cold air

A club foot shows under the robes

IV

Your passive kiss
and me not realising for more than a year
the magic of nakedness
we both wanted

V

Strings of a last act, valedictory
The railway-station, our fingers tugged apart
Ironic cadence from the overture

The telephone perhaps. Conclusion.
Jet of a match. Suitcases. Torn photographs.
A duologue alone in a rending world
                inspissating

Fatal t.b., a clumsy suicide:
flames in the gloom, no route back to choice

The first music of winter

VI

Absence now

The shadow of your hand
falls across my loins in the moonlight
as I open my lips
for phantom sweetness

VII

A half-familiar face
rounds the corner

                    Police-sirens
gashing the street open

A plastic skull
in a shop window

Headlines
mashed on to the gutter

            Who called my name?

VIII

Wearing to-day my dishonesty
at a less jaunty angle
I decided to commit
adultery with myself

Aftermath, my reflection shows
the face gone somehow thicker

And this time I can see your distance
increasing in my own eyes

IX

The tragic waste
A prince lugs off the corpse
mistaken murderer

Hero laments her own complicity
Leander lost because in love

Phèdre's passion
curdled to slander

Spring darkened
The sickness in the shoot
Doomed blossom

X

Like birds that die
robbing the day
of movement

Apples
as hemispheres in the mud
lend absence to the tree

You're leaving my heart

XI

Surface of the pool
re-assembling tree-trunks
after the non-perspective
of the storm

XII

My nakedness lives secretly
in the echo of a mirror
or against the bare walls

XIII

A question of desire

Meeting another you
black-haired this time

The past and future image blend
and memory's an expectation:
the electricity of skin

Wondering whether each cycle
of oblique relationship
leads to departure is
threatened by time

XIV

Alone again
            then
hands meshing in a taxi

Nighttime
the move to the mouth cups secrecy

        Fragrance of your hair

Having felt the
new dimension of your beauty

I build up disappointment
but your caressing my darkness
as the traffic flickers
forgoes compensation

        XV

Fugitive intimates
pursued by time, fidelities,
finding in the warmth of sexual touch
a brief unfruitful peace

        XVI

Illuminated bubbles
and the carp
lace fins floating

Pale beer in between
and what counterpoint of speech
is communicated by my glance

        XVII

Oranges,
green with a Friday promise:
will the rains hold off?

1966–1968

HALF WAY QUERY

The sudden tunnel: my reflection
in pale, translucent colours rides the wall.
I stare at myself, a somewhat pissed Narcissus –
and, taking in my dishonest, genial countenance,
a disappointed one. I'd come away
from the pool-test eager
for another face than mine.

An ordinary mask of flesh above the beer,
glum, slightly shifty – those tiny eyes:
concealing an intense and usually crestfallen
sexiness, concealing also
its thirst for humour, short temper,
dirty mind. Distorting glasses. Forehead
monthly larger. One twitching eyelid.
Red scars of drink that stain the nose.

Considering the flowers I've gathered,
shapes mouthed, torso, loins,
an oscular worship, call it my
lip-service.
          The train
plunges into late afternoon, a citron sun
illuminating rice-fields.

               Does time contain
more thrilled encounters, thighs touching in a bar,
hands dared to contact, brand-new kiss,
and the first wonderful unclothing? I'm
thirty-five. I must
once more abandon smoking (none to-day);
study the next Japanese lesson (something about
the potential form); finish that intermittent novel;
hone down this poem; read *War and Peace*;
see Angkor Wat; turn quickly into
a rather pouchy, unfulfilled old man.

So many films to see and all those bottles
to empty, cheques to sign. Records for example –
Bartók and jazz, The Spiders, opera.
Presents of yet unseeded flowers. Scarves.

More cat-food. Tickets to mapped capitals.
Some coils of celluloid to capture her
at forty near a crumbling church,
my teen-age daughter in some later morning.
Hubris this but love, hearing the iron wheels
punctuating rails. To-morrows hoard the grandeur
given interval and energy. That's it:
the will – not the desire; the need.

You whom I've just met, two-thirds my age,
don't sense a future breathing down your neck,
the empty weekdays being franked like stamps,
urging the calendar to silence, earth.
Half way, the road you're on starts tilting down;
you hear your breath, count heart-beats in the night,
study your palm for omens and relate
the symptoms in the morning paper to yourself.

The world could well collapse, those mad
old men in charge let off their bombs –
the value anyway disintegrate
as modish sociologists pursue
the smell of tinsel, more and more
illiterate critics start to rule the roost.

Thank God for up to now – for many friends
who care for wit and animals and beauty –
for artists with technique in awe of words
and images, for structures up against
the drab, brown mediocrity of most.

Others appear. My place
is obviously wanted. And
my wife is waiting for a drink. I pay,
and lurch off up the corridors to love.

The sun is lower, all the air
is turning scarlet, seated families
get solemn, peeling tangerines,
or, propped up, snoring by an empty can.
The children sprawl and whine; grey smoke
drifts from enchanting lips; I shoulder past
the guard, the magazine-girl; and apologise
to purposeful old ladies making for the loo.

The revolving power and what it doesn't mean
we take for granted, though
nagged strangely by its allegory –
deceptive speed, the crimson flag,
the gain of landscapes and half-noticed tension –
plus certified arrival in despite
of other figures yesterday at breakfast –
smudged glimpse of television, stretcher-parties,
breath steaming in the darkness through bamboo.
The ticket purchased means we meet the face
at distant barriers; guarantees,
meals later, safety: kisses: talk.
Disasters are impersonal, not ours.
Distorted metal and the voiceless scream
belonging to diurnal fantasies touch
the numbest fringes of security.

Blasé since cheek by jowl with danger all our lives,
we carry on a journey to the night.
Shadows stretch from all the unclimbed hills;
strange cuttings thundered through; exploding light
unfurling such last distances of grass –
one destination; many routes: time to assess
in artificial stillness hurtling somewhere
man's only question posed once more in hope.

FROM MY HOTEL TO YOURS WHOLE SEAS AWAY

Across the bay, from cape to mountain,
winter emerges from the leaves

The cold hotel is silent round my footsteps
Here at the off-season, in a way
under false pretences, having taken
one pace south towards your holiday

The grey sea here shades to your hand,
the warm front curved between us, flecked by darts
Now swirls of vapour thumbprint continents

I imagine you bronzing, my
temporary lover of the ebbing year
My glance goes down the sunlight,
turns after you on dreamed-of streets,
watches you run through breakers, dry on sand

The snowflakes land on spray near the volcano,
whirl round bamboo and palm
The year shifts, opposing climates vie,
eddies of cold drape the peninsula
Shops glow with presents, leather, silk
Crowds at each bus-stop, paradox of sleet
on a city built for summer,
and windscreen-wipers cancelling white stars

A rainbow slants over dark hills
The sun twisting through slow clouds
hints at your distance, my
sweet handler of the dying months

You limit me, I ought to try to you
The raw world gleams,
duties conflict as white piles up on green
The old volcano smokes and winter
sizzles into lava

You mould December to our shape,
lathe it to mystery

Clandestine inabilities
committed here and there from openness –
stirred masculinity appraised:
smiles only we can read: taste of your nakedness

Snowfall on frond and the exposed root
Old truths concealed, a recent landscape softened,
hypocrisies made tangible, gold
reminder of your skin shadowed by whiteness

The crater juts, smoke billows futilely
Your held youth allegoried, flame
and toneless foliage

Inevitable frost has no effect

The brightness lifts again. Snow lours.
A bleak marine wind chaps my face.
You'll walk in noon, rose shorts on,
dark glance weighing lust in others; letting no-one
past the opacity before your thoughts

The new year waits twice round the world;
jigsaws of development: snow: kisses,
deciphered only by eternity –
the way your beauty's to be found
in the lost interval between two photographs

The weather yields enigmas to a chart
No rhetoric forgotten, I relate
the past to climate and success to time
And vulcanologists as darkness settles
wait for the earth to speak again

SENTENCE

And so, meeting once more, we,
for whom at the beginning
only days divided
strangers from sex, having
a winter later forgotten
how soft our alien lips could be,
awakened thigh, the pressing closer
from proximity, yielding to yielder,
withdrawing in the emptied room
from solitude, half shadow
half neon, all we'd achieved
in a brief exposure of desire
the other side of frost, long twilights,
gone in the flow of the dark months
which equalled absence though
the same locale where you
continually came not to be
had coaxed me (the gap above your chair
investing the colours of the background
with a fading ghostliness of you)
to an occasional willed
reflection on your non-appearance –
why; not 'phoning; perhaps; best not to hope –
on jealousy, his nightly hands
frequenting my illicit memory,
to counting on it finally
while the space you'd blotted out
got real and ordinary till
the shock the hour before of seeing you,
kissed, starting the swift absorption,
the loosening from actuality
I'd stressed to my recent darkness
could never be renewed, until
a footstep in the corridor,
the rendezvous I'd warned you of
in the interval between the last
to leave and silence of our touch,
severed us to greet the opening door,
to drop ourselves to casualness,
banalities exchanged as your body
now yards away quivered on mine,

robbed tongues inventing clichés,
imagining all I'd been judged away from –
sense of your passion, re-discovery
of beauty, sunburn, sperm –
knowing at that just not forestallable
intrusion that you might
vanish this time for ever, bequeathing
a hint of what this evening could have done
which now's regret, a nagging rapture,
potentiality condemned
to probable non-repetition,
to us no longer held or hoped for,
a disturbance now re-introduced
to twist my resignation for a spell,
till the removal to a distant name, to
re-estrangement, anonymity.

for Christopher Headington

I.

Grey paper country
gazed at a second ago
through the three dark
indications of bamboo-stalks

II.

Ivory
and jet
dissolve into sunlight
A scarlet fin
brushes the glass

III.

The tempo hangs
clouds the colour of metal
and the haunted sea
lies monochrome
Silent gulls
skim the beach

IV.

Or autumn
The Italian wind
suggests radiance
to the quicker hills

V.

The wet
fragrance of a rose
hinted through mist

VI.

A stealthy moon
gives the ruin
back its secrets

VII.

White
and wine-stains
catch the glint
of the dancer to the guitar

VIII.

The colours flood away
at the afternoon's command
then garishness
wind-brought
blossom

blue clothes on a line
the shine of sand
sails berries flags
returns

IX.

A yellow rent in the weather
black and white
by ringing the grass
and seascape round
use for implication

X.

Curtains at a
southern window
lightly confer
impermanence
to the green façade

XI.

Eccentric lullaby
The silhouette
of Jimbo
and Mr. Pickwick
are seen dancing
Brief fortissimo

XII.

A lake perhaps
the ghost of a shore
a flower's shadow
in mid-air
droops and a boat
one lightening brush-stroke
seems immobile

XIII.

Black used
for zinnias stabbed
in silver
gardens having
a subtler beauty
under rain

(. . . Hommage à Debussy)

TWO POEMS FOR O-BON

(the Buddhist Festival of the Dead; midsummer)

one

Clean the altars.
          Scour
the wood remembering
dead next of kin.
          Their ashes
are gathering energy, emit to love
remembered presences.
          Let
the temple-bell vibrate.

Clean the altars.
          Prepare
the past, a welcome for the past.

And, waiting, pray.

          The ghosts
enter the garden. Familiar
features take shape on the
lamplit leaves.

A sad season (clean,
the altars; longing so,
the garden): chill
inside drab heat.

Make
the whole house an expectation, greeting
the long-lost and the brief-loved.

Who, lightly, blur
the polished wood of the altars:
departing,
move like the faint
shadow of rain across the lanterns,
among us if they ever were
no more again.

two

Half-seen
smiles unmet like mist,
maybe the touch of a hand
resembles dew,
their footprints tentative
cobwebs on the grass.

Spectres
in air-conditioned
cinemas and, suddenly,
footless, shimmering on to the stage.
Tales of melancholy love,
revenge, the green flame
signifying presence.

Phantoms
hiding behind peonies,
dissolving to hard
bones the further side
of tombstones at rendezvous.

AUTUMNS

The unreached peaks accepting frosts, now late butterflies
visit these lower gardens on shrivelling wings.
The fumes from August dissipate, a taller sky
drops clean heat through cirrus air, the absent wind
tasting of snow. Shops spill ripe colours. Youths stroll
in sweaters bright from moth-balls. Sun-glasses, gradually,
unvisoring candid eyes, grow fewer in the streets.

Cold spray these calmer days rolls on deserted sand. Spasmodic breezes
hiss through couch-grass, up-ended barkless twigs, the thorns,
whip crystalline grains around the amber scoop
of a bottle-stump, hone it to safety.
                                        Sinking, at first
an asymmetric sun poised in a lacquer sky –
soon liquid rim to a green, unyielding sea.

One stiff rose here, brown at the edges, lasts.
A nudge to the cherry-trunk brings down leaves.
                                        Fruit,
weighing in lit orchards: the jagged flare of a sunset
gives uncertain chill, the rocks across the garden's wet, turned earth
seen aquarelle.
                A sexless wind must shroud pale claws,
abandoned cowries, one dead hermit-crab, with night –
perhaps the impress our harder loins made on that beach
in an imaginary summer twilight. Now the moon
finds no response in an inked sea. The section of starfish
my raged glance saw then in the blanched darkness –
past your curved shoulder, scented hair,
(our thrown, gritty bathing-trunks somewhere, where) –
absorbed into dull winter.
                          Still thick-green, the heavy oranges
droop with unshimmered leaves; already inside the rind
a suspect yellow starts to flush, foretaste
of the midwinter-sweetened sun.
                                Rot,
hibernation, blaze of decay. October vines
drying to death. A full, puzzling moon swings past
the spurious hoar-glitter of telephone-wires.
                                        Half-light.

Unnatural tramp of a footfall past the bonfire,
ringed isolate in apprehension of the cold:
heliotrope charring their summer as the carp
resign their gayer flash to winter in the scum-dark pond.

Billowing grey of this autumn sunset, cold chip of a moon
through stylised pine-branches, innumerable needles
cracking the star-haze of a lucent sky.
                                        Late typhoons
flay the unseen coasts. Depopulated bay now fogged with salt.
As a three-quarter-moon burns through spread clouds. Time to
pull in one's dreams, a further birthday gone –
the gas-fire reddens, curtains drawn, neglected books
ranged on variegated shelves, the cat's fur moist with warmth.

Dull silver of jewellery below her smile transforms
the fear of November to a human conquest, acknowledged
and protected by each other, steel-cable-web
of a love beyond decision, every day a tightened sense
of the inseparable imposing loyalty.
                                    Frail walls
against the night, chrysanthemum vases, casseroles
spiced with turmeric. Apples throw off what tangerines hoard
of kitchen-neon. Beer gleams straw-yellow.
                                        Forgetting
promises of summer, hemispheres shift. We light
our fragile cigarettes against the cold, retire
behind scarves and thicker blankets, coat the nerves.
                                        Exposed to
recent sun-fierceness, unshielded, now the autumn-children
bring hot-house tokens, glow of ore, to domestic limits, fill
lengthening dark within the winter, prop
beliefs, like infants, in defiance of the frost.

METAMORPHOSES

Six poems on related themes

1   *Lines for Later*

The beauty went halfway. Old metaphors –
now blackmail, hemlock or a scrabbling hand –
no use. Gone, taste of roses, glint
on the eyelid. For wine read lees. As twilight
dividing melody from the usual spasm.
Dream bloodied over, scars
mock hieroglyphics to the pressed
fingertip. Flowers, seemed acrid. Henceforth
bought possibilities only. Musty;
a tarnished mirror in that
echoing house. Apple-cores
round the statue. The garden
of parched lily-ponds in the leaf-browned wind,
given on to. Hidden in scratched
mahogany, private dossier
thumbstained, and photographs
in sepia recession. The held glare
but key to chilly corridors.
Knowing. Watched magnolias
when ephemeral whorls, yes, cream on lip,
masculine twig defying sky,
grim khaki on the gutter. Contempt;
banknotes; third in succession. Crumpled,
dead for spring. A match flaring
again, again, armfuls prepared, what
gladioli even, sections of sun, other-sided
meaning. Cash emptied into the glass
relaying boredom of the stumble up
new and more sterile slopes. Interests crowning
indifferent temples. Contact? Filmed lilt,
the sway into each other's arms,
phased against by fashionable
dissonance: glimpse through the fog
of bygone tune, the acquainted
formality of shape. Years tolled.
Albums prove nothing me; long pause

attaining moonset and the game of dark.
Through all words, all yearning indicated,
hot mud that might heave similes
to alter daylight. Never. To
retire: black records; shelves in four tongues;
magazines. Goading the clock to synchronise
Schubert Lieder to one afternoon,
paragraphs to horizontal preludes, a comely
lead-singer semi-nude to certain
proscribed concepts: us and love
and liberty. Glance trails the nib.
Hands scorched by the futility,
star shoved beneath the flatness once again.
Short-circuit of explanation,
romanticism at last paid off, stubs
accumulating in the ash-tray,
another spring's farewell to rhetoric.

2   *Photographs of Past and Future*

Love's darkness falls. No allies. I'm. Again
the terrible lucidity. Since God's
condemned to death. Glimpsed, areas concealed.
A newer card-trick brightens up the baize.
Unseen excitements. *White boat summer.* Words
like tropic ivy smother form. Once more
now: armpits, arse-curve, hidden hair. Each page,
longing for revelation, turn, read on,
shows glowing food for peace-time, gossamer
on flesh. And ferns. Lay the long-stalked carnation
near the black wine-glass, enigmatic tile,
green steel. Rest from authority, the gods
vast photostatted creatures on the sky.
No notice. *Flap of glittering wave around
the silence.* Where? A conurbation. Each
responsibility. Ours. Tissued. Gaoled
but by ourselves (*shine of the offshore sail*),
the warder has our face, the -er ending
gaoler/prisoner, the same: outflying fist

strikes our own heart. Anew equivocal
the enemy. Have never dared, hacked through
the thrashing rose-trees, picked the wet toy up,
looked round, gone on. Unended book: the first
coiled sentences enough. The paradox
of ransacking the future for the same
dark daffodils we once destroyed. *Flicker*
of sea-light over nakedness. The laws
torn up but nonetheless obeyed. Their tombstones
grey, noble, flaking, choked, both lamp and angel,
by fancy-coloured leaves. Indicative
abandoned, premonition of the past
forlorn. The chill. (Or blasphemies to scare
the obstinate believer. Realm that each
perception maps.) *A pathless sea; the shoals*
not corridors; the signposts, cul-de-sacs;
freedom to stretch the unthronged skies on one's
own peril. There. And no reply. Felt object
to justify. And something knifes me off
from that, some nothingness. The orchids burnt
by frost. Conservatory forgotten, the
brocade now mildewed in the drawing-room;
the lawn is rank, the fountains smell, upstairs
the radiators permanently off.
Depart for the endless second. Once again
spray fanning slowly, frozen in warmth, the sun
immobilised. A June. The crowds who can't
die either, elbow abstracts, pelting with
busy, unseeing eyes for trains they caught
last week, the year before, a decade hence.
Roar of the surf unheard, weeds of the past
grip with tenacious celluloid, that house,
an uncle, when, what me was that, ahead
a sprint downhill, gash in the cinders, last
questioning glance of terror. *What white dawn,*
marine escape, captured behind what lids
before the emptiness. Extinguished still.

3   *Conditional Present*

'Rough gale rubbing the trees. Nose chipped,
the statue intermittently
perceived, bay, privet, yew,
copper-green. Once
focus, dead feet for rendezvous,
ground stained, world darker.
Steps dragging. Far. Too few.
If thunder. Wreck the coloured globe
of crocus, dog-rose, creeper,
last insult of chrysanthemum. So;
green. Brown. Estate denuded.
The harder task is grass and mud,
bark, handkerchiefs of sky. To clothe
with night, starless clouds.
The lamp's beam stops
on cornice, grubby mantelpiece,
bare boards, and panes that make
a limit for the light. Eyes closed.
Torch off. Wind sound. Proliferation,
locked up in one's own vividness,
of eddying dreams . . .
Child's hands part the wistaria,
in the fringed gloom femur, skull,
vertebrae; unseeing eyes
locate the tennis-ball.
Retreating laughter. Puzzled
to be here as the game
dies away. Cold silence falling.
Bizarrely, metal, gems,
scattered. Heirlooms lost from light.
Emeralds twisted round grey bones,
a battered crown, dun rubies
along the diseased knuckle . . .
Here in the half-light and not here.
There in the room's consciousness,
storm outside, lightning on rose,
and yet not there. If him,
here, then. Who never was.
Ghosting the self outwards
to printed lives, wreathing

old drawer of papers, younger garden,
clipped blossom shrivelled
in a former room. Whose
profiles, spectral in wrong seasons.
Snuffed. The black, commanded.
Whittling awareness down to here,
this draught, this emptiness.
And conquest partial only: night;
then; ever-present. Re-discovered.'

4   *Divers Gods*

In the ripped darkness, night's accretion.
Bloom still of self: the baseless nightmare;
visage caught curved on tumbler, a phoenix
circling round no centre.
Obedient camera tracing then
the movement of a thigh. Proud
mouth-slant. Waiting sex
that maddens with heaviness.
Invention. Depeopled street.
Glance clashing, etched smile,
façades, bus-stops, alleys,
a proceeded blur. Door-jamb,
pale carpet, curtains rasping.
Obverse, the truth. If eye unmet.
Absorbed impersonally in the throng.
The tensions of worship. Imply
a lone return. Paperweights
posed on a familiar desk
where recognitions still attend.
Imagined fabric forever
unstretched over naked loins. To
attempt again. Wind on the hill,
gorse sparked to sharper yellow, drop
of sheer rain from cromlech to a
disturbed sea. Stamped rituals
on worn moors. In the near-distance
bright cliffs of a retreating glacier.

Stained bones to hack out soil,
weird skins for clothing; ochre,
madder, prefiguring gods
on dry cave-wall, the presences
to come, swirled mist, dark sunlight.
Hard curve through cotton. Slightly moist.
Down on to it, fingers in my hair,
naked past my firmed lips.
Rough this or tenderness? Perform
the same, let him lead. This then,
mouth grab for taste. My hand
works in the sac, hearing
a protest moaned he doesn't mean,
go harder. Am tugged myself,
twisted, wrung. Across
aeons the summoned rainbow.
Whirl down through infra-red
from savagery to savagery,
dance after the ice-age, writhe
on a borrowed bed, the partner exiting
unclasped, never had, illusory.
The storm allows to intermittent silence
in-gathering of selves: memory
or fallacy. The same desires.
Eliminated self surprised
in words, *flash of sea-view from the train,*
advertisements for sunset, evocative
designs of rain. Softer questions
jigsawing more than physical
identities. White splash
on my tongue. What references.
Lumber of spare-rooms, china, astrolabe,
corded encyclopaedias, burst
hinges of labelled suitcases,
crammed escritoire, the aquatints
stacked face against the wall,
wax fruit, warped tennis-racquet.
His sleeping eyelids clamped
on what defenceless I revealed.
Blaze of the sky on furniture,
transfigured dust, random
litter in the unsewn night,
more words, more coloured

photographs, unfinished blossom. The
whirring of tired resuscitated wings.
Thus wakefulness, stirred penis from the scene
of its destruction. Tentative flight
migrates to nowhere. Glass
of garnet wine, brown fingers
on the stem. Skeining the self,
the metal hyacinth remains
diffusing dreams. And inescapable.
Reborn from momentary suicide,
enquiry close to unobserved
experience, constructing
endless futures, endless pasts.
In the ripped darkness, night's accretion.

5   *Some Definitions of Heroic*

Hemmed in by fire, noting
the appearance of the thing more than
the thing itself. Cut off, the whole
stage roseate, music pounding
as the free arc scorches
nearer, nearer. Heavy gold
ringing my finger, the voice of the god
punishing from the past, committed now
to what is being done. Given
identities based on feeling, hope
leaps from euphoria, humiliations
tempered by irony to a wry
success. Corrective view the product of
sticky day, article read, sudden
laughter irrelevant from behind
made relevant. Oneself that prince,
prat-faller, a pansy Siegfried
past it on a darkening earth.
Belief's ignited: rapacity beheld
as smiling. Tracked. (To where
the long tiger-roses proffer blooms,
maroon and cinnamon, Nile, jet-blue.

With equidistant dreams not quite
unrealised – both, groping in the glare,
have brushed perhaps the semblance of
a similar flower. Aching with sunlight,
loins hard and naked, dazzled,
hair matted, unhearing, encased
in crashing brilliance, and
an inch's separation only
of coursing gold. Impersonal.
Fluent in fire a brighter danger. Leaving
charred aces juxtaposed on forgotten teak –
since trumped by unexpected jacks,
crimson, flaring. And defeat, if that,
prophesied for ever on drab
cyclostyled instructions from
a bureaucratic angel.
(Return to the land of bronze dreams,
mouth glittering with night, my back
beaded with gold dew. More likely,
mordantly, in the blazing garden
a solitary figure shouting
messages to himself; unseeing; risible.
The space for unpaid freedom shrinks.
My heart, reviewed, disjoins.
The profile vacillates, transparent,
and, as I gaze, you go. Nurtured,
suicide growing day by day
in the hot-house of the lungs.
Objects themselves take on
positions of command. Geometry:
existing only at
the intersections album
to red midsummer cherry-leaf
makes with the line
from record-sleeve towards
discarded underclothes,
imprint of sex's heat
imagined on the linen. Talk, dead.
Some cool jazz on: in-turned
acidity, the brass and darkness
revolving; development
inside the circle as sound
evokes silence. Whose house

a thought gone always. Again where.
Dared, the doors of mist,
each vision on its own;
oolite and fissure; glimpsed,
the woaded dancer and the rain-god,
boy actor balancing
on slender shoulders what
invisible to him oppresses
adults with the words of tragedy.
And a solution beyond us still
in our control. Fighting down
superiority's arias. The dark
lyricism of hatred. No time
for heroes with their blackjack
of honesty. Discretions. Round
the corner of the yard
sub-tropic leaves provening.
And disallowed. The orchestration
brushed on, soft note on note.
(Following an anonymity
for all the minutes of a street,
tight cleft below canvas belt,
uneven corridor of day
between his legs. The table's
borrowed calm, svelte nouns,
long quiet from trumpet. By-passed
the problems of involvement,
self-respect curdling, their fault,
no guiltlessness, keep the connections clear,
the sudden afternoon, child
and wife asleep, curved on their side,
sun dropping, neighbours' chatter,
trees heavy with summer.
(Hand's-breadth of soft hair between
the jut of collar-bones, in another
thoughtful room, smooth otherwise,
the two coins of flesh dark on his chest.
Legs faunlike, feet uncloven,
languid tool at the end of daylight
a challenge for heroes to unsleep. Guide
to the joy of nowhere, aimlessly;
a honing-down of moments
to extinction. Onus of

step taken, wedlock, issue. Matched
metaphors by themes, the two
irrevocable; ironic
bridges (game and iron thoroughfare)
coaxing duets to yet a re-want;
palmed aces and bribed guards,
the same ingredients of
a different patience with
one flame-singed pack. Shuffle.
New pattern: tramping to and fro. No
exit, despite the use of currency,
past either frontier. Underneath,
the sunset torrent foams. Poised
on no-man's-land. Gossip
of integrity with similar
wanderers. Fugue and shift.
And overlapping time
subsumed. Thickens now
within my grasp. Desired
expense achieving
nothingness. And his. Dissolved.
)Blond)period)wig)doffed,
the silk-lined wolfskin changed.
At last the lights extinguished
to an emptied theatre, no tickets sold.

6   *Climbing a Volcano*

Justification. Or bygone epics
that support a previous
ignition. Lava-stone
culled over mist, sulphur
dyeing the sun above the crater,
clamps dog-eared notes to a deal
surface. After evening,
grey television-light
and neon couched in plastic throw
illumination on scrawled dreams.
Wind takes the smoke. Perfection,

killed each sunset. Interpret.
Words in no language, perhaps
adulterous thoughts, him gone, explanation
deriving from outdated themes. Getting
merged with other difficulties,
vases and photographs and myths,
such meaningless significance,
the quickened image to belie
a subsequent collapse. Soft rock
and shifting sunsets. Ash all round.
A yellow falsity of light: what was
shored-up romanticism left
menaced. Can who proclaim
without a wound, badge
glory with no relationship
untouched. God's orphans. Stumbling.
The place for wet bracken, noon-coloured
hydrangeas drooping in the green
above, the sundial, gravestone, all
crisscrossed to by questioning feet.
Inside the emptied drawing-room,
phantom of concert, fibres of waltz on waltz,
blare, gloss, as the 'cellos the
tone of exposed chestnut
alter under arc-lights. Weave of past dust.
A burnt twilight. Still
sexuality of filched autumns.
Erotism in black and white.
Boy masturbating. One cool flower,
the purchased vase a coarser blue,
transposed. Private, the sweetness shed
in nervous indulgence, drying
on your cloth, my flesh. Fold
of carnation on itself,
the ceiling darkening, sunset
required. Alone. Extension
nowhere. Rainfall
on non-existent earth, senses
shut off from twenty years ago,
blinded to next year's diary.
Petals now humus. No
welding offered between
the game that might have once been played

and the strange adult streets
you pace on when you've seen
parental corpses lying in the bleak
provincial morgue. Where back to.
What electric thread. None. Memories
disallowed and on to some
ever-created kingdom. Surety
slain, links rusty. Pronounced
guilty of deicide in
the interim between the touch of flower,
the glimpse of nudity, proof of now.
Beneath, always, the piled
mountain. In dark water, shaking emblem.
Areas of love. Interrogated thought. If I
has been destroyed who am.
Débris. All wanted,
vision gone, the orange sun
rules light on every other stair.
Patterns. Cold well-chain pulling up
from nothingness the subsequent . . .
taste over, slackening . . . still . . .
heaved range on the horizon
unassailed . . . forever . . . the stone
unrobbed . . . yet. Frontier closer.

May–October, 1968

A House Against The Night
(1976)

TO MY GODCHILDREN

Robert Leach
William Johnson
Harriet Bakewell
Philip Reeves
Madeleine Lanzer
James Reeve
Katja Weitzenböck

CLOSING IN

das aussichtslose
ist keine karriere

— HANS MAGNUS ENZENSBERGER

Winter comes on and I am trapped.
    Long lyrics
that coil their sameness round the day.
    The town sags.
A last boat linked the harbour.
    To the north
the frost is splintering escape.
    Rust-darkness.
Signs creak in a blade of wind.
    Pointless tasks
on quay or side-street make up a career.

The cold sea organises its blockade.
    Noon now a
mockery, sail, martin, sapling, emblems
    of the gone.
Time hangs behind its cobwebs. In the wings
    a figure
absent at rehearsals waits his cue.

All whys proved cul-de-sacs.
    The darker
birthdays stack. Blunt pencils, dust, as
    said before.

ANNIVERSARY

We smile licitly
in a hired house,
aliens by a dying
Christmas tree, the dust
accumulating
on bright ornaments
and paper angels.
You return for the
moment to your book;
cat sprawled and glinting
in my lap; fire-quiet;
early Schumann on –
the madness waiting
at the long end of
a black-cut spiral.

Winter shaking the
windows, night displays
no barbed branches to
our met gaze: children
in cold sunlight, pram
and trailing plastic
dog. A hard red buds
on empty twigs of
japonica; cards
too remember prints
of another scared
maternity made
poignant again this
closing year that needs
such ambiguous
promises of peace.
Dilemmas of food,
pollution, torn hints
of war, diurnal
reminders of guilt
at being happy:
guilt at giving life
threaded as often

with improbable
convictions of hope.

But when, cancerous
poisons dropping with
the rain, can ever a
swollen planet have
looked darker. Affirm
with what small comforts –
teaching, giving, up
over the stretched wires,
concentration-camps
of doubt. Belief in
what?

      Easy, darling,
in one spent gesture
of love, ivory
of your nude body
on cushions, the room
silent to a now
humming gramophone:
I, damp and ebbed, watch
radiant our peace,
thinking once more of
effortlessness or
of private concern
in this area of
apparent safety.
No answer to that
iron question, life
for any quartet
having the nature
of evasion: shared
harmony while the
records last and then
the pressure of fear
beyond frail walls.

          Back
to a glittering
insanity a
century ago.

Incarceration –
captive, imbecile –
related to a
general problem here
and now: convenient
polarities of
schizophrenia, once
fertile tenets which
allowed commitment
cheek by jowl with dream.
Till as at present
the proportions go,
the split widens and
into the made gap
drips lunacy. No
longer both contained
separate in one,
the extrovert in
fact the obverse of
the same damned coin. The
two selves match, the wry
perceptions curdle,
spinning imbalance
into terrified
sunlight, flickering.
Superimposed, the
sombre personae
blur, identical,
divorced for ever,
with Eusebius in
the end becoming
Florestan. Alone
with the demands of
social being. When,
unreconciled, a
darkness edges in,
the heart contracts and
sections of conscience
start to rot.

       Where is
belonging on a
globe of unmet friends

and set against an
ever-cancelled past?
Contraceptives may
in theory form a
reply to fingers
levelled at famine:
despite the edicts
of crazed celibates,
a two for threatened
two seems reasonable.
What help though can there
be in stressing mere
consolidation?
We are, have, knew. And
yet what illnesses
privately prevail.
Wishing mankind can
live one day by some
love, some beauty, we
try to juxtapose
the scent of memory
and the colours of
tomorrow, plant bulbs
in lengthening autumn
or watch our children
dreaming their silence.
The future stops now
where my pen concludes.

This rented place with
oranges falling
loans us asylum
on a dual journey,
the blank pages in
unbought calendars
noting the mooted
quandaries from next year.
Romantics had their
own limited pain;
ours should reach out to
the rent corners of
shot–up villages
and dying mothers

in a wilderness
of tortures.

Yet love
subsumes what's here or
was, continued yearn
for a tomorrow.
If this is nonsense,
if those who know none
but the normal dreads
are presumptuous,
unorthodox, then
what remains? The dark
equation only
easily foreseen.
Insanity of such
a world, wars all our
lives, a weary list
of greed, bombardments
and the public wrong.
Improvements read in
the palm of history
(and clung to in my
innocent youthtime)
unfulfilled. Ancient
proofs of Roman games,
of inquisitions,
a bracing saga
of the fall of man
retold as gradual
rise. Each chronicled
brutality weighed
cheerfully against
what's dubbed a growing
moral consciousness.
Such tired debates
holding no holy
water to our time.

Or take in their lieu
a Brueghel landscape
in a gilt frame, skaters
caught transitory

on some red evening.
The tenor lists the
ironies of spring
and lovers in an
August garden leave,
the sequence over,
pledged flowers on the lawn.
A woodcut mist like
spray fans over sharp
peaks dyed with maples
as we synchronise
our more fortunate
watches to other
menaced scenes.

         Inside
the gloom, tentative
movements day by day
are dared despite what
prognostications
soon and dead achieve.
We pay, along with
many, penalties
of ordinariness.

Textures of horror
coloured like our own
guilt blanket a sky
once white with all the
aspirations of
eternity. No
more. The universe
shrinks to the evil
neighbour in our heart
and atavistic
mirrors of knowledge
show us ourselves.

         Here,
with a confined flame,
not unaware of
tonguing shadows in
the square of family

it illuminates,
we emphasise, by
living by it, its
light worth: to have our
problems offered here,
concrete, is something,
tangible ogres
to wrestle with. Cash,
a baby's mucus,
heartburn, injections,
one's health fucked up, a
ready grave – cosy
finalities not
able to touch the
newer night-times man's
ingenuity
thinks up each day.

    Doomed
wish to share in one
sublunary map
of terrors still a
shone belief. Leaving
heroic tales to
literature: as Brecht
said, Woe betide an
epoch in need of
epics. Newsreels each
evening unfold
appalling tests of
bravery required
over and above
the still too normal
heritage of ills:
un–run–from facts that
inescapably
urge major memory
of the uncured sin.

Our skulls unable
to contain light-years
of space, exploding
stars, the absolute

zero of anguish,
statistics tell their
interesting lies to
sated consciousness.
No balm. And charity
must, in self-defence,
dwindle honestly
to such unselfish
precision. Living
eighteen hours a day
with data of this
breaking magnitude
proves ultimately
negative.

     And so,
our daughter on my
lap, primaeval son
lifting a wary
head, you clothed in blue
hanging sheets up in
a sparkling garden,
linger cherished and
untypical. Gone
in their way the days
of faith, a fragile
thanksgiving remains.

Five years, two children,
recollections of
three continents, one
love.

     All we can do
after a thousand
lost arguments, is
limit, cultivate,
the tried humanist
panacea. Brahms
and cakes. The minor
risks posed up against
shrivelling days of joy.

Kugahara, 28 December 1968

SPRING 1604

A new land or
the same land reached
in negative.
                    Dark blossom.
                              Near
the now silent sundial
a trio plays, faces half-hidden,
a sour deception.
                    April arrives
and all the green's one curse.
The gangster and the pimp invade the courts,
force innocence at knifepoint and convert
pavanes to blasphemy.
                    Purpose
of magic now to sever friend from friend.
Daylight's a spill of mist, and night
is absolute between the sputtering torches
glinting on shed blood.
                    Pierced
memories of other Mays,
the wonder echoing from seashore
and riverbank and glade. Dazzle
the one ingredient of all,
each kiss was rimmed with sun,
disguise postponed delight.
                    That gold
has hardened to a killing blade,
the poisoned rain
leaves iridescent pools in ditches,
rots the rose.
                    Beyond the future,
unconsoling now,
what unimagined island may
blend fair with foul, bring what's thought lost
back dripping radiance from the sea?

CONTAINERS

Denn mit Göttern
Soll sich nicht messen
Irgend ein Mensch.
— GOETHE

Paring it down
to skins of crystal,
the clever shoals of winter —
unseen sands
dragged to dry patterns,
ridge and furrow,
contour-lines wavering —
an unshook heat
quivering with fuchsia.

Water fluted,
the bent pale stems
upright in air.
This side, the substance,
dimension and thickness,
self known as well
as what's apprehended
in an occurrence
reduced to cold canvas,
unreachable gleam
ghostly in pane
and a surprise
ambushed in mirrors.

Description, correlative,
lucid and lying,
faking results
from the transcription,
chance juxtaposed
only as long as
distraction allows,
ellipsis of circumstance,
surface depicted.

Time fleeces the blossom.
Moving the object

subtracts or increases
pigment or shadow.
Altered relations:
discoloured the leaf
coming to terms
with the intrusive.
Offered again
a novel decoding;
lens picks on absence,
fixes a challenge.

Kept, the flower dying
vased in the darkness.
The warm air is locked
a hair's-breadth from blizzard.
Trapped, the split second –
impermanent print
already receding
from what it had imaged,
the still less immortal twin
shreds to finality.

Since we reside
endlessly fictive,
fleeting assurance
feigns a repose: –
thus a device
relied on for truth,
as tarnished and flaking
silver eventually
loses its gift,
and while we stare
we are discarded
fibre by fibre
bringing lacunae,
shattered, disfiguring.

The fresco's designs
robbed of precision
fragments of scarlet
litter the flags.
Praising a depth
we know's non-existent

still as we gaze
space is revealed
within our reflection
and the bare patches
expand by default;
limitless, terror-filled,
unstarred, despairing,
all we achieved
questioned by method,
caged in a cell
of ephemeral glass.

THE INHERITANCE

for Christopher Hampton

Comes into the room. Entrance
centre left. Fairly rapid. Limping. Stops
three paces in. Early sunlight though door
kept ajar, straw gel, angle ten degrees.
Pause. Jingle of carriage departing.
Moves upstage, draws back heavy
floor-length curtains from french windows.
Late March landscape. Flat meadows. White effect
on cyclorama. Flood of light
opening the stage. Mahogany furniture.
Dark red wallpaper, floral design.
                                    Frock coat,
black hair, cravat. Takes in the room,
noting big portrait of a man, middle-aged,
over mantelpiece back right, gilt frame.
Sofa up left, overstuffed chairs, occasional
table, silver-mounted miniature,
bric-à-brac. Crosses to harpsichord down right.
Plays, facing audience. A Rameau piece.
Woman enters silently through door right.
Long grey dress, cameo. Watches him.

Count five. 'You're back.'
                                At first
no reaction, then, speaking over music,
'As you see.'
                        Piled blonde hair, taller
than him, beautiful. Moves to door left,
looking out, full light on her. He stops,
fitting cigarette into ivory holder,
lights it, observes her though the smoke. Then,
'You haven't changed.'
                                'I know
(*Back still towards him*). From
the pier-glass, that is.'
                                'But it has been
difficult?' 'Yes, difficult.
The long snow. The suicide.
You know.' 'And you resent –'
'What?' (*Turning*).
                                'My absence.
Presumed lack of interest.'
Shrugs. Breaks downstage.
'The boredom of it. The length
of winter. No-one to help . . . (*Pause*)
He was here.'
                        'Who?' (*Fingers
the keyboard*).
                        Gesture of impatience,
'Do I need to say?'
                                Half smile,
'Not really.'
                        'Well he has. Been here,
I mean.'
                'I see.'
                        'Enquiring.'
'About me?'
                        She stretches, inelegantly,
'Was the train crowded?'
                                '"Enquiring",
that's good. Yes, very: no seat all night.
And they lost a trunk.'
                                Exiting abruptly,
'I'll go and see about some breakfast.'
He stubs the cigarette and rises.

Drifts centre undecidedly, shaking coins
in the pocket of his plus-fours. Young man
appears in the embrasure, brown hair,
very handsome, silhouetted against
the low hills, thick foliage
of July. Warm midday tones.
He hears a step, turns, 'My sister
said you'd been here.'
                Pause. 'Did she?
(*Comes down to him, leaving*
the dozen roses he'd been carrying
on the arm of the sofa). And how's
the thronging capital? What was it
The Gazette said of the new novel?
"An artist of sureness", yes,
that was it.' Laughs. White flannels
grass-stained at the knee. Bare arms.
'I'm glad you found it funny.'
Faces him. They both smile. Long
passionate embrace. Young man
breaks first. Sits in tubular steel chair right.
'Perhaps I should marry her.'
                      'My sister?'
'Of course.'
          'Keep it in the family anyway.
(*Moves to ornate cabinet up left*)
Cocktail? Just time before lunch.'
Studies his nails, 'You know,
your father's . . . death was –'
'She described it: "difficult".'
'Something of an understatement. I did
naturally what I could.'
                Flashed smile,
'I know that.'
           Door left, thrown open,
'They've found it. The trunk. (*She sees*
the young man) Oh – hullo. (*Impatient again*)
It was at the station all the time.
They're bringing it up on the bus' (*Touches*
her shingled hair).
              'Oh good,
because . . . (*Shakes the cocktail*)
there're valuable things in it.'

Pause. Then, with a light sneer,
'New manuscript, I suppose?
Don't be too long, I'm – Oh
(*Moving to the sofa*) what lovely
chrysanthemums. Thank you' (*Takes them up,
stands a moment awkwardly, goes off,
slamming the door*).
                        The high slopes
indicate autumn. Sunless day.
Vase of beech-leaves on the
white upright. He crosses to the stool,
maroon smoking-jacket, paisley
handkerchief spilling from top pocket.
'These damned Octobers. A wait
while the year prepares decease.
Nothing to do.'
                        Young man to him,
padded shoulders, gaudy tie,
signet ring. Touches his arm,
'Play something. Chopin. Lament
for time. (*He starts the Third
Ballade*) There's no hope, you know. None at all.
For us, I mean. Never was. It's all over,
stillborn.'
                        Pause. Music only.
Sudden smash of hands on the keys.
'Over! To hell with that. Unbegun.
(*Rises*) Oh . . .' (*Takes his hands*).
Pause.
                Tear-stained, 'You see, it's not
possible, we'd –' (*Runs off
on to the terrace, vanishes left*).
Fade FOH. Cyclorama dimmed.
Patter of rain. Landscape beyond
the windows sombre. She re-enters,
brown jumper, rope of pearls, tweed skirt,
'I can't help missing him.'
                                Attempt
at tenderness, right centre,
'I know that.'
                'He used to come here
almost every day. I mean, he came for you,
there was never any chance . . . He would turn up

hoping it was one of the rare occasions
you'd deigned to put in an appearance.
(*Siren. She lifts her head*) The third
today.'
      'I thought it'd be quiet
after the capital.'
          'No, they've started here.
Every afternoon about this time. It's
the new armaments factory
down by the weir.'
          Drone of aircraft.
'When did you see him last?'
'Just before he left. In uniform.
Joking. Saying he'd be a field-marshal
in no time.'
        Pause. 'I had a letter.'
'Of course.'
         'Saying I was missing a lot
because of my gammy leg.
(*Explosion off. Slight hint of a flash
outside french windows left. He shivers*)
That was near.'
         'I thought you'd be used to it.'
'Up there I am, happens every day. Somehow
here, I didn't expect it. The more
frightening.'
      Sudden
access of gentleness, 'I wish
you'd come and live here. Just
the two of us.'
        Turning away right,
picks up suède jacket from the chairback,
swings it across shoulders. Green polo-neck.
'I'll go and unpack.'
         'Just
the two of us.'
      Stops, practically
a whisper, 'I can't.'
        Sighs,
'No, I understand.'
         'I really can't.
It – it'd be – no good' (*Quick exit*).
Long pause. She moves up centre

out on to terrace. Bathed now
from an amber flood off
upstage right. The mountains
dark at the foot, peaks
gilded. Stage in shadow
save for flicker of grey
from television-screen, the sound off.
Young man enters centre left, khaki torn,
bandages smeared with blood, the stains
black in the light. She concentrates
on the sunset, eyes puckered, never once
turning to him through the whole of the scene.
He seems to look in her direction, 'It's cold.'
Pause.
   'He's been here.'
        'Bitterly
cold. I'm shaking. (*Pause*) Who?'
'You know. My brother.'
        'I can't see
anything. It all hurts. And the cold.
Where are you? I can hear a voice,
woman's voice.'
      'I remember
so many tentative moments, walks
on the outskirts of the forest,
reading his books together,
commenting.'
      'Who are you? Please
(*Hand groping*). Take me somewhere.
Into the warm.'
      'Wishing
he were here. And laughing together even.
Sometimes at any rate.'
        '*Please* . . .
The shrapnel. Blood.
A film of ice over the bandage.
I can't see. Listen! I don't know where . . .
Just pain. All pain.'
        'I miss you.
I miss you almost every day.'
Blackout. When the lights go up
snowscape under moonlight, the room
in semi–darkness, most of the furniture

gone, squares of darker colour
where there were pictures on the white-washed walls.
No curtains. He sprawls in the one armchair
centre left, visible in the bright grid
of window-frame thrown by the moon
across the floor. Steel-blue gels,
frosts on them, 1000 watt. Right hand
in jacket-pocket, large shiny photograph
lying in his lap. Shirt unbuttoned,
threadbare jeans, unshaven. She enters right,
soft yellow flood off illuminates her;
pauses in the doorway, flicks the switch;
standard-lamp comes on left of chair,
big light on table centre. She leans against jamb.
Noise of a jet-plane, high, fading to silence.
Pause. 'It's late.' Quilted ankle-length
white dressing-gown.
                          He stirs; removes hand
from pocket; tears deliberately the photograph
into tiny pieces, littering the floor;
replaces right hand. She comes to table;
picking up travelling-clock, adjusts the hands
glancing at her wrist-watch; winds it;
sets it down. Takes paperback,
'Why do you stay?'
                          Tonelessly,
'I've unpacked. At least,
taken out the things I need.'
                          Flicks pages,
'God, this was a bad book, one
of your very worst. Can't think
why it's been reprinted (*Throws it down*).
You'll have to get out eventually. I've
decided to sell, get rid of it all,
move, go somewhere else, try
(*Hands pressed to eyes*) to begin again.'
Silence.
          'I hear you' (*Withdraws
revolver from righthand pocket,
examines it absently
under cover of the chair-arm*).
Hands down to cheeks, 'What
are you doing?'

'Nothing' (*Calmly*).
Replaces it. Rises. To her.
'I only wish –'
                    Uncovers her face,
looks at him, almost
fear in her expression, 'What?'
                              He takes
her hands from her neck, kisses her
on the forehead, 'Nothing' (*Limps
quickly right, switching off the lamps
as he goes, shuts door behind him*).
                              Gesture
of impatience. Then, moves slowly
through rectangles of moonlight to the armchair,
kneels on the floor beside it,
picks up the shreds of photograph
one by one, reassembles them
on the cushion. Long pause. Gunshot off.
No reaction, simply carries on
gathering the fragments as the curtain falls.

THE CHARTS

Your tenderness
enquires of me
certain truths, a
strangeness.
            Knowledge
of want perhaps,
limits of a
greyish square, streets
radiating
to shadows of
other districts,
herbs in window-
boxes, figures
posting letters,

hose glittering on
grass, and ploughed fields
glimpsed past sparser
houses.
          Each time
illuminates
elsewhere, marble
steps, clock by the
mirror, summer
curtains gauzing
damsons in bloom,
bookshelves, other
geographies
of absence to
be shaded in.

We meet and love
and disappear
again, no kiss
providing more
than a report
on the moment,
lovers in touch:
melting then to
isolate times,
a shred more of
evidence for
the spread map and
the gentlest of
missives left on
the table for
perusal at
a later date.

LACUNAE

White wind
incessant over moorland.
Figures in a cold ache of love
unspoken.
                    Thus
the premise. Add
restraint. With a fourth figure,
inexperience.
Such ghosts to blow across the past.

Who may forgive beyond the grave
although
the rent in innocence remains
distorting the reflection.

Winter. The dance haunts memory.
Fox-tracks on snow,
the rime-stiff bracken,
a blank acknowledgement of widowhood,
her son to run with.

These distant images bring pain.
The tors stood out,
first greyness on the silence.
If there was laughter,
the echoes carried isolation,
companionship
struck stone.
The sky unyielding soon became
the wrong familiarity,
mirrored a lack.

And now apology.
Stick fast in recollection
to the plea unuttered then.
Grafting experience attempt
a vanished prophecy,
lend a maturer glance.

Of understanding. Or
of tolerance. Who can condemn
the youth I was,
the need of unfulfilment.
Cling hard to undeveloped moments
baffled by change.

And grasp this later spring
before the bloom is spectred
past recall. From loss;
from knowledge of this mute
late-realised compassion try
no further error, but
placate what went
and was irrevocable.
The burden stays, its weight
eternal warning.

One other scene
years earlier although
mimetic of the same.
A childless couple at the gate
dividing the white August château
from the cobbled square.
Their invitation to the callow boy
refused. The dust.
Dry trees. And churchbells.
                         Then here too
a reticence obtrudes,
pulls out the guilt
and substitutes a pattern for
what I would not recall.

Lost masks receding,
frost whitening the traces by the wayside,
though the reproach
yet glinting from the eyeholes
still pursues.

The August Notebooks

for Lynn, every season

The Place

The maps, studied beforehand
in the shut city, as always
were misleading –
heights decorously given,
inlet, afforestation,
settlement: offering no hint
of what might not be there –
a darker isthmus, low green island,
toothed rage of stone.
                  A laziness of form
the words surround, changed lace
to splay and pull eventually the seaweed;
black contour-lines,
clustered, dilating,
invisible on tree'd irregular slopes.

    2

    A thin grey road
glimpsed mounting from the bay.
    Lush the unseen highlands
snowbound in four months.
    Today's easy descent
infrequent as adventure.
    Familiar sporadic faces
and local gossip over wine.

Return, once summer landscape getting colder.
The safety of an untried habitat.
This August way a source for casual glamour,
unpeopled now.
                The blizzards swirl,
the line back to the capital cut off.

3

Mirages in the sliding north:
a sprawled arm of mainland
detaches to open sea.
The sun–glow on roan stretches –
yachts – underwater shadows.

Never to know what works.
Effect and fingered colour.
This tinkering with weather,
nudging the unsought phrase aside,
then, now.
   Re-punctuating.
Place of tenses. If
the apparent meaning lost,
arranging fatal.

4

Clouds crown a new-found sky.
(The rain came later, squall
thrashed upon twilight, lining
inaudibly into the sea.)

Routinely, a half-empty train
brushes the undergrowth
from yesterday.
   And tilts
after the watershed to more sedate
farmhouses, sudden
surprising garages, the terminus.

5

Futures at last reduced
to luggage, midday sweat.
 The crowded bus, at swaying
angles hillside, drop to surf.
 Dumped at a crossroads nowhere, slog on foot
and two sides of a room on to the bay.

All afternoon sea-falcons calling.
Sheer vegetation and the high
yellow needles of rock
dissolved in mist.
This could not have been foreseen.

Vocabulary
that traffics in precision.
The certain heat,
reek, squabbling, asylum,
escape a winter annotation.

6

Thereafter only
waiting for the rain
as inky localised haze
beyond the offing
from far pale fangs of rock
sweeping closer
unease of problems
waiting on departure and
encouraging departure.
Ever impatience
otherwhere than here,
treating by the moment
moments to recall,
life led in the fore-reckoning
of retrospect,
deduction never though
in that explaining
masks the excuse.

7

Maybe the circumscription is
too soon envisaged, drabness,
poverty. What's done disliked
or gone through passively,
the summer at an end,
the brightness over.
Tortured perhaps only
unconsciously, something

pressing on the awakened
dream. Landscapes
to a slower repetition,
knowledge of fear and ageing:
tawdry contempts, willed
shelving, such
cold elbows from the past,
and all the few
recapturable lights.

8

Intimations of peace –
an isolated house, high view,
locality to dwell inside,
as ideas trick evasion
round the core. The love
deals merely in the obvious,
the major snags jut through the dream,
are never faced.

9

Home in its adequacy far
and the familiar closer.
All lesions of the hour and place
are healed through distance;
tensions created
unbearable politeness
that grates on love.

10

An afternoon sea-feeling.
Brown sunlight lazy on the floor.
The three of you post-prandial.

Salt atmosphere
blurs the lugged notebook.

Dichotomies the autumn
will unravel.
A strained decoding,

sharpened, falsified.
What was delved up
melts into morning.

11

Rain on a dark tide
and arrival. A distant
spray-silent cape
and the bare islands.

12

Too pink for these middays, my son
squats white-hatted on the shingle,
and finicking picks only up
the paler stones for hurling.

My daughter takes my hand,
marches me past the harbour to
a minimal point she's eyed.

Stepping (occasionally) over
the cables that maintain the fishing-boats,
we wade ungracefully through swirling water,
creeks that could nurture limpets, corsairs, mermen,
and scramble up a sharp, adventurous rock
that's meant for waving.

                        Too far
to shout and hamstrung by embarrassment,
we semaphore. He doesn't notice,
over-preoccupied with choice of pebbles –
he's probably myopic too
like both his parents,
both his grandfathers.
She sees us, lifts an arm.
My daughter, distracted by cormorants,
looks in the wrong direction.
My wife and I signal alone.

13

The rocks
grow pale at nightfall
and the horizon lingers
a strip of glow beneath the rain.

The saline feel,
unlikely light on cliff-face;
the far-off camps are sending up
brief fireworks before dark.

14

The night is moist.
A shrouded sky
pricks the attention on to sound,
the restless sea.
Invisible the tug at isle and shingle.

Dumbfounded love,
cool smell of salt all round,
her mouth at evening to my own,
touch of her body by the open window,
silence before the rain.

Moods of the year accounted for,
slow peeling-off of clouds,
the stars soon hard on black.

Shift of the ever-feminine sea –
reduction of it all, ebb,
meteors, erosion, wheat,
to certainty:
a woman's month
and a man's need.

15

The quiet stirs. Inside
the night-time water is
perpetually at work.
The hawk is roosting. All

the infrequent cars
have ceased. Tomorrow is
uncertain weather coming from
the peaks behind us. And today
a lucid beach,
inevitable tantrums, also laughter.
Now in the room beyond
my wife has joined the two of them in sleep.
I sit, the damp around me,
brooding on nemesis and fearing
luck. The waves
reject all surety,
all hope, their noise
has been will be perpetual.
I write alone and timorous,
left contemplating darkness and the sea.

Parables of the Dark

The problem when ideas
of peace occur divides.
A novelty of quietude.

            And
varied splits upon the clock-face
separate, say, the forest
or the jammed rocks. Blurred also,
messages from yesterday:
the green-robed priest's
odd drumbeat in the shrine –
the frond first given, then enclosed
in sacred paper, handed to
the kneeling mother and her child.
We stood barefoot beneath the eaves.
Gongstroke. Conclusion of the rite.

A lackadaisical involvement.
Amateur. The subjects
wait there in the gloom –
lost kings, arcaner
texts, such tapestries.

Shadows of the event
drag on the gravel,
interstices unguessed at then
stridden across.
The seen world halts,
a seraph's wing
impatient
brushes the pattern off the dust,
is gone again. We want
to hold what is not, supplement
the non-existent by desire.
The lag, the fault, the wish-fulfilment,
ours. The structure,
noon, syllabic
utterance unheard,
elsewhere.

      Distracted
as so often
by passing splendour, quick
naked thought of youth,
unloving torso, cool
unreached magnolia, summers
of willingness.

A lacked perspective that ignores
inches of dark,
the heat reflected topaz in the pool,
incalculable bloom.

        A curious
depeopled art. The things, the place,
remain. Children observed
and praised in racing, their
unshareable games,
a restless scattering of doves, these
wait for inclusion

in airless cells of memory.
The easily inanimate
veer off
and phantasy alone
smokes from the lit, the seen.

Partial Recall

At sunfall than
the zenith west-
turned cliffs though the
horizon than
the sea.
       Features
via a smoked
pane brighter. Duped
as to values,
the quality
prefiguring
the dark to come.

Now everywhere
impossible light
provides the tones
for memory to
encounter: half-
translucence as
the glass adds an
extra note of
colour, stripping
the form aligned
for inclusion
in the aching
gallery of
recollection.

Clear wine-cold taste
and vivid still that
sensual movement
on forgotten
headlands framed and
chosen: seabird
and tamarisk,
the fallen surf
one splendour.
                    Years
muddied, the tide's
plash, censored flowers
dying, the touch
richer in dream.
All paring done,
the tremor past,
what's hard alone
remaining, calm
the essence if
all else is lost.

Nichol

Winter-noon eyes
defiantly half-open
see nothing, resisting sleep.
I stroke your back
brown from the unprotected
seaside, memories of pebbles.

Your flat, crinkled feet
work a concerned tattoo.
I croon throatily
hoping to encourage rest
after bad temper. Nothing
seemed right all morning –

the train too hot, that soft blue bear
rejected like an insult,
your favourite biscuits even
hurled aside.

The tear-blobs dry to salt
on fevered cheeks. Your gaze
at last shuts out a strange midday,
the swaying curtains introduce
warm gusts of trees and sand.

One final leg falls heavily. My hand,
loving, impatient, parental,
spreads now a waiting inch above your back
which is at last shelled over you in sleep.

The Shifting Stones

for Niikuni Seiichi

You look once.
The perceived
is lost – stacks
out at sea
have shifted
and the north
is forfeit.

You try then
the unmoved
enquiry –
mere clifftop
again: where
initial
placings were
has gone un-
remembered.

That there'd been
a logic
seemed certain.
Rooted in
heather or
silky foam
the solid
monoliths
offered no
problem. In
using the
compass there
were no snags:
the needle
wandered to
no lodestone,
the weather,
hazeless, was
favourable.

Not shadows
either for
the sun's un–
wavering:
a steady
drench of the
copper light,
no cheat of
cloud, eclipse,
on moor or
water, all
conserved in
the normal
move of day.

We cannot
chart this far,
gorse-strewn, sea–
blackened place.
Others may
come and test
with brand-new
instruments

what we have
also been
unable
to record:
the puzzles
that exist
and won't be
solved – the weight
that's there yet
isn't, the
angles that
abound but
change.
          The rest
is child's-play.

The Temple

for Peter Gamble

Moss. And cicadas in huge trees.
Rocks half my size deployed inside
a rectangle to make an ideogram.

Silence. Except for dripping water,
insects. A sudden crimson lily
hides in green.

          The calm
a challenge. Procuring, hoarding,
schemes made for each indifferent year,
the hectic move from work to holiday.
Correlation in summer
of lichened village churches with
the voices of the dead imbued in stone:
as here, word-patina
from those time-distant throats –

the morning ritual in mist,
bell echoing to moisture.

And here now, genuinely interested,
we're never likely to return.
So many places on a hemisphere
talked of imperfectly on casual evenings,
and checked by postcards that record
another arbitrary quest.
                    Asking
if faiths have gone peripheral,
if sacred buildings turn aesthetic only:
posited as rain in copper gutters,
on the aligned, disparate tiles;
house-leeks, gardens, a graph of mould,
commercial maintenance, graveyards prepared
for non-believers.
Not wanting to revere finality,
all the cremated loves unmet forever,
our own existences a few scrawled words
and meant for fading.

Perpetually there in intervals
the hope: the energy of being
must be and is immortal,
all the unwasted love
eternal present as what's spent
in wonder, caring,
saves their enchantment.

Contingent when alive, creating
any preferred relationship, locale,
by glimpse, by touch;
unmisted; past, not gone.
The stone, the rafter seen
remain in me and I in them,
plunged and irrevocable.
To leave, even haltingly,
to waiting car or bus, is to bequeath
something that's valid.

The place retreats and other
localities beckon. In the rear-window

are only dust-clouds, foliage. A summer visit –
the spot, the date, always irrelevant –
once cut on time, enters
on definition.
             To move
mayn't be progression but to stay's
no answer as the millions of us shift,
despoil. Response perhaps
the tracing of a pattern, limited.
Recall
the form of holiness on August noons,
half comprehended, magical;
the moss, the leaves, the structures,
the resonant sound of bells unheard,
dwindle to tourism
but hauntingly.

Takidan-ji

Inland

on the lake
poppy-coloured light
storm flickering

the rice-grasses
in the noise
swarm with wind

to cower naked
under shelves of thunder
cool stabs on our skin

Mallarmé's Blank Page

for Miyoshi Toyoichirô

The scaffolding of the day
is visible only
as spars of pale wood
on every sunrise.

Inside, the darkness lingers.

Cage of shadows.

                    The months circle.
Nothing occurs to alter waiting.

Martins flick in and out,
secrets clinging briefly to their wings.

NOCTURNES FOR THE DEAD OF WINTER

for Lee Harwood

I

Blood round the tooth,
each melody
lassoed by midnight.
                Dawn
from sunset lengthens.

II

Scrape of a record; even,
stylus encountering dust,
explosion. . . Then not alone – a
switch flicked in a nearby room,
the set not earthed.
Poring meanwhile:
chronicles, dead insects
staining maps, the crease
of other fingers, former comments in
faint pencil, shapes
of adjacent blossom
faded now. The music though.

III

The grace gone by.
Exploratory notes are ink-
marked on a stare. As clocks suffice
forming an angle to disparate
lusts. Who then between the eye and page.
The questioner remains,
crouched in a chair with
atlases (the wrong
initial flags), outdated
lexicons, involving . . .
Such tediums of distance,
memory. To decipher
old meshworks of reference,
when, how. Enquiry

ending in the blur
of senses, adequate,
confused.

IV

        The scroll
intends chronology. Somehow,
encircled in the wrapping past,
all time's simplicity is not
cloud over peak nor firs nor slope,
edged wanderers between
abyss and overhang.

V

Past fingers
recreate the pace:
reality
at three removes –
composer, player, marketeer.
The staves only
at the corner of hearing,
caress of tune and concentration,
pain of age.
Ignoring now
the colours on a plan,
the shirked interpretation:
writ battles, epaulettes,
incitement, boundaries
relaid. The arbitrary
politics of place. The chair.
Ghostly piano. Record-cabinet.
Exposure to an autumn light
not gone through. Only studied. Later.

VI

Reiterated theme, on water
proffering the bloom, a
laziness with decorations,
self-excuse. Not being here
what latterly seemed viable

so deprecating all:
preoccupations, hazard, contumely.

Excluding love
from an infertile hour,
examination of
the cold whorled roots of motive
disallowed.

VII

The woods rust.
                Playing out
greasepaint convention to
a minuet of winter.
                    Torchlight,
forest darkness, youth and age.
The loneliness. A tender
sufferance of connection. That.
No more.

VIII

Chessboard of night and frost;
and pick one's way, a spectre
over darkness, patch of moon
to next, distinctions chanced.
No project. Truant.
                    The leaves
snap like twigs.

IX

Argument in whispers in the bound
garden. Words
smoke, the hedges crack
around them and alone together now,
no light falls from the house, the
chimneys cold.
              Solution at the end
apparently unfound, the gate
creaks open. Shuts. The lawn
recrossed in solitude. Hard

worm–casts, white, forlorn.
                        The terrace,
urns with brittle stalks,
years wheeled, the same
retracing steps in pitch–dark winter
to the ice–held pane that's
groped again for, forced.

            X

The library. Racked shelves.
The windows mirrors, naught
beyond them.
                  Chill.
Gloved hands to folios.
Impossible enchantments
culled. Making
connections where
there were none and
inventing systems . . .
Touching, unfulfilled.
                        Dust
everywhere, wires trailing
aimlessly, the power
cut off. Unshaded
light. Green, shifting,
drowned. The search.
Rustle of pages, silence
otherwise. A cough.
                        The lost
nenuphars of history.

            XI

New calendar however if
of incompletion. To
plot out the wastage, threat
of each recurring year.
Paralysis. Loss
after equinox, decline
to now. The thought
of midnight, memory
of splendour, fire–bar dead.

The room
ceded to stillness, wrenching
selected help from print
and blankness, all the rest
assumed. And where
the consolation, tonal,
irises, the pictures
shining from the wall.
Filled glasses, touch,
companionship. But
partial currents as late months decree
tensors incapable of
venture. Limiting.

Daylight contrácts, the shedding
of opportunities gone frayed.
In exile, craving still
a distant hearth.

XII

       Smell
of cold ashes in the grate:
enclave abandoned, now
the metal, plaster, wood,
upholstery, infected
by winter. Clock-face
immobile. Frame too,
the nerve-ends severed finally,
benumbed. Remembrance altered via
the nadir of cold, the credence
taxed. Red spit
streaking the basin. Hurt
and silence.

XIII

       Standing-stones,
glazed stretch of ice
on the north side. Whine
of black air past rock. The night
no longer guidance as
the shapes revert now

cancelling the blaze, spilt
shimmer, hurtling pattern:
shivering, alone. Footstep crisp on turf,
stamp round and round invoking
summer memories. On horseback.
Shirtsleeves. Such
bland distances of moor.
Brown rivulet, cloud–shadow,
poisonous gleam
of bog-grass skirted. Laughing.
And circling now, in danger,
night-lost. Under
the similar constellations with
each step equivalent, downhill.
The stun of cold. Awaiting dawn.

SHORES

Broadstairs 1951–Miura Kaigan 1971

Brief winter's day,
the quality of faces
etched on dreams.
A street of tears.

Tarmac,
assembled images,
the sea:
bleak, wind-scraped sand,
starfish, east-slanting rock-pool.
Spray-roughened wood
boards up the summer.

Another February beach,
low sun, discarded shells,
unmarried silence
and conjectures
of a discrepant now.

Cold terminus, but as
the mordant air is darkening
return is plausible.
All other futures branch
their gleaming limits,
shunt time and opportunity,
are hampered or enhanced
by what's been proved,
what forecasts are rejected.

Hard nightmares of the afternoon.
The platform aches with bare sun.
No evidence the hour it is
hangs between trains. If
here for good . . .

Walking by tides again,
scuffing the unremembered grains,
to find assumptions of what's known
conflict. The smell
of this horizon falsifies,
the guesses from those eyes
are laughable.

Between the empty station
and the abandoned shore
a garden juxtaposing
last autumn and today –
ripe oranges, plum-blossom.
Another season lost and found.

THE LAST SCENE

came through the door and watched
the sunlight drifting off the leaf
before addressing   . The garden lay
in summer to the sky. 'When   first
arrived . . .' The voice lingered,
a fingerprint on silk. A time
for reconcilement, blaze outside
darkening the strictures of the room.
To broach then. If only   .
'All   can say. . .' but which is known
not all. A gesture. Glance perhaps.
Eyes searching the impersonal
evidence of love.   shrugged
in an intense predicament –
no longer   or   , simplicity
reducing this duet, this triangle,
to movement without substance,
dislike, gained jealousy,
gone unpossessed. A cooler
version, civilised, the jade,
the pearwood, Aubusson,
no thought of claim, no question
of what   may redeem, a mere
existence vis-à-vis, at least
a tolerance. No passion though.
The light goes gliding past the rose
with no involvement. Safe
the bright garden, safer   caught
in a relationship that could be none.
Watching the curled grass-blades,
pale iris, shade, the business of the moth,
at last   felt a commitment
lain beyond, left abstract, comment
on what had never been achieved.
'   'd better . . .' Thus departure.
Decision stemming from a lack,
blurred statements, the unsaid
coheres, irrevocable. Planned.
Vacating rooms never inhabited.
The failure, the success remain
unspoken, greyer. Whose?

THREE LANDSCAPES

I

The winter nearer as a region here.
Known.
        The snow escarpments . . .
And the living-places
tilted towards the feebler
summer.
        Rare sun,
the noons close-fisted,
grudging.
        Late spring:
the shivering flowers
overnight between the snow.
A sudden flowing of pale green,
the rivulets tug grass-blades on the rank
hillsides.

        September
closes the high passes.
Ice deployed.
        The claws
unflex of winter, threads of snow
drift into the villages,
gust southwards.
        The threat
moves in, areas
tighten about the city.
Time to leave.

II

The nomads, with their mares,
the gaudy plaids, skin-tents
on hollow struts, had left the valley
now that spring was offering itself
on upland pastures.
        Glimpses
could be had of them on the new running slopes –
a flash of spur or waggon-shape

seen through the fresh rowan,
fording a swollen torrent.
The whinnying of the herds
was sometimes borne on the chilled breeze.

Up past trickling overhang,
shale where the final tongues of snow
recede and some,
dirtying in the careful shadow,
last until autumn.

       Their embers
cool now on the valley-floor –
scorched patches to be pricked by grass-leaf,
traversed by brambles.
            This winter
others may be here or none.

III

The sand has no boundaries.
Trembling, it dilates
between hot swords of sea-water
and the clumsy brushwood
choking with shadow.

The forest itself is hoarse,
restless under the matted roof:
a garish bloom a rarity
in the quiver of twilight.

The mountain quickens its angle
shrugging off the big trees:
charred rocks, grimy soil,
scrub making headway in the interstices.

The crater is not even smoking.
Innocuous, the sulphur colours
muted to ochre, rust,
blue as though seen through onyx,
cobalt, grey.

The whole island shook this morning.

MINIATURES

to my wife and son who were
unable to share our holiday

I

Its farness widowing
             Sunfall and
the distant ranges
a lazy brushstroke
             Earlier
one floating triangle of snow
above the air
         Smooth
on either side greyblue
belying hardship
           A small disease
is left behind
         Nervous
reflections of our wake

2

The phone's a link
a mockery
         Your lips
I do not see
form words and love's
ghost voices cupped in blackness
relating illness
sadness at parting
all that's missed

3

An island word recurs
             Landmass
the earth itself
suns
galaxies
        Offshore

diminished archipelagoes
to rocks invisible at high tide

4

Deserted town
            The lights
halt single cars
shops for the most part
shuttered
            Breakers
November-tamed have left
foul tokens of the summer

5

An evening message then
the fever's down
                  Too late
activity repairing
listlessness
             Both absent
our delight
connection
merely sound
and undersea

6

As well your love
the syllables pronounced
recall
         My fingers ache
for your soft nakedness
in autumn
            For the
each evening new enigma
wisp-light along the cavern
and rich
annulling peace

7

Here where the smoke drifts up
staining the sky
you were to be
            The mystery
its origin below the bay
a distant blur of mainland
hiss of the surrounding ocean
yours still
apart

8

The crater's outer lip
achieved
         Slope of clean sand
precipitous
          Slide down
and shake our clothes
              The grains
patter all in silence off

9

She laughs her way up dunes
as dark as negatives
            Looks round
light–footed
encouraging her slipping
father
      Notes though like me
no symmetry
two absences

10

Translucent
fumes race the confusing
cloud
     Split rocks
that crumble underfoot
           Stones

lack almost weight
deceive the hand
                    At night
a pink irregular mist
curves flaring
              Drips
its swathe through vegetation
                          Smears
the mountainside and cools

          1 1

The dirty ebon sand
laced by the waves
                  Forms
thorn the water and the cliffs
note recent strata
distorted
unreliable
          No fossils
                    The earth
though slowly chilling
here's still young
correcting shape
in more dramatic ways
than wind-erosion
sea-devouring
rainfall

          1 2

Camellias show roots
above the ungrateful ground
and some fantastic birds
hide
cower in the dappled
foliage
        She stands
between two peahens
and the grey trunks
frame them unevenly
                  Such
beautiful fragility

Bright
marine autumn all around
with down the offgreen slope
the shore
            End of a moment
and the camera records
nothing that was
something that wasn't

            13

The comic geese
squabble for food
                        She threads the shadow
chasing a white
reluctant rabbit
                    There are swans
black redbilled ivory also
goldwinged ducks
                        Her eyes admit
brief
vivid yet unmeaning
snapshots
            The moment
whipped away
replaced perpetually
by surprise
                    Awkward
fowl leave the pond

            14

Bearing
no misplaced adult centre
                        Here
the island the
immediacy
with shore-walks or
the mountain
and at nightfall coloured
grotesques on television
                        Mother
a quick remembered voice

nice doubtless to get back to
not offering though
diurnal problems

      15

Fatigue
        But not her frame
which obviously lacks
resilience
        More
the mind allowing
just so many novelties
past the swift shutter
past awareness
           Hillside
shade–zebraed zoo
a coach that harried us
from the crater to the bay
               Thereafter
nothing
but sullenness
digesting all

      16

In shells the alien black grains
hide longer
        Gone
since never there
the genius of the sea
           No wash
inland of fictive waves
           Select
a husk
what vibrancy there was
departed
        In these blank words
no echo from the crash of foam

17

Leaving an island and each time
the flattering rain occurs
                        As tears
from nature
              No
                    Unseen
the pressures veer
                    The clouds amass
uncaring as to voyages
                    Each drama
yellowing nimbus
wrack upthrust
the surface changed
is there for someone
there for record
                    The peeling diaries
agree that it takes more than no-one
to make a storm
                    Prehistory
a stone reminder only
of the cataclysm

18

The plastic filth
an August memory
                    Fringes
the wearying tides have never reached
stay hideous
              We may well be
the last imperfect race
to value imperfection
                        Now the sun
through fitful mist
occasionally gilds
wet cancelled sand
the further swell
the offing
              Watch and know
                        The waves
look spuriously clean but are

contaminated
filling

19

Indifferent
all majesty still licks
transforms
            A child
lives in the moment in the faith
the next
will also blossom
                  Adults know
the present leaves a rind
or should
            Tomorrow's still
controllable though left to chance
is nothing but disgust
                        What is
our legacy

20

The photographs recur
spaced out in time
                      Frequent them
and faked–over light
can give them oceans that
they never had
                  From underneath
tinged currents or
from unimaginable sea–floors
alteration
shift

21

The ullage of a growth
through wilfulness with none
except in general terms
to care
            A century ago
the shores were freer with

the laving given only what's
destructible
        Now crammed
with permanent disgrace
            The gain
is only gain if you and I
can hanker back
to tenets that we have
perhaps unfounded that
things were
things could be
better

   22

Cite comfort then
           Or speed
convenience
       Cite health
penalties for sheep–stealing
or spools of opera
obedient in the drawer
           The dirt
remains
increases on a dying planet where
cleansing by fire
brine
compost is
undone
     The laws defied
to make unnatural things
that will not die

   23

The marrow of creation
must be death
        The indestructible
a figment of the proud
or worse
a diabolic image
          All that's made
in reverence must wither

gain its patina
and die
        The dance
the wooden statue
gardens
tableaux
invented not to last
                        Language itself
degenerates to footnotes

        24

Impermanence as well
is valid
        x and x
or I have messages
corroboration
that must wait
still to intensity
and fade
        The water's
longer than an empire's span
and falls in whitening
to chaos
change

        25

The wind again tonight
and panes are rattling
                        An island
swirled in salt
                Tracing
these lost words
between the cream of tide
and the potential lava

        26

Desire
        They marshal past
in myriads unmet

Want
        The remembered leave
a residue
caress

Love
        And you
ineffable are there
                The words
assemble and elucidate
because they're here
your absence

        27

A definition not
a fact
        You are say
and I am
                The children
mercifully too
                A wake
traces itself greenwhite
on limits
        a and b
have met and therefore
c and d
        Not that
though that is true
                What is
                    Which
phantoms nonsense of the symbols
                        Is

        28

Explaining is
a problem given is
reduction
        Marks put on paper must
you say
diminish
        But

you where in time with me
intensifies to something
glassburn
gigantic fibres
what though
                    Signs disperse
                                There's
you not here and loveliness
                                A
partiality with all uncaught

            29

Posit the leaves strewn
round us
            We remain
                        Or daytimes
reddening and dropped
                        You're
there and therefore I
however ludicrously
was
        Defining love's to tell
what isn't and our two clasped forms
were there

            30

Not even an embrace which is
since past
approximate
                    What's indefinable
is true so words are
                            Leap
in my heart at seeing you
                            The
waking by you
                    Shared
laughter
            Now so
missing you
            So many
indications only
of all you mean

31

Leaves whirl wherever
and the colours fall
                    To catch
in middle age
the relish of impermanence
and feel
belonging to a world of shift
                            The children
losing a charm to gain one daily
blending if they're allowed
into a transience

32

The window gives
on to a straggling lot
the sea however toneless
lies beyond
                Control
the tiny landfall
and the scope
                    Salt here
and damp
                Clothes toys
and nursery-rhymes
the thrillers
your scarf included by mistake
toothbrushes and notebooks
shaving-kit
                Hotels
afford a temporary order
lend to those
unsure of whereabouts
security
                Thus this
truncated family
forms something of a whole

33

She wakes at an insanely
inappropriate hour
                   Plays then
the dawn all whitening
with variegated paper or
designs subjective
alphabets
              I lie
warm lazy and inadequate
attempt
my desiccated mouth
at various jingles
                   She's there
in independence yet
creates a world that I would like
unshaven to live up to
                   Animals
are colourful and kinder and
the universe is lit by better rainbows
and I can't go on

34

Then what
is innocence and did
I lose it
           Is
all that white thrash of tide
tossed shells
the silly group of rocks
for nothing is
hers here
mine then
              Myths are
for our own making
always
           Start
from such perfunctory
beginnings
              Await
the visitation of the seer

sunsets
volcanoes
cheap playthings
boughs
rocks
       All in
the making

35

From far away a speck
the haze delineates
to something recognised
                        Disembark
the shape is walkable
the strand
the rise beyond the scrub
the cone
            Spot on the map's fake blue
become familiar
a lesson taught
we could have learned
but here
            Surprises and
foreshadowings
                What was
inevitable because
arrived at

36

Whisper of night-air
and inside the dreaming skull
few memories of day
                        An anger
for the garbage
disfiguring the sand's
a filth on love
                Sun-orange though
is there
her father's long concern
and through a mouthpiece
casual tokens of

her mother
            Now as darkness
batters the pane
she knows inside her sleep
she is
        Tomorrow
we return

Ôshima, November 1971

DAGUERREOTYPE

It was either, all unclear now,
that you did or did not desire
me, a room somewhere, chintz perhaps,
p.m. I think, the place getting
more detailed, yes, last sunlight through
half-opened curtains, the corner
of a print illuminated,
tendril of a flower, coast-line,
bird's claw, imprecise, something curved,
coloured, fragments of a décor
for but no sense of you, burnish
on memory, gradually the
postures of remorse I take it
more developed, shadows on the
wainscot under closed windows, you
in recollection beyond that
clothing yourself slowly smiling
after sex, can taste you even though
the contours of you uncertain,
smudge where the dazzled eye took in
the definition of you on
all backgrounds, focused edge of flesh,
the eagerness of want gleaning
exactitude, sieved later to
this clarity lacking as if

seen through water, emotionless,
spectrum cast by the paperweight,
noise of a car on gravel, that
scene though, conversation was it,
idle, no hurt, the affair such
as it was over, or wait an
intimation now the room was
empty, a feel of disuse, I
reliving a recent evening,
long interval, unthought of, there'd
been others, you spent the night, while
there we'd talked of impersonal
things, this side of the words perhaps
an exploration, is it worth
or even possible, revive
vague passions, anyway nothing
came of it but the letter, yes,
I was standing, the dahlias still
fresh, one petal on the rosewood,
my novel you'd been reading left
open face downwards, the air stuffy,
door closed behind me, ripping the
envelope, yes the clock striking
five, I'd just returned, your writing
on the carpet in the hall, the
kettle on, a late October,
upstairs, dark landing, studying
the postmark in the sudden gold
from the open bedroom, turned the knob
of the other door, closed it, yes, shut
in there with a two-day memory,
alone with your fading presence
uninterrupted, can't think who
would have broken the spell, lain on
the shadow of your weight, certain
then anyway was solitude,
but the message, what inference,
regret was it, confession that
you wished you'd persuaded the hour
a little further, paragraph
of warmth, the tables turned from days
of my humbler ardour, or a
cooler intonation, drawing

back even from what ambiguous
sketches of intimacy the
night had indicated, maybe
it was that, a confirmation
of the end, whichever way the
mood of writing tended, it was
some years before we met again.

REQUIEMS

in memory of Vernon Watkins

I

Already early Easter and it's
blossomfall.
Chord in the bonfire flickering,
of pink, of ivory.
Charred manuscripts that are
altered, perdurable.
A scattering along the bough
branded for wastage. Fresh,
young, and dying as the sunlight
describes ellipse.

To record the sound
one dropping feather makes,
the nest abandoned
in increasing noon.
Rats skirt the gutter,
and a darkness
hangs in the lizard's eye:
the lacy, issued wings
crush in anticipation.
For fodder, predatory need.

2

Perfect, full-blown, as now
the natural man
enters on trespass –
knife-blade, defoliant.

The gift of self-destruction,
tasted fruit accruing venom and
ignored as relevant,
a pride untouched.

The combines work through wheat.
Bent women grope for rice-plants.
And from the dusty road
cattle motioned to shambles.
Morbidity of August thoughts,
out-edged and willed.

A meadow's corner,
and the blown, protected hedgerow
moves shadow over poppies,
compost, beer-cans. Torn shreds
of aimless newspapers, somewhere
a guiltless citizen
bleeds out his pain.

The crows are raucous;
new, indifferent cars
whine on to motorways;
thumbs of clover unpricked
swing back in fouller air.

3

Descent.
Concentrating on Michaelmas
in foreign darkness –
ploughshares, steel surface showing
greyer bristles, seagull.

Wind.
Dropping now, the air

gone stagnant. Pause
and still regeneration
unbelieved in, there.

Weeping.
In furrows, blood, loam, and
an augury. Swelling,
a stranger womb, next year
the purging. Whiter flowers.

Knowledge.
Eternal fugue unfolding
newer stamens and
discarding, always drumroll,
the expendable.

Together.
Ash of a life mounting.
Unclaimable,
if not in love, considerate,
disclosed by drying leaves.

4

Cold blazon
of an empty sky, the factories
unravelling smoke.
Weeds in a vacant lot,
the barbed wire rusting.

Withered the skin, to now
the sole observer
April incredible
as ponds begin their hardening,
the goldfish trapped.

Cleanness again, the picked earth
equalling imposition –
tidy, as always, death;
the stucco monuments,
trim squads of soldiers,
numbers, delight
in answering, squared off.

Disorder mercifully
inside the root;
wayward once more desire;
dormant, perpetual,
the benediction.

Birdskull and the acceptance:
bone-structure fumbled to mould.
Ceramic seasons adequate
when fragile, glowing,
taken from the kiln.
Daubed, used and broken,
never the whole.

Midwinter birth as northern air
inscribes the count of breath
on nothingness, on faultless wind.
Axe-stroke unsounded and
scrawled autographs on frost.
The anguish drained
can only squeeze what has been
down to here – old age,
reduction, saplessness.

No anodyne though on
sparse and unworthy twigs –
ancillary – unlikely
salmon-coloured bloom,
or, hellebore,
a Christmas rose.

Embattled void,
and these chapped hands
of no account. Low suns
burn off the crystals
and the sad name melts.
Behind the spikes of loss
another affirmation and
trouvaille – dust,
denigration, pain: a
temporary supposal that's
eternally
provisional, achieved.

HALF-ISLANDS, ISLANDS

for Annette

Mesmerised. Each mountain, faded,
    rears dispensable, piled
on the far voyage unfolding.
    What was potential once
rocks by: familiar beaches
    craved from headlands of clear
childhood, never walked on though loved
    in the high caressing –
sand framed in needle grass, the slabs
    of limestone sheer, fossil-
bearing. The blue lost summers – caves
    just inland, each gaping
mystery fringed by berries, orange,
    poisonous, and a boy who
followed his torch into darkness
    already beyond him.

Early days in wrecked castles, stone
    shapes on green lawns, clambering
sky-empty chimneys. The gained dunes
    still scorch bare feet trudging
past rock-faces splintered with grey
    coral, fangs, vertebrae,
whorled with ammonite. The hard wind
    flowed always by us, rain
sometimes, erosion proved, the bite
    of the long tides.
            Our boat
is thwacked between the islands, jars
    the unseen from the seen,
the ends of each peninsula
    now isolated. Fogged
beautiful peaks merge to their half-
    suspected mass. Nothing
is lost, the absent evidence
    proves nothing, here a trace,
a telling nerve, the whole rich love
    can be reconstructed.

A rusty buoy bobs on a new
        stretch of the enclosed sea,
the cape now slanting to a bright
        gully leading sunward.
The glitter blames the eye, calls back
        a dry far noon vibrant
with insects. Shade patterned the walls,
        arid riverbed where
silence began its slithering.
        I'd wandered miles from yet
another temporary home,
        sweat–terror breaking out
of rattlesnakes concealed.
                        Panes strewn
        with foam, prehistory
is smeared again with fictions. Hills
        tree–blurred jut graced with farms,
leave supple terraces though glass
        annuls their relevance.

Years back I squatted down to watch
        the ebb in the salt–creeks
glide past intricate settlements
        in my mind's view. Tug of
the grass–blade where the jungle caught
        on mud–banks, the wayward
voyage of a leaf round eddies
        my canoe. Lonely hours
spent practising my power upon
        geography.
                Brief halt,
the further islands veer, a fresh
        course taken for the new
harbour. Now all veiled scenery
        is higher, tortuous,
with sudden fields more complex in
        their colour.
                        The ferry
starts hurrying description past
        its speed. The children dance.

I pray they're on their way towards
    a similar set of
uncontaminated futures.
    The piers approach, the past
already frozen in our wake.
    Tomorrow's menaces
evoke the raw material
    of dreams. We plunge into
each maze, star-haunted, unaware
    of what will be redeemed.

Shôdoshima, 1971

The Don Juan Papers

1   *Lord John Looks Forward*

No longer then romance
the dream replaced by rain
Spatter and chill against the glass
grey scudding air
Formed for a time delight
the curse of fragrance round the rose
sheer excellence of flesh
Count now alone the grains
allotting the fatigue,
a strategy involved between the kiss
and getting dressed again
That inch of time though sunlit
no different in texture
from other moments littering a day
Pacing the noon gravel near the lilac,
decanter, yellow apples, cigarettes,
the calf-bound memoirs opened by oneself,
the medicine to sleep, the touch
of sweat and slide of mouth on skin,
appointments made and broken,
made and kept,
the music and the coffee and the talk
Such strata in the hourglass merely note
the past increasing,
oxygen inhaled,
night on its way

2 Lord John Looks On

The jewels I gave her –
green edges refracting
the naked firelight of our heyday –
cold in their velvet now
as crystals of the dark.
New heady blossoms
madden the same alcove.
Gilt mirrors that tarnished
the frequent ache of our love
display anonymous hands about her.

A visitor these days politely
turned from the white threshold –
told she's out while late lamplight
stresses the upper windows –
my exiled weary ghost
steals through closed doors,
examines their act,
lift of her breasts,
the quiver as she's taken not by me.

Her half-closed eyes
as he works to perfection in her
ignore me at their bedside,
the fact I once was
unimportant like
the colours of her privacy.

Past his bare shoulder
an area of slate gables
lichened, correct
A seagull wheeled
One hardly moving cloud
Perhaps the same vermilion one
that hangs above the darkening elm
Strict view of roofs, strained winter sky,
an alien afternoon
Trapped, his embrace protecting
a memory of need
Short-sighted eyes that furtively
longed for release
Before arrival, in
intricacies of love, a marvel, if
afterwards with age
increasing disappointment, tact
required to disentangle the spent limbs
The mirror catches my grey hair, his blond,
each time we clasp
It all must end
I kissed him rose moved to the window stretched
stood naked for a moment looking out
shivering
picked up my glasses dressed and left
already now hours later
wanting it again

4 *Lord John Looks In*

This drawer like a cemetery
retains my guilt. Letters
in faded writing still possess
a flavour of the past
which can't absolve me nor can I recall
the face behind these old endearments and
the anguish mentioned. It seems
I stole a lover, was unfaithful,
left with no warning – actions
of years ago and other lands.
At one stage I'm accused of making love
to a couple, telling neither: if so
what harm was done and did it last?
I visit now this landscape of remorse,
foolhardy or compassionate,
invite the wronged to come and have it out
amicably some evening over supper.

5 *Lord John Looks Back*

Lines written
     to the
memory
     of them.

Such grey moss
     governs
the sundial,
     numbers,
precision,
     gone, mere
tracings, blurred,
     who, when,

a kiss hung
        in air,
a sweetness.

        Dark casts
unbelief,
        sense of
grim wonder.
        Vestige
remains of
        form to
tantalise –
        name cut
the bark has
        started
to misshape,
        flowerbed
running wild
        or the
footprint I
        try my
returning
        one by –
fossil hours
        with no
meaning, the
        texture
has changed past
        recall.

Night now. Pace
        the ground
turned frost–black
        round me.
Star patterns
        offer
only the
        senseless
glitter of
        distance
cold and lost
        in the
sharp branches.

        Bronze ghosts
departed,
        all that
lent purpose
        gone with
the magic,
        nothing
but dead thoughts
        staying
to comfort.
        Walk back
alone now,
        spell past,
woods empty.

6   *Lord John Looks Round*

The dark descends. Earth shivers. In the hedge
        the holly turns to iron.
The brown untidiness of autumn fixed
        by cold. My breath alone
moves to evaporate in silence and
        the fallen sun has left
the year behind. Increasing twilight, one
        crow winging home, the red
on flecks of ice dying to grey. Move on,
        steps echoing as in
a corridor to hell, the distance shows
        no light, no curl of smoke,
the sparse fields all deserted, heading for
        what refuge from the night.

7 *Lord John Looks Through*

The fire near extinction
earlier flare dropped to a glow
yielding to moonlight
Tall windows
indicate the abandoned garden
A gale smacks the panes
holds the house in sudden silence
shakes it once more
Today like yesterday contained
no lover or companion
The decanter stands empty on the mantelpiece
At midnight wide-awake
Tomorrow's calendar another void
The bathroom then
the sleeping-pill
Trembling in the bedroom to undress
Cheek on the cold soft pillow
eyes open
imploring sleep
Silence and repetition
Night
Played out
Alone
I think I'd almost welcome now
the final visitor
stone handclasp

Exeter, 1973

Lost and Found

(1983)

LANDSCAPE, SAINT-JUST

Rock falls sheer to the brown water.
  In one south-facing cleft
bluebells are in flower. A high breeze
  moves in the opposite
larches barely in leaf. We walked
  here in love through still air
to look down on the lily-pads
  though now a cuckoo sounds
hollow across the heath. Beyond
  those Bronze Age monuments –
tall blocks of quartz isolated
  among the gorse – sprawl tombs
from an earlier time dispersed
  and open to the clouds.
Fragile I feel your hand in mine,
  its warmth, until the first
rain-drifts speckle the pond's surface
  with a warning of change.

'A LANE NEAR UPTON'

for R.
25/6/50

I could never find it again.
My diary says
we left our bicycles at the gate
then walked between barley and hedgerow
till we came to the place beneath an oak.
You'd brought your own enchantment
yet the day
matched youth with magic,
lent our love
that sense of a still unencountered world.

Three decades intervene. It proved
the final time we lay in one another's arms.
I search the book of spells in vain.
The skies have changed.
Indifferent seasons sweep the earth. I've seen
the light of sorcery sinking from the fields –
although your face –
its beauty as I kissed it –
stays unforgotten.
I can still smell the fragrance in your hair.

Where the place was
the diary doesn't say – there's just this phrase
'a lane near Upton'.
Bright corn was rustling in a summer breeze,
slow June clouds never hid the sun,
the strip of turf felt smooth, swaying foliage
dappled your bare skin with shadow.
No bird sang and no insect whirred. Once,
a goldfinch passed. All this,
the detailed sweetness, I recall.
Before or after, hours lie in shreds.

The map we used is lost. Memory begins
at a five-barred gate of grey wood.
There were dark nettles and sprays of cow-parsley.
The back wheels went on ticking

when we'd laid the bicycles on their side.
Touching your hand I knew
a sharp foretaste of joy.
The secret quickened in your eyes.

One last caress,
the empty lane,
late afternoon,
the ditches thick with grass –
then nowhere, there's a blank
where sunset should have been,
midsummer harvested and gone,
each signpost wiped out with a rag.
Did we stop our bikes,
linger in twilight,
one foot on the pedal,
one on the tarmac? We must have planned
to meet again, our lips
with their imprint of pleasure
smiling . . . no,
I cannot see that far.
There's no path back from paradise.
The way that leads there has no starting-point.

June 25th, 1980

HAND

I am hand.
There is no sin in me.
I grab what I need –
stem, pebbles, fur.

Angel stricken in the shade
was mine.
The juice was mine,
those curves of fruit.

Wind, mist,
unseizable,
mine too.

Cobnuts are mine,
sweet roots.
I hold the husk, the thorn.
I use an edged stone bright with frost.
My palm bleeds.

I rummage,
probe,
crush woodlice, slugs.
Nothing eludes me.
Fingers scrabble on rock,
inch forward,
reach soil.

I grub up bones.
They stink of then.
I had forgotten.
I'll bury them once more,
scour further.

I am hand.
A smear of red marked yesterday.
The air is still.
His feathers do not stir.
As long as I am I,
am hand,
there can be
no trespassing.

THE EMBASSY OF HEAVEN

The light of sunset
down one side-street
strikes the façade.

Flagpoles
slant empty
over the pavement.

The brass letter-slot
in the high oak door
stays closed.

At nightfall the curtains
remain undrawn. Passers-by
catch a glimpse of mirrors.

Or see through shadowed rooms
to the garden transmitting
a tree in flower

where a building's
transparent heart
baffles the sure.

LOVERS

        Where are they now, between
what sheets or nowhere do they have
        their way? Unwearying
my memories range back whose bright
        disturbance brings comfort
in the small hours – flurries lasting
        a week, a year, the form
caught sight of, bronze conquest at first
        a dream. Calmer after
the sweet effort at times I find
        the wrong profile by me
on the imagined pillow – blond
        mouth turned to kiss, church clock
striking two, avenue of limes
        rustling with moonlight, dark

hands discovering my skin, voice
     husky with invention.
Scenes from those days drift past me, drift
     on windless plains where ghosts
of loveliness gain shape, disperse.
     Where are they now, desires
which harboured me? With the half-light
     as ally we made up
such supple contours interlocked.
     Do any sculptures carved
by our passion gather cobwebs
     in some out of the way
warehouse? My fingers attempting
     their salvage have been gloved
in stone. The muscles stiffening
     have taken their revenge.
There is no thread that leads past blind
     alleys of lust on down
the corridors of remembrance
     to where the lovers stand
trapped in the labyrinth of time.

QUERCUS PEDUNCULATA

There's been a wood here since the last ice age.

Daytime is always twilight,
soft. The branches, swaying, sift
what you think you see
from the perspective of a different world.
Changes occur behind your back
no matter how swiftly you turn.

The glaciers did not reach this far.
To their south the land was treeless.
Cold mist hovered above standing water
and boulders were scabbed with lichen

then as now.
         The ice withdrew.
Another springtime repossessed the earth.
Men wandered through warmth, through brightness,
hunting the red deer.
Oaks spread, their crinkled shadows falling
over moss and curled ferns and dry twigs.

Air sweeps the high moor.
On cloudless evenings stars
spurt from the north and east.
The mare whinnies to her foal.
New frost glitters.

Here, the river
slides into silence.
Pale trunks distort the slope.
The valley is hidden,
dense with leaves.
You heard no footfall but there's been
a movement over turf
yet what you're staring at is only
space, greengrey, shade–dappled.

Piles Wood, Dartmoor, 1980

KILLERTON

Grey light is driven from the west.
        The rare flowers lose colour,
lean fluttering against the slope.
        A March wind chaps our hands.
Here there is little sign of spring.
        Song-birds are silent. Day
is a few minutes longer now
        than night but across blurred

fields comes a hint of the late snow.
      With dark glee the children
show us where a dog is buried.
      Rooks fuss in their high nests.
The grass is white with their droppings.
      No one else is abroad
this afternoon save for the ghost
      of a man out walking
his retriever through rain that fell
      a hundred years ago.

MESSAGES

to Lynn

After the yellow lava
has reached the trees in the orchard
twisting them up in a plume of fire
words burden the ear
for what can redeem the fruit-harvest?
But the hand taken and a thumb
gently smoothing the palm,
one kiss, the unkempt hair caressed –
then the demons leave
that were locked in the single body,
and the fears bound taut round the eyelids
start to give. At such times
one statement placed in the silence
'I love you' may be less true
than the fact of skin to skin,
though realler for a moment
than savage photographs showing the torn road,
the farmhouse threatened by molten rock,
the red glare on the skyline.

LANDSCAPE, SOUTH DORSET

Unclouded dawn. Mist streaks the rose-
         glitter of the Channel.
A hen-pheasant scuttles beside
         one pale lane ascending
the down's sheer green. Under mounds smoothed
         with grass kings lie, their bronze
swords mouldering. The dew is spread
         in silence. Six o'clock
rings from the valley. We came here
         once when the land held less
detail – neither had yet found out
         what the other noticed.
Not that these sites or contours were
         harder to decipher.
Our eyes beginning to focus
         on new textures of love
stayed memory-blurred since they contained
         too many pasts to share.

AGAINST THE COLD

I

Soft mask of winter with the eyeholes shut,
the mouth a slack grimace:
                    we watch
its semblance puckered, swelling with the fire
and changing.
The cinders drift to form a dune,
lie flat till the greasy ash
crumbles to powder,
rises as an unsubstantial pillar
and spins itself away to nothing,
falls as haze.

The particles increase,
scurry to the brink
of some achieved design – a map,
the outline of a bird of paradise,
bars of a prison cell.
The breeze stirs fitfully,
unseen fire crackles again
and the scheme such as it was
is nervously erased.

A far-off April rebels
and embers from an autumn strata-deep
disturb it, but the surface holds,
retains the pout of self-deceit.
What was the pattern trying to convey –
a system of geometry perhaps?
the explicit gesture of a god?
Too many plots to overcome it
though few work. So we return
to those high constructions of wet twigs
and a complex grid of canals
with thin and distantly placed bridges.

II

The forest is
November, leaves
cobwebbed with fog.
The rides criss-cross
far apart in
areas of
dripping silence:
soft underfoot
with all the waste
of foliage
brown, fallen – spruce
or the other
dark conifers
merely adding
to the effect
of loneliness.
None can be sure
which direction
leads back from fear.

A horse whinnies
but there's been no
sound of hoof-fall.

In this sudden
clearing stands one
lichen-coloured
fountain never
there before, set
with grey statues
of men and beasts
life-size.
        Behind
a rotting tree
this granite plinth
is wreathed with dead
bryony. Herbs
are stuck upright
in crude glass jars.
A slain bird lies
in the centre,
blue feathers still
sticky with blood.

III

Dark leaden sea
one cloud to wedge
the harbour-mouth
with gold the film
of midwinter
everywhere dun
smoke obscuring
what colour there
once was that picked
each item off
from its neighbour
roof hull chimney-
stack white crates piled
on the quay patch
of lawn glimpse of
distant hill *gold*
breaking become
the same and cold

the wretched cold
of winter weight
of mist to press
all gaiety
forever from
the world without
the *hint of gold*
behind the grey
that bursts as sun
beyond the shroud
that curtains off
one object from
another *blaze*
of gold having
to grope through haze
the blind façades
unlit and bleak
the gardens with
still half concealed
the *radiance*
that stars the grey
and shatters walls
of fog until
the winter makes
a heap of drab
fragments lying
underneath *this*
triumphant shine
of final gold

IV

i

Mahogany
reflects her brooch
those dark garnets

her wedding-ring
worn to a thin
uneven wire

ii

Morocco sets –
each shelf displays
a different tone

of leather, black,
olive, snuff-brown
and indigo

Sunlight glancing
off gilt edges
refrains from proof

discarded facts,
old wars, a dead
man's enterprise

iii

Autumn oak-trees
towering by lakes
of glass present

as light floats west
a double mass
of heavy gold

V

A crinkled rectangle
limits the scene –
column of black trees,
ragged flare of sun,
pale green of that receding meadow.
Dusk falls. The gold
withdraws, the wall
seeming to absorb the frame.

Some eerie willpower
keeps the landscape alive
which glows unaltering

long after the real day
beyond the uncovering window
has yielded to night.

VI

Behind the rain an angel waiting,
muscled, wingless.
His bare flesh, rounded perfect limbs
gleam, like a lover's, gold.

A winged cat sprawls lazily
on the turf at his feet.

The rain falls noiselessly
on the discoloured forest,
falls on the far pool knived with reeds,
falls on the yellow slope littered with rocks,
falls here where I wait by the ruined terrace,
falls in the gutted house at my back.

No rain runs off his naked skin
or seems to affect the cat's smooth tawny fur
though my hair is drenched and the cold
downpour trickles into my ears and mouth.

Inside the rain an angel waiting and the sense
of nothing wasted, nothing trivial.
He smiles, for the touch of his outstretched hand
would unshadow time, desire
increase with each fulfilment, spring
be born transparent, hold the world
in one bright weightless moment
and sweep on.

              The rain drives down,
blurs the superb dimensions of the vision,
smears it out. Now nothing
but the usual contours under rain.

Depart without a further glance
at where the magic practically took place.

Depart swiftly with its unearthly gold
stamped on the back of the eye.

For though the symbols of splendour
are one by one pulled down,
there behind each failure,
behind the rhetoric of loss,
behind the spread of winter
and the coils of smoke from charred buildings,
gleams what has been to prove
it may be broken through to once again,
even surpassed.

COMMUNION

for Tasha

'We love we know not what
and therefore every thing allures us.' — TRAHERNE

Fourth after Easter. My daughter and I
set out together obeying a bell
in the north tower. Rings of time melt,
travel the speeding vapour of air.
Mid-May. The blossom shaking. We breathe
a far tang of the sea. The sculptured porch
muffles the sound (chime, breeze) as masons
long-dead draw the stone fabric over.
Saints piecemeal round God in glory
replace the sky. Any building, finished,
changes. Altars. Charged with spring flowers.
Books with silk markers. Colours go
from violet round to green – herald the grand
arrival of judgement, blend the three aspects
back into one. Here, touch the future,
tapping the past. At these tables certain
phrases are needed. As is silence.
Also company, you kneeling by me.
We've entered this place so we can peer

inside our hands at questions. Baffled.
Consoled. For mysteries loop, return.

Approaching, chastened, the rail, we reach
a barrier that's been breached between
our fragile pulse-rate and eternity.
Life is offered where amid murmurs
we clutch the fearful permission
to starve. Or feel unscorched the blaze,
rush-past of splendour unmoving. Stand,
not a hair out of place, expectant,
there in the holy cascade – self lost,
though never so wholly oneself. Dear girl,
trust the experience of the jonquil –
midwinter's – furled inside black soil –
parched – forgotten – trusting in brightness,
the proper moment. For something tugs us.
Into light. All our knowledge
must be partial. Hear that piping?
The swifts have arrived. Bringing news
from an unseen country. In this life
we face a tapestry hung with the wrong side
always towards us – yet those threads,
the hints of pattern, tantalising, blurred,
are the loose ends of paradise.

THE ENCHANTED ACRES

There could have been no time in Eden
merely
      days
when the warmth is a mist of blue and gold
along the blossom beside the fruit
or rain slants
while one five-coloured arch
spans the bruised cloud

    and nights
when starlight detaches each leaf from shadow
the air holds memories of mint and lavender
and drops of water trickling from the ledge
flash into the pool

Beyond the gate
the pulse ticks out its warning.
Trees calculate the loss of autumn.
Suspicious children
compare one pattern with another.
Every white flare of dawn includes
a flavour of remorse.

Back in the lost defended garden
then and now
were pleasures still to come.
There
the heart inscribed
remembrance of the present
while regret
was like blind eyes
when the spectrum throws its glow.

NEAR CARNAC

Smell of hot gorse
and larksong
embroidering the silence.

Far sea glittering
with no horizon
beyond pale dunes.

The stone avenue
lifts along turf to
a broken sanctuary

pointing to sunset.
The grass darkens.
Shadows link stone after stone.

The pile of air above
accepts the change,
the winds of evening,

the chill, disturbance
of a last bird winging home,
eventual starlight.

MAGNOLIAS

Curved shell of a soft red petal
on the stone path.
Grey river:
one small craft becalmed
catching the dawn–flush.

Desire alone cannot explain
my presence here, the rage
to hold you naked
before the freezing mirror,
kiss your flesh.

Above, white blaze
of premature magnolia,
motionless,
regal,
starring the boughs,
the silence.

I long for your touch,
for the depiction of loneliness
to glide downstream.

And higher still
another system of twigs
whose scarlet flowers
resemble the parrots of fantasy
perched for a moment
like a sanction
against the unfriendly blue.

FOUR HILL-FORTS

for Michael Bakewell

I

Eventually
grass-green aisles roll down
on nothingness:
here is length light.

Eggardon Hill

II

Conquest:
a darkness brimming
under royal yesterdays.
Careful ascent
seems to lose exactness.

Cadbury Castle

III

History's echo muted
beyond unseen
resplendent years:
flourish
of receding trumpets.

Hembury Fort

IV

More an island –
dunes undulating,
numinous.
Can age
settle these long enmities?

Mai-dun Castle

THE ABANDONED

A temporary god departing leaves
a blankness to accompany your walk
that falls across green barley, cancelling
brick house-front, sky on elm –
a grace or focus lacking
robs the distance of its light.

A gap in colour measures all that shone
in those weeks when the god strolled at your side:
horizons of stone and nightfall
leaped at the mind's eye, steppes of sun
shook the discovered pastures, you approached
the same lit millpond again,
again.

Now what's beheld is a space dissolving,
ragged ingredients of foliage or cloud
stir at the corners of the glance,
the sounds of May arrive distorted,
the long tombs
send rivulets of darkness over the adjacent crops.

Displacement since that loss
has been recorded in real time;
the causeway you might take on any Wednesday

can never again
echo in that forgotten way beneath your footfall
since the clock commits all trivia to the same
buff file in the same abandoned warehouse.

Gone now forever the frequent gold
that ringed remembrance before it struck.
Withdrawn the god's
bright forefinger piercing the scene.
Failed his enchanted guarantee
that held the next suspended in the last.

Mislaid that formula which led
to gardens out of time
where sprays of blossom hang in azure air
above an unmoving sundial and each kiss
shivers with youth.

Now the insipid waves
lap round an empty pedestal and wash
the faintest hint there may have been a radiance
away.

GYNĒ

to Lynn

1   The tides shift
in and out
of your skin.

2   You tug at the moon's
orbit with your womb.

3   You know the way
lace ghosts move
through old houses.

4 Eyes gaze at themselves
  in every pair
  of mother and offspring.

5 Shadows of herbs
  brush your fingers.

6 You hold
  the young
  of each species
  roughly
  for their own good
  and watch
  them sleep.

7 Love
  contains them
  strong as an eggshell.

8 Your milk
  lifting along the veins
  of April
  nourishes
  the summer foliage
  with light.

9 Silence recalls you
  as the night dissolves
  about your beauty.

10 You listen
  and the unseen attends
  or dream and the unknown's
  remembered.

ON THE PRESCELLIES, JUNE

for Lee

The most difficult thing
is to stand on the spur
while a late afternoon
unfolds the haze or strikes
the distant lines of hay
and omit nothing, no
note fallen from the high
lark, no grey lamb bleating,
no tang on the faint wind
of clover, the day's warmth,
salt and sheep's dung nor yet
the open taste of air
that has picked up nothing.

A clutter of blue rock,
dark curve of the mountain
lifting towards the east
and the indolent fields
dropping away past green
clumps of oak and hazel –
to record these things now,
not for the future, not
as ingredients of truth
but as lights or textures
deployed round the moment
sufficient in themselves:
that is the hardest task.

A raven flaps its way
downhill and the harsh cry
drags silence behind it.
Small yellow flowers shiver
among tufts of coarse grass
and white stalks pierce the moss
round a patch of cracked mud.
Each detail must be placed
in time – this beetle, two
red moths fluttering apart –

till miles beyond the mist
blurring the plain the sun
lays flat gold on the sea.

Mynydd Preseli, 1978

THE MAGICIAN'S TABLE

for Tasha

On the ebony worn into grooves
    a cup half full of quicksilver
    the map of the stars of the north
    a raven's skull
    dried rowan-berries in a jar
    a pair of dice whose twelve sides show
            a black crescent moon
            a cobweb
            three diagonal lines
            an eyeless face
            the pawprint of a wolf
            nothing
            two sycamore leaves
            a needle
            a spiral
            an axe head
            a hollow rectangle
            four crowns

If you use the proper words
If you have brought coins of the right year
If you can solve the five questions

Then he will bring out the fragments of magic glass
and place them apparently at random on the table
with none of the small irregular pieces
fitting together in any way

One showed branches waving silently
Another hands on a yellow keyboard
Another numbers written by the dead
Another salt spilling slowly from a tear in a sack
Another someone who walks on sand
Another smoke obscuring a room

Some though inches apart shared the same scene
for a cat might pad across one
vanish
reappear on the other side of the table
and vanish there

He passed his left hand over the fragments
and glass now
reflected only
blackened beams of the ceiling

THREE SONGS FOR OCTOBER

I

Brown water laps
at the abandoned boathouse.
Days grow old. I close
the windows earlier and deflect
those few enchantments inward
stretching parched hands
to the blaze of apple-boughs.

Decline and solitude. Drawn curtains
sadden and piano-music
merely reflects the dark. Tired eyes
to gaze at nothing. Whirr of the clock
and one chime hourly. The chessboard
blooms with dust and a cobweb
trembles between pawn and pawn.

Sparse flowers dry in the vase.
The same admonitory shadows
expand the cold to glass
and wood and china. Tearing up
your final letters I recall
one evening when there were
lanterns across the river.

2

You turn to me and bring
a rhetoric of autumn
                              Voice
that belonged elsewhere
as the weeks here go to waste
the garden falls dishevelled
and past the thorn–hedge
tidal reaches flatten
steelgrey after the gale
                              Your touch
held comfort as the year dissolved
blocked in the space
between the saffron roses
and dangled silence from eaves
now choked with rain
                              Whole memories
of racing sunlight
dropped from your kiss
                              What can
resemble these rooms in winter
where portraits stare at nothing
and where the clock between empty lamps
points to the past
                              A white gull
curves by the gold file of birches
on the landward side
                              The colours
drift and fade
                  An ardour
that descends to tenderness
or worse
              There have been
no messages again
                              Where does

236

this strip of path lead
under frost
          The dark
is gathering in clusters along bare twigs
the way the pool
brushed by the wind starts calm
to collect the night
                    The few leaves stir
rasping on the flagstones
and it seems in terror
I have imagined your hand

       3

The chain holding the gate to
is brown with rust and a dry vine
lashes it to its post

I walk there once a day
and pick the last of the marigolds

Glance up the lane and see
a tall cloud on the brow of the hill

Nobody comes to revive the year

In wet grass along the hedgerow
the berries swell with venom

The hours lie sterile on each other

Apples fall sour and hard
from branches grey with lichen

No letter from your new address

Rooks drink the twilight
and in the empty house
one stair creaks unnervingly

Moonset and eddies of cold
though nothing moves outside

My face grown pallid in the mirror

DEATH OF A FRIENDSHIP

I mourn, now that your house contains
such fractured shadows.
This wine you've handed me
tastes sour. I joke and you do not laugh.
When you speak, assuming my approval,
I stare into discoloured
depths of my glass, longing
to get away.

Rain drives against your walls. The few
shrubs you have planted shrink in the cold.
Where there was amity, questions
echo between us. Tufts of dark
lilac branching from tall vases shed
minute dry flowers like grief
for a lost fragrance, leave
on the smooth piano scattered omens
neither of us can read.

The past is empty of romance;
its summers flecked with heartbreak
and its negatives destroyed.
But weren't there moments when
the blue sea glittered, when the lithe
curve of a diver forged another
link between wave and cloud?
I wonder, though, in fear –
were those young grinning faces always
plague-marred, was the fun a lie,
were dreams we've jettisoned
mere husks about this dirt,
dislike? One fiction may
have replaced another for
wherever I look with you I find,
instead of light, a slyness.

We could not name the truth. What used to brag
lies in your cupboard under lock and key.
You care no more
for angels or the underdog,

translating all the terms we used
into intolerance. Your world
now clusters round
the emulation of the rich.

I can't feel glad about old times
because I am afraid
that what I see here I suspected then
but shunned the knowing.
The tarnish of this has rubbed off on me.
The years we shared look counterfeit. If so,
more than affection died today.
What hurts perhaps the most
is that in you as in a mirror shows
not only what I could have been
but what I was or am.

LADY CHAPEL, ELY

Grey sunshine slanting
in a cube of light.
Mid-May. The paved floor
holds on to winter.

Ferns of dry coral
bleached by the ages
sprout curved and brittle
from fossil-branches.

Clarity fills all
available air
and pushes space back
against the four walls.
The building is steeped
in lore of radiance
cherished, remembered

under the criss–cross
threads of an anthem.

This box of thin stone
presses dark soil while
remaining in touch
with elsewhere. This place
created to track
the flight of angels
acknowledges one
pigeon clattering
by that bright window,
and those who enter
with the right purpose
are borne unwinged past
the places and years.

NATIONAL GALLERY

The forests of another world
      glow on a background mixed
by night – lit trunks, hot foliage,
      each fruit luminous. Sound
comes muffled. Through thin trees, winding,
      one horseman approaches
armed. The blackness stirs as when draughts
      ruffle tapestry. Here
pollen from an unearthly flower
      drifts over vivid glades
making the grass, gold skyline, one.
      Neither picture is ours.
That path leads under the blue threat
      of June. Barley rustles.
Cumulus shadows come, go. Gulls
      cry a warning. The breeze
caught brine, caught soil. The red cliff's edge
      is crumbling year by year.

ENCOUNTER

Unseen your skin
with its pleasure
taunted my hands
while long moments
passed in desire
gazing at lips
curved in a smile
and at your hair
catching the light

(Sound of the rain
striking the bright
tufts of apple-
branches in flower
and in the room
reluctantly
day doling out
saffron shadows)

Your fingers were
bound too briefly
around my own
to allow time
for the charming
guesswork of sex
so I stand you
poised in the dream
sun-tanned, naked

LIGHT GROWS . . .

Light grows and in the stealthy room
        the lovers are revealed –
one full-face, one tanned in profile,
        the eyelid clamped trembling
on both the victories traced by night.
        Soon now, too soon, parting
means the harsh taste of the last kiss,
        beauty locked in mirrors,
bare skin traded for a world where
        lies thrive in sunshine, bronze
statues of triumph in the square
        prance their indifference,
fountains aim at clouds, the lavish
        flowers for sale catch daytime
from the crowd and two who have known
        in secrecy such paths
along each other's pleasure must
        tread pavements as strangers.

EQUINOX

The hills
tug at one another
capped with beech

A pared moon swings
uncanny
in the copper sky

Each blade of grass
is now a magnet
and the dew
falls as sparks

Ears of corn
silver beneath the soil
begin to sway

The bedrock
sings with tension
and a pebble
held to the cheek
whines

The air splits in two

Out through the new
fissures of darkness
tumble the rose
the pear
the hard holly

There is one clap
of bright
inaudible thunder

The night closes
sealed

Earth has crossed
the threshold of summer

ADVISE ME

You sit up late
in your house on the estuary
while the thorn-hedge
sparks into flower
and cold stars swirl about the tip
of The Bear's tail.

Ten years. Ten years
without you when I think at one
          now legendary
          time five minutes
apart would have been too long dragged
          from your kisses.

          You re-appeared
out of some unmapped place. Poems
          describing you
          went humming round
those grey concrete walls. You were still
          slim, still charming

          as when pressing
against me, eyes moist, you'd pleaded
          with me to stay
          but lust is such
a fickle master I stood close
          by you unstirred.

          Drink wine alone
for night flattened on your windows
          will not betray
          secrets we shared
and treasure still although we own
          them no longer.

NEAR AVEBURY

Beyond the field one block
rears taller than a man.
The lichen makes green stars and noon
scoops at the surface with shadows.

Ripening corn
flows past the plinth of turf
where furrowed soil

bordered the dry
stalks of January.

Bright axe,
the flakes of healing leaves,
antlers,
jet bead –
what mysteries were found
gripped by the skeleton?

Along this hedge
note the convolvulus,
whitened,
dying.

DOCUMENT

I changed my flag and fought against
        the stars, but still you haunt
me with your dark hair, with your blond
        hair – nor have I forgone
allegiance to a time when each
        white bud unfolding meant
a catch in the throat mimicking
        desire. The foreign braid
glittering on this uniform
        proclaims my loyalty,
conceals the cost – an ageing heart
        in conflict with itself.
I walk beside this canyon where
        grass-blades on the further
lip show gold in the setting sun
        for fate baulked of her prey
confuses what I glimpse beyond
        with boredom, with longing.

PELLÉAS AND MÉLISANDE

They met in the shadowed garden.
                Between the trees, far off,
lay the last of the shining water. It was
their first encounter. They were alone.

Cries from the crew and the great
                sails hauled aloft. Brightness
withdrew from the high gold span of day.
Hissing against the waves the ship entered

a stormy sunset. A lighthouse blinked.
                The castle, her new home,
unseen. Only the one glimpse of sea. Elsewhere
dense tree-trunks, vines, flowered shrubbery.

There were no words as darkness thickened,
                leaves swayed and a salt breeze
brought the cold. And still she did not move
looking through twilight at her husband's brother.

ST. JULIOT

Thomas Hardy, Monday 7 March 1870

A stile of vertical blue slates,
ferns licking them.
The churchyard starred with snow,
still falling.
Scrawny daffodils bent
over a cast of snowdrops.
Steep field.
Below, a steeper wood,

leafless, sleeving the torrent
tumbling, tin-grey.

Snow blown from the south,
bruised wall of sky.
Flakes circling an unseen centre.
Snow through bare thorn,
lying as powder on the flat primrose leaf.
Snow in the gale hissing among branches.

Beyond the wind was silence.
Then the boy coughed and the door creaked open.
The nave was cold where the girl prowled,
read the carved tablets with no excitement,
turned to her parents again,
smiling, impatient.
                    Who would not swap
wisdom for youth, being middle-aged,
yet have traded firm thighs for understanding
in our spring years?
In this place once regret was focused.
The splendour here was celebrated late,
perhaps not even recognised as splendour
till the chance was gone.
What mapped then – think, compare – our meeting?
A chalk lane and a shingle beach,
the cropped grass of the high down,
far glitter of the sea . . .

He came here alone
with the green beginning.
Flowers sparked among the gorse.
There was salt in the north wind.
He came expecting nothing
and what was there he did not see
until long afterwards, again alone.

The vision, elusive along these lanes, was irony.
When he re-visited the place and found
even her ghost a teasing absence, all
he had ever written about tricks life played
seemed cruelly confirmed
near the waterfall and at the turn in the path.

Gusts bring more snow. It's time to leave.
Our son sings to himself and our daughter
asks questions ignoring the answers and we nod
and try to explain, holding chapped hands,
laughing together,
not without reverence, no, with awe
at such wry gifts, at that
embittered passion, at the waste,
the grief remembered and the love
known at the wrong time and set down too late.

AT THE TOMB OF CHATEAUBRIAND

He recommended
a blunt grey
cross stuck here
against the north.

Green sea
hisses beneath on granite
and the unceasing
gales bring mist.

Under the stone slab
a fleshless head
stares into earth.

Ear-sockets
of crumbling bone
catch the pointless
noise of the living.

Nothing excludes
the tide's return
or the black wind
or the seagull's
questioning cry.

Saint-Malo, April 1978

ZÉAMI IN EXILE

for Keith Bosley

The Nô poet Zéami, banished to the island of Sado in 1434, is reputed to have written there one of his greatest plays, Yuya, *the story of a courtesan made to dance for her lord even though she has received news that her mother is dying in a distant village.*

Wild island
and the north too near.
I walk among sparse colours
hearing the gulls cry above the rocks.
Endless the black foam-covered waves
that bar the gulf.
Through far haze sometimes
I glimpse the mainland,
blue mountains where the road
starts for home.

Impulses spurt in the heart –
old plays danced by brocaded actors,
court-ladies veiled in perfume,
the ache of distance.
What crime, what fault, what slight?
Displeasure and the lord's command.
The journey here, brightness dwindling.
Silence
after the salt crash of history.

The fishing-boat is a speck in cold sunlight.
A hawk grabs something out of the sea
and dropping it again
screeches, wheels.
I alone
not free to leave
this island that hangs in the sunsets of other men.

I pace the shore
spattered by spindrift,
murmur my prayers
in the smoky hut at nightfall,
wait for news.

And the gift falters.
A plant uprooted at the wrong time,
fixed in another courtyard, shrivels,
dies. My brush
suspended over this coarse paper
is laid down again.
The gale tears at the shutters,
flecks the ground with snow.
I read. Outside,
the empty speed of air,
the cold like cruelty in the mind of power
and the classic texts
do not spring into images,
offer no song,
no pattern.

Days change into one another.
I visit the shrine,
rinse my chapped hands,
stand by the vacant gate.
Or, in the frozen gloom of the temple,
repeat the proper words, eyes downcast
like the saviour's. He said,
The house is on fire for threescore years
and still we are reluctant to escape.

Bright ghosts tug at the sleeve. Tall grass
hissing in the palace garden.
Memory wears a painted mask,
speaks with a borrowed voice.
Lost passions drifting
as light depends on autumn or a stone
is dropped in the quiet river.

Darkness arrives and the wind
pours unabated from the sea.
A letter perhaps.
From an old woman.
Ill, far away and by herself.
The daughter pleads in vain
but has to dance.
Flowers tremble on the cherry-trees
and she weaves the call of conscience

into the dance, her steps unfaltering,
longing to be gone.

A light shower falls along the branches.

The brush
makes shapes down the damp paper,
each line
spreads sideways to the next
blurring the picture.
Cooking-smells from the brazier
sting my eyes and nose.
The waves
smash against the twilight
and I shiver in the gusts that jog the door.

Rain then on the fragile blossom.
A few petals fall, the dancer
catching them on her open fan.

And does the lord relent?

MEMORIES OF THE SINAGUA

When the mountain thundered
        and black ash hid the light
our people fled the anger of the gods
        ran with their blankets and pitchers
ran till far ahead a line of sky
        turned dark but not with smoke
darkened with night and there were stars
        stars only opposite those fleeing faces

When dawn yellow as a flower showed
        in a wider line of sky the roof
of smoke seemed thinner and not so dark
        nor was the roar of the mountain so loud

nor did the ground keep shaking under their feet
        shaking as they ran so that children stumbled
and the old had to be supported in their haste
        while the mouths of all gaped with fear

Our people came to the bank of a river
        a small river sluggish and winding through bad lands
where the water often failed in the hot season
        and no one could save the stalks of corn
 that withered and rattled in the dry wind
        without coming to ripeness

But there was nowhere else to go for the smoke
        covered the sunset and at night
distant flames flickered in the darkness
        while beyond the river that became our river
the many-coloured bad lands spread
        where nothing grows and the soil is poisoned

There was no other place so our people remained
        digging the pits in which to build houses
growing cotton and jointfir and green beans
        and many died in the parched times
when there was no river and the sky cloudless
        and the ditches cut through our fields held dust
though we sacrificed deer to the gods of the place
        and danced beating the soles of our feet on the earth
as rain beats down from the fat white clouds
        so corn can grow tall and the saltbush make its seeds

Our fathers and their fathers kept watch
        while the mountain spat fire
and the darkness that was in the sky
        dropped on the ground so that too was darkened
turned dark as the black ash dropped and lay thick
        till the land they had known as a good land
sloping red and ochre away from the mountain
        became a black land that was soft in its blackness

And then we are told the mountain fell silent
        the flames died the ash stopped drifting
and the sky cleared the way the wind
        combs away smoke over a cooking-fire

Seasons passed with rainfall and snow on the mountain
    the land stayed dark and silent beneath the wind
and our fathers saw green shoots on the blackness
    wondering they saw flowers
speckling the soft blackness like blue stars
    marvelling and thankful for the gods had sent them
had sent them flowers as a sign the ash was good ash
    sent flowers to show it was time for us to return

Our buildings stand sturdy and square and red
    the corn grows high and green in the fields
our women weave bright clothes from the cotton-plant
    our granaries are filled and our men squat at leisure
throwing their gaming sticks on the hard floor and shouting
    while scarlet birds screech that are brought by the traders
from a land to the south where such birds are common
    flashing their plumage in a place of many trees
for here a man may hunt all day with his dog
    and see no more trees than his hands have fingers

We are safe at the foot of the silent mountain
    tilling black earth and watching the breeze
drive a black haze over the fields
    for summers are dry now and the dust
lifts and spins taking the form of a wraith
    that runs dark and shapeless in front of the wind

NOTE *In AD 1065 a volcano erupted in northern Arizona, driving
the Sinagua people from their settlement. When the eruption ceased it
was found that the layers of ash had made the ground more fertile
than before. The Sinagua returned and farmed the land successfully
until in the thirteenth century a long period of drought forced them to
leave the area forever, though the splendid ruins of their villages still
stand in what is now desert.*

THE SISTERS

Luke 10.xxxviii

One sat in wonder while the other
went to the well,
fetched oil and salt from the storehouse,
dropped plates, scolded the cat,
chose wine in jugs, set fruit out.
And no one
crossed the tiled floor of the kitchen,
nor at first
did she ask for help,
just muttered underneath her breath
and felt hard done by.

The cat climbed in the visitor's lap
and Mary listened to the wry
glowing account of the way all things could be.
For food and drink
at this one time
were of no account.
Hospitality
for once
lay in the ear and heart,
not in business or display.
They were for later.

IMAGES OF CHRISTMAS

for Nichol

The tavern yard. And snow.
A heap of broken jars. Rakes leaning.
Stone trough bearded with icicles.
A disused shed,
laths showing through the plaster.
Inside, the mother in the hay

and Joseph, hand to chin, watching
while she attends to songs from another world.
Angels stand daylong on the peeling thatch.
The ox stirs,
the ass stamps a grey hoof
and the stable cat yawns in the straw.

God is a baby
and these stars, this frost
glitter forever at the core of time.
A king is born of a realm that has no name.
A priest is born who gives
transparent as a window on to truth.
A victim is born
to hold in wounded hands
the doom of all who suffer, all who die.

Three sovereigns kneel by the manger.
Dazzled, uncomprehending,
they lay down their gifts –
gold for the king of a land without frontiers,
incense to wreathe the priest who walks
as simply with the dead as with the living,
gold for kingship,
incense for prayer
and ointment ready for a sacrifice.

Bells ring in the unbuilt cathedrals.
The holly sways in the trackless wood.
And candles light the way to leave
the dark in any year.

BRUTUS IN HIS ORCHARD

Lull in the storm. Between these walls
a sense of time mislaid.
No moon.

The constellations blurred by cloud.

The trees hang heavy in the dark.
An owl's note shivers from the distance.
Drenched grass. Spread cobwebs here and there
catch at the glimmer of a falling star.

The hours drift to a standstill.
Night. And somewhere. Does the way
lie in this direction,
that or this? And dawn's
grey knifeblade at the east
behind which branch
leafless, invisible?

Meteors pierce the mist,
leave red tracks on the sky.
The cold air apprehensive
and the compass gone.

Far thunder.
    Still
the time seems ripe. And death
at this extinguished moment
logical, not to be feared.
A step towards oblivion.
No more.

I am not I. And nowhere. Am
a process of thought
lost in the darkness, dark mind
without position, past or action.
Inside the night. And by myself.
What I must do is harm. Now.
Either way.

A light.
The boy approaches.
Perhaps a message or reprieve.
The wind gets up once more, some rain
spills on my hand and I'm
no longer quite alone.

ANTINOUS

His beauty stands between two worlds.
    We picnic here on scraps
from private islands, half sunlit,
    half in shadow. Hadrian
banqueted. Live flesh absconding
    bequeathed the emperor
nothing but a dream of youth, sweet
    sweat, bare echoes above
the great river. Statues began
    kindly imitating
the past. In vain. Can a chipped mouth,
    blank eyes, the block of throat
dovetailing awkwardly with robes
    of stone, convey the loss,
that alien fragrance needed, gone?
    The drowned don't pose. Tribute
frequenting empty rooms is no
    match for the vanished kiss.

A SENSE OF THE PAST

Two eagles in a cleft of the sky above Delphi.
We trod rough grass in the stadium.
Thrasydaios the swift boy ran here
praising Apollo. The centre of the world is close.
Immortal light fell on the victor's limbs, his hair.

HISTORY OF ART

Art
like alchemy
waits for the full harvest

Smooth wheat
flowing pale and silent
into the storage jars

The smith with scorched hands
tempers the hot bronze
and the masked priest
dances amid fiery leaves

Leisure to trace
the twig across wet clay
and see each thing for what it is
as well as what it does

Whine of a swan's wing
across the flat spaces of the estuary
or sudden
orange on the swerving kingfisher

Watching till waves
cover the thorns of limestone
or adapting the night sky
into triangles and legends

When the grain is threshed
and the fruit gathered in
when the animals have bred
and the stockade's been secured
then images may be carved
of a world that never was
and the bright deer painted

Now is the time
to mix lead with sulphur
and from the cooling ash
draw the dry useless gold

GRAVE-GOODS

Spain, c. 29000 BC

They stayed in the shadow of the overhang
to watch him die.
There was no room for grief,
barely enough for a grave.

He gazed past them into daylight.
They were only shapes that stood,
presences without feature.
And in their stillness they knew –
even he had to obey that quick
choking, stop of the heart.

He would soon be a part of them.

His eyes lost life as the sun
reddened the far side of the valley.
A wolf howled close to the cave.

The elder son cut off the head,
scooped out the brains.
All ate solemnly
for he had read the scrawls of lightning,
set broken limbs,
found hidden water.

Apart from him they were afraid.

The pit was shallow.
Bending down they laid
his stone knife, still bloodstained,
across the ragged neck.
Then the dog-fox and the ewe were slain.
He would need patience as well as cunning
stumbling among the dead.

Mixing ochre into the soil
they heaped it over his wasted body,

over the slack animals,
over the knife he had made.

They returned to the cave each autumn,
chipped fine blades and hunted,
built fires.

Then they did not return.

The valley
thickened with trees.
Centuries were measured
in rainfall and avalanche,
the movement of herds.

Then others came,
took shelter in the narrow cave.
His spirit was strong.
They lived there many seasons,
tiptoed past the mound,
and left it untouched.

Lithuania, c. 6000 BC

When she was dying
they lashed her legs together.
She must not be allowed to walk.
They had all seen those who were dead
loom threatening like strangers.

A stone axe lay under her neck.
Between her knees was a bone dagger.

The boy pointed at the dagger.
When she stirred again, after the death-cold,
her fingers, groping for it through loose soil,
could cut the thongs that tied her.

The man nodded
and fetching more strips of hide
bound her wrists.
Straightening up
he spat on his hands
and cast the necklace of boar's teeth
into the pit beside her.

Hastily they scraped the earth into a pile.
Her skin seemed to flinch.
When it was all covered
they gazed at the mound in fear.
Her eyes
were pressing against the dirt
striving to see them, the buriers,
those who were still alive.

Muttering words that had to be said
they backed away.

Mist hovered by the lake.
The hillock with its raw mound stood empty.
She lay there, trapped, newly dead.
The air above
quivered with curses.

Brittany, c. 2300 BC

Using bracken and thorn-branches
they swept the floor of the chamber.
The dry stone blocks, carefully fitted,
gave off a smell of earth.

The narrow entrance allowed
a far-off flicker of the sea.
Wind hissed over grass,
brought fragrance of gorse and hawthorn.
Inside the tomb the air was still.

It was time for the offerings.
One box made of oak
held bronze axes. Another,
flint arrowheads. Another, made of elmwood,
was crammed with daggers.
All were unused.
A ritual wound nicked each blade.
They too had died.

When the gifts were in place
the tomb was sealed.
They buried the chamber with clay and pebbles,
roofed it with turf.
Time in utter darkness
slithered between the boxes.
The captive air grew stale.
There was no sound –
save from time to time a chink of bone
as the skeleton fell apart.

THE EASY DAYLIGHT . . .

The easy daylight
unrolls over soaked farmland,
cold stain of ponds
edged by the leafless alders.

Unmapped perspective
whenever the crinkled steel
of some unlikely river
seems too close.

Beyond the tall shadows of the winter
where sunlight is loosed
in green and dark mirages and in cloud
a hint of snow-flurries far away
is leaning against
the enigmatic hills.

STAND CLOSE AND DARE TO DISBELIEVE . . .

Stand close and dare to disbelieve
in the ghosts of departure.

I hear your breathing measure what remains,
a stir of dust behind the photograph,
the stone steps by the terrace
preparing their echo.

Sundial and urn
continue their disintegration,
months of your anguish
shred into the dark.

All we committed here
hangs in the growing shadow,
trails at our heels throughout
the time to come.

Rose light and the westering day
suffuse the clock face. Hold my hand.

CHALK ESCARPMENT . . .

Chalk escarpment
and the buried river.
Lost ritual –
the braided cloths along the bank,
the sun's disc sliding in pails.

Picks formed from elk-horn
littered the dry valley.
Brambles, a scooped-out quarry,
flash of a green snake
and a smell of spark around those flints
like glass.

Here in the morning light
stand on the sea-bed
while the frail
skeletons of extinct creatures
come drifting down.

SUMMER IS ONCE AGAIN . . .

Summer is once again
my inability to love,
an empty table in the window
and readiness for scorn.

Who can survive among
these pyramids clipped from box
or peacocks spreading dark foliage
down narrow alleyways of turf?

The marjoram succeeds
and songs of triumph
are shaken from the lilac.

And if I chose
to turn the fountain off,
lock up the herb–garden
and the peach–trees?

Abandoning starlight
and the heavy scent of earth
to memory or
the incessant rustle
of the hour–glass.

NEVER AGAIN . . .

Never again
to see this length of water
or the fields
descending from the distance
to the further shore

White sails
on the tides of April

We turn indoors
to the bedroom full of photographs

One evening ahead
to start unfastening
the thorn-shoots tethering us here

Faint gauze
passes across the sun
and I watch you in the looking-glass
for the last time

PRECARIOUS TOUCH . . .

Precarious touch
as often before
on the iron cord
bracing conscience.

Four metal pennants
hold the prevailing wind.

The limestone buckles,
swells. The tower
impenetrable on the sunrise
poises against collapse.

All too soon
releasing from the crypt
such whiffs of resolutions
long concealed.

REDDISH NETS . . .

Reddish nets
dry on the harbour-wall
where spheres of pale glass
put off the sunlight.

A trail of smoke
from the departing ferry
hangs in the sky.

I leave the deserted quay
hearing the seagulls
and cross the intricate
reflection of the town
in the wet sand
composing the first of many
unanswered letters.

NIGHT THINS ALONG THE VAULT . . .

Night thins along the vault
and praise
tugs the reflection
blue and gold
along tomb and stall
and kneeling figures
in cloth or marble

You are here
though you won't believe me
via the force of love

Silver morning
tentatively
highlights finger
and open book

The altar
stands out from emptiness
fresh statements in a bygone language
inhabiting the ear

WOODS DENSE AND THE OLD . . .

Woods dense and the old
brick buildings hidden.
Roar of continued
water, path and trees
in an unseen mist,
a dank smell hanging
on the windless air
like iodine. High
walls run from the house,
enclosing a dark
garden blocked by one
yew-tree. Neglected,
a long lawn shows yards
of daisies, plantain,
its borders always
in shadow where flowers
fight the way noon mutes
them all save one white
lilac with such shapes
of blank fragrance that
momentarily
assert the summer.

THE GOD HAS ENTERED THE SEA . . .

The god has entered the sea
like a spread darkness
although my skin
is dazzled from his touch.
Elements of air and landscape
are one by one ticked off –
the samphire, hollow in the sand,
curve made by a grey gull on the wind.
The world brought down
to the sound of night,
to recollections of what thrilled
and therefore is discarded.
I apply
the acid-test of dreams
and am left with
strange detours round the past:
transcriptions, five-
finger exercises,
the shadow of a kiss,
one colour and the blemished gaze
from an ironic looking-glass
stuck in a previous year.

WINTER . . .

Winter.
The lamplight.
Black third-floor panes.
My thigh beneath your hand.
The portraits avert their eyes.
We commit love.

Nemesis.
Can thought bring on the end?
Old stone flaking.
The roof glistens under dew.
Thrush-song and a May sunrise.
I leave your tousled bed.

DESIRE IS WHERE YOU WOULD HAVE BEEN . . .

Desire is where you would have been,
love where you are.
Shock of his mouth on me,
the cornfield stretching round us,
and his sudden taste. Daylight then
span with stars as the texture of July
clung to our palms; bared skin;
caress. With those forgotten hills
jutting above the dry gold stalks
dark on the west. First
ebbing of the summer and the boys
get up reluctantly, stare
at the altered fields their eyes
wild with a silver focus, dress,
walk hand in hand across the frontier,
kiss once again more absent-
mindedly than to confirm, gaze back
at the lost enchantment under cumulus
and we are pledged forever you and I
to that long private look at that
receding memory. Desire's a land
you think you visited,
love solid ground.

ROMANCE . . .

Romance
A table-top littered with amethysts
Your hand on the faded map
deciding

The islands again
Dark leaves
strewing the inlet
And the memory of you
standing naked
in the tumult of summer

The firelight trembles and the gale
shakes in the chimney
Your eyes elude mine
though your kiss
was shot with salt light

Those cliffs relinquished by the sun
and the purple flowers dying

Chill sand
beneath bare feet

The imagination of your love

HIGH LEAVES ON FIRE . . .

High leaves on fire in the evening light
The valley blurred with gold
Dark lilac casts
a shadow on the stream
Silence
Save for your presence
hawthorn, may,

beside me
We talk intermittently
of the fading day, your hands
the shining grass
and in your too briefly
repeated glance
the way the dying east
withholds its stars

YOU HAUNT THE ORCHARD . . .

You haunt the orchard
and the telephone
kindles your silence

The greengage bowl, clothes
you once wore, comment
of the dark hillside,
vetch and pimpernel,
the locked desk, one book
with the place marked and
a dried-up inkwell

You once said when we're
older dreams between
embraces would go
but recollections
throng the deserted
galleries and warp
pure lines of the stream

Banish your shadow
and the willows shed
their silver
            Love once
more and your return
naked, indifferent,
through mist, through autumn

SOUND OF THE WEIR AGAINST
THE DISTANCE . . .

Sound of the weir against the distance,
clematis
starring the grey wall

The black tom cleans itself on the top step,
pauses as a bat starts hunting

The landscape adjusts to twilight
gilded by air that flows
from the slopes of legend

Paragraphs of the past
ablaze with woods left by the axe,
untouched parks strolled through,
love never spoken

Beneath lost colonnades
those lips not kissed
kissed hard and again

The sunset draws the evening away
and colours now diminishing
turn cold

NOVEMBER AFTERNOON . . .

November afternoon
The first frosts
I remember
your body underneath my hands

These spare boughs
separated by mist

Few gold leaves

Deer pick their way
over the hard grass

The clock
painstakingly
works through the white day
as I move in wonder
further from you
wherever you are

STAINED SUNLIGHT . . .

Stained sunlight
falls through prayer
dry sand
crumbling past shadow

Agreement whispered
and the time-dark pew
reaches through granite
to the scarlet winter
touching frost

Jackdaws spilled wheeling
where the half-hour
collides with dawn

Stone lilies
and the immobile
angel's wing

The mutter of lost hours
and dead hands
in harmony
smoothing the page

Victory

Kneel on the cold
so many lines of soil
above the past

EACH VANTAGE-POINT A MEMORY OF LOVE . . .

Each vantage-point a memory of love
once shuttered houses open to the day
and the dead sit there contentedly
in armchairs warmed by the falling sun

The stone goes yellow, holds the heat
this side of darkness where
I invoke you
                By the pool
the rhododendrons withdraw their bloom

Love meant for evening
questions each former kiss
with dreams of re-discovery
                        The voices
plan delight
        Or else rejection

You opened the piano, smiled and played
The window indicates a moon,
black roses
            Cry of a nightjar
The distant church counts nine

Furniture, velvet, leather bindings
show best by candlelight
Your profile now transparent
trembles, departs

CUPPED HANDS . . .

Cupped hands

Gold water brimming

A kestrel hovers
somewhere in the depths

Slow clouds passing
miles below the backs of my hands

The magic trembles
and the colours out of time
tarnish

Open the fingers
and spill forever on the ground
what seemed to be

Elegies

The First Elegy

The area was overgrown. Brambles and fireweed
had to be uprooted before a boundary
was agreed upon and the last pale
driven in next to the first. Sometimes
the acreage is complete before pen touches paper,
at others the map only remains itself and the final
shading contradicts the outline made at the start,
for example a grey summer's day and on the lake
hardly waves only the slightest folding
over of water on water with nothing reflected
though the hills enclosing it were purple
and on three sides trees came down to the shore.
Adults were elsewhere. We skimmed stones or sat round
in the gritty boat-house. What furniture I remember
appears scoured and cheap. There was a gramophone
playing swing. Unheard mosquitoes
stung our bare legs. Today we stroll beneath lime-trees
in another garden that does not belong to us.
At that time we could not have known each other
even though in a sense sharing the same time-zone,
privation, absence of sunlight, for war
had removed our fathers. The faces are unlabelled,
those melodies possess only a period texture.
I cannot recall who owned the property nor where
we went later. There was a small rocky island
but no boat and I couldn't swim in those days.
The dramatis personae were children on their own
for an afternoon and you and I increasingly
find ourselves left behind as they run over stubble
where the last swallows flash or enter gloomy
chambers in some ruined castle where the lintels
are too low for our foreheads. But a chipped stone egg
on my desk admonishes me for change
emerges from the air and colours the thinnest
depictions of the past. Late June there. Few flowers –
the one rhododendron flecked with unclenched scarlet

shows by its listlessness it has fulfilled
a yearly duty. The blinds are half drawn though only
on one far field where the hay has been cut
sunlight, slanting, picks out yellow among the green.
Knowledge of being alive at a given moment –
given if not taken – has details of heat and shrubbery
absorbing the past tense before we exclude them.
On the ground floor, there in the room forming the corner,
two oil-paintings, each about the size of a postcard,
display these illusions: one, a path through a wood in spring,
the other, a slow stream broadening into pools
under brown foliage. Both show what was needed
though neither comments on anything here
since the brush-strokes limit the scene not for the viewer
only but for the dead painter himself.
The way they've been hung would imply that it's the second
picture that holds autumn replacing April.
It could though be the other way around.
Take a day, any day, says the old fortune-teller.
It may be one that rises with indifference
to the surface, flicks the merest hint of a red
fin, gold scales, one among others, but at that time
you sat and read or went upstairs in a house
that has since been destroyed. You showed me the place,
now asphalt, near the church we were married in.
A copper beech spreads over this wall
and the dead elms show stark amid all the green.
When you were ascending that stair you saw
floor-boards stained dark, a carpeted edge of landing,
no foreshadow of a wind with dust and fumes
blowing across a sunken highway or its intrusion
years later into our talk. You stepped into space
going perhaps from one high room to another
and the crunch of gravel is cancelled under
our shoes as we leave this path for the lawn
but where I wonder will the two of us be when this
is remembered together or separately. The sun by now
has closed the last of the distant hay-fields though one
shaft of light sinks through green water in the estuary.
The open sea is concealed by the long shoulder
of the foreland. In theory you can walk round any lake.

The Second Elegy

Locality is present in the curve of a bowl
and the style has lost all heritage, all sense
of place, gone nameless, international.
Geology though cannot be flouted and subtler
changes happen in the quality of clay
even from village to village. The water, pigment,
wood-ash, flowing through space, reach time. It is hard
to detect lost sunlight or lines on the potter's hands
but soil round the roots of the plum-tree still
matters when fruit is eaten miles from the farm.
Some years ago now, on a walking holiday,
I encountered the whereabouts of a ghost.
At a threshold in the centre of the manor-house
you moved three centuries. The owner's voice
went on explaining but now there was a sweet
illness in my nostrils that got stronger
as we mounted the stairs till in the narrow
bathroom overwhelmed I had to lean on the cold wall
hearing words with difficulty through a smell
of rotten flowers, vase-water, meat going off,
and it was there according to the legend
that the dead monk had lain. There are also
the books to be chosen when one is about to cross
a desert. It is important to know something of the rocks
as well as the living things – rare blooms, the snake
coiled to strike – for there are bound to be lodestones.
Before selecting compass and penknife
one is strongly recommended to make a note
of one's own name and address, even mark the house
on the map for mirages occur and time-slips
and people have been known to stray far from the dusty
water-courses. No one belongs in an airport.
We motored over with rugs and a wicker
picnic-hamper to watch the fragile planes taxi
on the flat grass. Mechanics and travellers seemed
to have a place there but then that was an aerodrome.
We lay together at the foot of the slope discussing
desire in whispers, the dew was tracking the sun
as it diminished, the busy or languid players
cast distorted shadows on the field and the bat

struck the ball a full second before the sound reached us.
You watch lightning flicker over the tossing trees
and count five spaces of time as one mile. Today
the bar of twilight stretched between pole and pole
travels as fast but we adjust our watches
without winding them. Many have died since that time
and I have mourned them, attended the funeral,
grieved for the unseen smile, the dependable love,
but then dry seeds dropped in the earth give no
indication of stalk or flower, no glossy
berry or flourish of leaves, if a pun is not flippant
there is no hint of the yew-tree, indeed
looking at a corpse one would say, This is nothing.
The soul has begun its journey. You listen
to a record with the cat on your lap, the sounds
pass her unheeded. We also fail to intercept
movement of angels or the clamorous sense
made by the dead we knew. Other examples
demonstrate time – petrified sea-shells clinging
to the mountain-top, cold accumulations
of lava carved by the endless wind. A grouse
scuttled over the heather and I searched
for the nest without finding it. Unseen, always,
the wonder of speckled egg, of shrivelled leaf
and the seed-case is matched by the wonder
of fossil and rainbow. This is the interchange
of faith and belief. A sandstone escarpment
drops almost sheer to the north. Far below
in the green cup scooped by ice is a round pool
and sheep are grazing. In better weather
you could see more but at noon sudden spurts of rain
blur even the near-distance and grey shreds of cloud
pass level with the summit. It is politic
to keep out proper names as far as possible.
Poems aren't works of reference. They provide
the interested reader with the kit he needs
for an excursion into the uncharted hills
from which he'll come back tanned, unfocused, acquainted
with other ways of expressing each pavement or garden.
And there are as many editions of poems
as there are readers because *house*
will have a different shape for each of us
and *apple* a different taste. What do you see

when the word *red* is mentioned – bricks, a cock's comb,
the Whitsun altar, part of a flag, a judge's robes,
last Wednesday's sunset, blood at the dentist's, flamingoes,
garnets, a pillar box, fuchsia, morocco leather,
a pimpernel? What is selected will of course
isolate you for nobody includes the same
objects in a suitcase. Only music perhaps
can command the logic of its ingredients.
Wherever painting is involved the room,
the air dictate their gold, their mistiness. Glitter
of flood-water gets into the simplest paragraph
of a letter home so how can a poet say what is
or is not present in his poem. Fixing the terms
is the first task though organised with dangers
like opening windows on the cold side of a house.

The Third Elegy

Reality never gets into the newspapers.
A snapshot or a television programme
are most remarkable for what they leave out.
Swann said, 'They call our attention each day
to insignificant things whereas we read
three or four times in our life the books in which
lie the essentials.' Outlines of metaphor
rest on the map and the rain falling so quietly
is not the real rain. Water-lilies bloom now
in the pool, wax-yellow, scarlet. The dragonfly
we saw yesterday darts, a bronze flash among reeds,
and I stroll twice a day down to the post office
and collect nothing. None of this is correct
though the truth is present as a tight bead of water
among the hard petals. You took me by the hand
and told me of your unhappiness. No phrase,
no caress of mine reached the boundary of sadness,
altered it. This won't work either though reality
sometimes occurs in a poem just as it's only

in examination of time that eternity
makes any sense. If on a journey you stay
obsessed with the contents of your pockets
you will not be touched by the development of space
and space is the protection of the infinite.
The bird sang deep in the forest, the horseman
galloping up the ride did not hear its call
though later that evening when the rain held off
the crescents punched by the hooves brimmed with water
and perhaps the same bird went flying across
its own reflection. Wonder is a faculty
many do their utmost to smother in children
but when the pear drops on wet grass and the moon
urges the tide among salt-flats, the world
declares its magic the way in the silent garden
the figure walking by the tall box-hedge
was not there at the turn in the path. Two people
in love who share the same interests – films, coins, wine –
disagree over the method of pruning roses
and fascination with cut glass or prehistory
may appear uninviting. But poetry
is neither a pastime nor a public act.
It is an ordering and from that rearrangement
each reader extracts another. In among
the gestures of the orchestra a music emerges
that was not the composer's intention.
You can train the intellect as you would a retriever
or a sheep-dog but it is only one of many
apprehensions – there are also the five
senses, instinct a sixth one, emotions forming
a barrier like intolerance or else a dye
like joy, a soul that teaches us to love
and the spirit, atrophied in many, that holds
relations outside time. It is as absurd
to limit response to reason as to obey
a tone-deaf man's view of a concert.
I do not try hard enough to see through your eyes.
And I know, dear, I bore you. Once, years ago,
an archer entered the mews where dusty windows
brought in the morning and hooded falcons
gripped their perches. He chose ten arrows.
Dew glistened on the short grass for the hay
had been stacked the week before. He set the target

clear against the darkness of the forest.
Stringing his bow he shot the arrows one by one
which missed the padded circle and stuck like a grove
of leafless saplings bent by the wind. How else
can I define my love as the words employed
replace my passion with the unreal events
of metaphor? How may I leave my love for you
fixed on the fields of time if I can't
convey the unspoken except with words.
Others have painted the conquest of death and shown
the calm Christ stepping over the sprawled soldiers.
Others depicted the blaze of recognition in the inn
as the travellers grasp the fact they've been walking
along the edge of two worlds. Reality lies
in the empty tomb, on the road to Emmaus.
What will convince you that this is not blasphemy?
Love must go beyond the here and now
if it is to be anywhere. I think I tried
to read the misery in your eyes that day.
When you cross a familiar room in the darkness
the table you do not brush against is still there.

The Fourth Elegy

The starting-point may once have been a rose
or a rose-seed or, as you watch through glass
burnished by autumn, one petal falling
and striking the thorns as it falls. An age
of lyricism can be said to have ended.
He stands there, flushed and starlit before the mirror,
uttering cryptic phrases, for instance, 'The well
is fed by a spring on the highest point of the island'
and the reflection laughs back with Arcturus
studding the bare shoulder. The finest of all
influences is memory. Zophar, the third
of Job's comforters, says of the secrets of wisdom
that they are double to that which is.

A new enigma is detected gliding
under the surface of words where dark alders
hang low and insects form a dancing cloud.
There are times when no phoenix rises screeching
from its charred nest and the day leads dry
and unconsoling in every direction.
In exile however he gets up early,
breakfasts alone by the sunny window and watches
the lines of snow-capped peaks above the pine-trees
forming the frontier, for here they speak a different language.
He spends each morning at work on his masterpiece.
His hosts are considerate – he has this house
rent-free plus an income. And he is at liberty.
At evening, alone, a sense of pointlessness
enfolds him like smoke. Why pin any hope on the next
generation or on the next but two?
Those who might find these pages scorched with his indignation
of interest, even of use, are distant and timorous.
Sales of his work in translation grow less every year.
He was once a wonder, his books, his integrity
valuable fodder for speeches on freedom
but now it's the tenth day and the world has changed.
This cool gallery is lined with ancestors
of a total stranger, some in armour, some in orange velvet,
proud or stupid or handsome, having one thing in common,
the gift of death. To pass dutifully before each portrait
is little good. One is sometimes in too much of a hurry
even to examine the curl of a peony,
the gleam of light on a far pond or the cloud
whose summer brightness holds a dark blur of rain.
A glint of silver among the shadows of rosewood
recalled that room, do you remember? and the sunset
lighting the end of the street while the high gulls
drifted. The questioner remains austere
in the very centre of recollection. Logic
must never be ignored but cannot equal
conviction like a radiance behind the eyelid.
At rare moments of revelation there is only
the state of being as foliage is in gold air.
I know because I can't be sure, I am aware
but locked in rings of iridescence that conceal
time. There are two kingdoms. You belong in both, the one
where you degenerate and where all paths

must peter out in grass or stone or other paths
and the other where the moment stands
weightless in splendour. The platform was empty.
Milk churns were stacked in the warm shadow.
A smell of haycocks came from the near field
and a score of caged pigeons waited murmuring
for their release. When evening comes you sit
reading and the book falls to your lap and the corn
left by the harvesters sways with ripeness.
Or I watch you sleeping. Every frontier
is made up of such moments. It is a question
never of place but of time. The mirror as well
holds danger especially when, fringed with dusk,
a white face flickers behind you, vanishes.
The future too has barriers between room and room
but at times it is enough to write letters
as the moon's course slants across the square of window
and offer a few friends who may never read them
the chance of sharing in a borrowed midnight.

The Fifth Elegy

Airs of summer wind their way through the empty chamber
for the skulls have gone to stare behind glass at a crude
map on the museum wall. Perhaps the bones
were removed piecemeal when the mound fell in. The sun is low
and slopes of tough grass fleeced with hazel
repeat the fragrance of the day. High stone slabs
freed from burial by five thousand years of rain
stand in the light and frost. You do not like these journeys.
Along a green-sided estuary where the tides race
hedgerows are twined with dogrose and stunted
apple-trees crowd against the white-washed farmhouse.
Fuchsia blooms by the gate until late November.
Beyond the water, fields lift towards the sunset where bare rocks
are whipped by the fog. The ferry would take us dryshod
past a brown seagull floating. The brasswork shines,

flush with the fine red wood. Each screw is countersunk.
Blue leather cushions are spotless and the rowlocks
turn silently. Art matters as itself, as structure,
as joy in its own structure though the function
may be to get something across. You must remain
conscious of the surface, its music, the promise
of another world even when the devil is muttering
lacklustre words. The worst is to be tempted not to try.
Better to scoff forbidden fruit than offer
the easel for sale. You can't make money the way
you make a sonata, make a field give grain,
make love, unless the coins are counterfeit.
The unimportant aspects last each day
from nine to five. It was a still June evening.
The guests stood by the open window. When they'd gone in
to dinner, glancing round the table, she asked
my cousin where the grey lady had gone, the one
all by herself in the other room. And her host warned her
by kicking her under the table for the grey
lady was seldom seen indoors, preferring it seemed
narrow paths of the garden, the scent of stocks
and warm brown bees working among the lavender.
Old houses like churches find it hard to exclude
the bruises of memory and layers of atmosphere
placed there by prayer or perhaps incidentally
because of a quarrel never properly made up –
year after year some grudge against destiny,
letters unsealed that glowed with stale
impressions from abroad. You'll find a lace fan
and a jigsaw in that cabinet – also
a pack of cards with the nines missing. Sculling
on a foreign lake the son who'd sold the estate
heard distinctly the stable-clock chiming. There's a green
cul-de-sac lined with the graves of dogs. The hill
looks over glittering beech-trees to the moor.
You climbed a different path, one that seemed easier,
and we met by a bed of yellow roses
twisted by the wind. The children were there already
pretending to be horses. We saw the white half-moon
and the distant colours of the sea. Naturalism
is an outmoded form. For a millennium
those who were buried in the shadow of that church-tower
have known of life what we know, that reason

reaches only so far before the truth
takes over. Listen now to the first birdcall
as the trees show a barely perceptible
shiver of green. And water too is sacred in well
and trough and font like hawthorn-leaves and the red
cord that links the child to the mother. You struggled
slipping on greasy chalk in the lane that autumn
and your beauty, flushed, laughing, was such that my heart
was seized with more love than I had imagined possible.
Who though can put a face on words or claim
to interpret the sundial? All we can say for certain is
there was a house, a tomb, a copse, and beyond
the land sloped to the river-mouth. This journey
will take its place among the many ways
of identifying movement. The portraits have arrived.
So have your books. Look at the distance. It has been
a cold summer. I was told in the village this morning
that the old man who rowed the ferry has died.
We could hire a car and drive inland to the bridge.
It's not on this map but would you like to go?

The Sixth Elegy

The track, cut in the yellow stone, runs straight
between flowering shrubs. To the left the ground drops,
the trickle of a stream is clearly audible. The southern sky
is hidden by the slope of trees, green upon green,
swaying. On the path it's still, sheltered from the wind.
In one room only, though at frequent intervals,
the furniture was shifted, usually at night,
but not always. This is a fairly well-known
phenomenon – like the spare needles
twisted out of shape inside the sewing-machine
or the pair of scissors found in the empty scullery
with a black zigzag running the length of one blade.
The horse was discovered kicking, terrified,
in a disused room with a door so narrow

they had to break down a wall to get him out.
Puberty seems to provide a focus for these storms
almost as if the child hitherto controlled
by other forces trembles between two
contradictory poles. One often uses 'it'
for a child and perhaps absolute possession
of gender, fixing the young man or woman,
atrophies other powers. What was glimpsed, once, no longer,
between the fickle leaves? A king and queen,
their naked bodies the colour of wild flowers,
stroll laughing and the sound of their laughter
is shrill, anarchic. A fairy huntsman pursues
the unwitting adult and transfixes his head
with a silver lance that vanishes. A tall figure
created itself out of dancing shadows and moved
across the wood like details of another wood.
The house shook slightly. If you treat the symbol
as a screen before an object claiming the thorn
indicates protection or the ruined barn
the failure of the old ideas you reduce the painting
to a work in code. The hills of allegory are real
hills, stars burn and the lion stalks among high trees
lashing its tail. It is often an effort
to look north and south among the images
and those who translate the poem into prose
are praised for having found the solution
for the achievements of intellect are the ones
that seem to count. Lip-service paid to dead poets
or to the statements of religion is as much as most
are prepared to pay. But Blake not alone knew
it's the other way round. What the narrow-minded
conceive of as reality is only the first step.
We have lived elsewhere. How otherwise explain
the shock of recognition at the gap in the hedge,
that day high on the downs when the sun led you
to a place you knew though it was your first visit.
Each dawn renews our loss. Half-creatures, stumbling,
seeing through a divided eye, we slip
from plane to plane and walk bewildered as the light
rises and shifts the distances round until
we are uncertain of our whereabouts and wonder
which one is our companion, which the ghost.
The cuckoo flew hooting above the rowan-tree

where the stone avenue points downhill to the spring
that trickles from the grass. You have seen this
and gone over marshy ground in winter to find
the last brooklime unshrivelled and the crow's
shadow on a litter of bones. The danger
lies not in loneliness but in absorption
leading to self-absorption. This was never meant.
There is the need to be kissed and the need
to be by oneself. Our children called out in sleep
and my own nightmare put the wrong faces on friends.
No comfort issues from the dark. There is a splendour
inside the heart that cannot be challenged.
Who is that pale woman with grey hair standing
silent in the white room? She smiles as though
she recognised who we are. The moat is frozen,
the orchard stark and bare. If we are patient
there won't be time for questions at the end.

Coming to Terms
(1994)

DESCENT

Into an area of stalactites where children venture rashly
and silica glints above the eyeless fish in their pools
lead me who am equally lost, equally in peril.
I miss the stars. This stone warren, lovely in torchlight,
has nowhere for a horizon. Slow, cold, the stone orchards
swell with petrified fruit, the narrow fields grow rough with
     stone barley.
I knock my head against hanging columns
or stumble blindly along a mineral world.
The roof here is beyond the reach of your lamp.
We have threaded the twists and turns for so long
I cannot point back to the entrance. There's been no north,
only the shuffle sideways up an uneven ledge
or the crawl down slippery tunnels which join two echoing spaces.
When we stand silent there is the drip of water,
the faintest whisper of a distant stir of air.
Don't turn off the torch again. That utter blackness
squeezed against the eyeballs puts the mind out
and a man's dissolved to terror, bone and skin are shadow,
black blood pounds in the veins, the breath you gulp is black.
Why have you brought me here? Where are you taking me?
There is no end to these paths through cold limestone.
In such deep caverns even the ghosts are dead.

NOON ON SUNDAY

a portrait of the poet's wife

Shadow of you
on window-pane
profile among shifting
leaves dark green light green
flickering with silent
silver of rainfall
while a quartet
composed across centuries
comes from an old town
over a hundred
miles away and still
listening I ponder
the chance of our meeting
unique counterpoint
of movement and luck
though your reflection
lucid on foliage
hangs unreal whereas
by turning I behold
your beauty blonde
sun-tanned with no
complication
of rose-bush or hazel
to lessen the lovely
presence of you

THE GREEN CHILDREN

for Joan and Jack

They were just there one day,
two of them standing by a clump of bramble.
'Where have you come from?' we asked.
They shook their heads.

Their skin was the colour of grass,
their eyes, and hair, and nails
resembled early wheat, or mint, or shadows among ferns.
When they opened green lips to speak
their teeth, their tongue gleamed like the stripes on a marrow.

They could not take our food at first –
only the pith of beans, that they devoured.
Slowly they grew accustomed to our ways,
drank milk, ate bread, lost colour.

When the boy died he was hardly green at all –
just a glimmer from a summer wood at dusk
each time he tried to smile.

They learned our language, told us of their land.
It's always twilight there, the sky
pricked by a few elusive stars.
Otherwise it seemed a country much like ours
with coppices, slopes and meadows
bordered by a wide river.
Beyond, they could see bright trees
and the air above them showed a mistier gold.
No one had ever crossed the water to that further shore.

The girl lived on among us for many years.
She could never explain how she and her brother came here.
Sometimes, deep in her eyes, you saw leaves stirring.

*(The tale of the Green Children is told in Woolpit Church, near
Bury St. Edmunds, Suffolk)*

'OUR HISTORY WAS LIKE A DESERTED STREET'

– Dmitri Volkogonov

The parade with flags and cheering faces
passes across a scratched newsreel
in silence. No echo was caught on the soundtrack.
Events that mattered took place offstage.
Machine-guns stuttered from distant squares.

Families in that grey block of flats
were all taken. Some screamed for mercy.
Most went in sullen obedience. One by one
the little shops closed down.
The postman became a rare visitor.
No one wanted to set down the past.

They shut the newsagent's. Then the library.
Perhaps, behind that neo-classical façade,
the books are still gathering dust.
Probably not. They'll have been destroyed
along with the archives, for history
must be a series of blank chapters.
Those who could have testified will never come back.

It's not a street now for the living. Bare pavements.
Bare roadway. No hoardings or bicycles.
Uncurtained windows. Windows boarded up.
Smashed windows betraying darkness,
glass splinters glittering in the gutter.

The men and women who belonged here,
who bought their bread and cigarettes
and waited for trams chatting by the kerb
lie tossed in an unmarked pit.
Some ended as cold smoke
spewed from chimneys above the ovens.
Others sprawl as bones
among a handful of metal name-tags
in a ditch near the battlefield.

It took a lot of lead –
and chemicals – and paperwork.
It took determination as well as an unswerving
loyalty to the cause. It took time.
It took shoe-leather and medals
and throats gone hoarse from shouting orders.
It took cordite – and barbed wire –
and the axe-blade. It took persuasion.
But in the end it proved worth the trouble.
The street lies deserted.
It need never be peopled again.

THE BIBLE IN CORNWALL

for Jack Clemo's 70th birthday

The headstone leans.
Blurred angels, garlanded,
grin under corrugated rain.
God's acre tilts. Weeds trickle into fissures.
A mineshaft slants beneath the graves.
Dead families hear the chink of ghostly hammers.

Hell may lurk inside a cliff or kiln.
The damned themselves must be man-made.
Where there's life there's sin. We sabotage
our own attempts at holiness.
Christ wears a crown of gorse.
The tin nails are hourly driven home.

Hymns falter.
The board with the Commandments hangs askew.
Each bride and groom can if they will
prove love a suppler thing.
We turn our backs on dawn – unlike the moors,
the spoil-heaps, etched relentlessly.

God spat on earth.
He moulded Adam into a jug of bone

and poured life in.
We're smashed. The soul runs free.
Salvation's still at hand in bread and air. We find
the impress of the Pietà in china clay.

STOKE WOODS, NOVEMBER

The autumn slope
under tall beeches, unmoving
and golden, stole
into twilight, mist and shadows
creeping like webs
from branch to branch. Dull pools of flood-
water darkened
along the valley like mirrors
in a widow's
bedroom. My shoes crushed unmourned leaves.

No stag would pound
uphill towards me, no child's voice
break in wonder.
The last blackberries had shrivelled.
Hours of night hung
waiting. I was unwelcome here.
The marauding
blackbirds chinking in panic left
winter to turn
solitude into loneliness.

A far gunshot
warned me it was too late to walk.
Other concerns
tugged at the moment unable
to snap the spell.
Who can wake the past from its sleep?
My melancholy
would not relinquish the attempt
nor did I wish
to leave the precincts of the trees.

LAZARUS BREAKS HIS FAST

from the painting by Sickert

What could it have tasted like,
that first mouthful of life again?

Aridity of the tomb,
faint start of disintegration,
throat hardening,
palate dry –
then to be
jerked back again from darkness,
from the quiet,
back from that slow
place of mortal rotting –
air gurgling down into the lungs,
sunlight
clamped on eyes that had learned not to see.

He's sitting by a table,
awkward,
not used to anything,
cutlery, chair-back, floor.
His own room has now become
a blockade of strange shapes.
He's gaunt, unfocused, clumsy.
His tongue is still clarty with death.
He cranes forward with little interest
as his hand brings food near his lips.

MAP REFERENCE 553746

Sparse rocks of a triumphal way
once led to dawn.
Horizon battered into shape.
Bleak sky. Wool rags for clouds. Grey
interruptions of rain.

A theme for jagged watercolour. Add
a disturbed grave, traces of huts
confused with poor grass,
a ring of stones.
                    Though now
the avenue trodden in wonder
points to no red beginning –
nor to the goal of time well spent
when fading light brings one by one the stars.

Hope may not crack its shell again
to launch aloft that rough fire-hawk
whose wings flash gold.
This circle's a spent battery.
I've lost the touch.
The site no longer
tingles with mystery.
My tongue spells facts.
A rusty chain binds my eyes.

ARTHUR FROM SILCHESTER

The road that led from here is lost.
This gateway makes
a breach of grass in crumbling flint.
Grey walls ring a space where barley
sways among pools of shade.

No echo of splendour
stirs across fields
where the bright youth was crowned.
Calleva's streets
now guesswork, no mortar juts
above tilled earth. The careful grid has been
mislaid in time.

He rode out
via these thickets of ash and holly
amid cheering, reek of sweat,
clouds of sunlit dust.
He was frowning to recall
what he'd been taught –
that order lay
behind the semblance of things.

Turning in the saddle
he watched the town diminish
till rampart and mansions
vanished for ever in the dry
haze of summer.
                           Challenge was waiting
by wooden chapel and holy well.
A blank shield hung near a ford.
Smoke rose far in the forest
and a wounded man crept from the shadows
to spill his message
from a mouth full of blood.
The new king and his dragon-hunters
scoured the cold parchment.
They bivouacked by faded farms.
Weeds burst through the mosaic of a floor.
Setting his teeth he clung on tight
while his country bucked beneath him.

The darkness of a friend
fell between him and his bride.
Reproach stayed in its sheath.
Some twist in his flesh
kept him on guilt's side –
when younger he'd been drawn
to his witch-sister's bed.
Pale glimmers of her magic
licked round the throne.

He advanced unblinking to that last
encounter on the bare chalk hills.
The outcome was predicted,
cut in stone. A shaft of light
skewered the death-wound.

His bastard nephew-son
smiled under the stroke –
he knew what worms were at work
among the timbers of the realm.

Survivors dug graves, set limbs.
The sword was drowned. Such days
would never blaze again.
The land, rearing,
had thrown its master.
Flanks of the downs
quivered with shame.

The widowed queen,
her lover exiled,
knelt in the white
brilliance of winter
hearing the wolves
howl on those uplands.

In this green bowl of history
no legend has taken root and the tale
lacks a beginning you could point to
for here are only walls
and a gate
and fields under wind.

ORIEL

Inside this cage of light
where memories preen and flap their wings
visitors pausing catalogue in hand
reach back impersonally through time
finding consolations that they can
by wine-red glass that stains the sky.
Crash on a harpsichord deflects
attention from the coloured shields –
lucky the rapiers that slid along

each other with electric death
are locked away, though late
summer lances of radiance
stick quivering in the floor and one
vapour-trail between the clouds
advances like a snake of blood,
for we too have our violence,
our tricks of international deceit,
whereas this sun-greyed stone –
annexe to shadows in the hall,
half-circle stolen from the lawn –
protects now barely visible
spectres of rage or laughter
as ages ebbing left behind
of fame or secrecy but this
bright space unpeopled, emblem, sign.

Athelhampton
August, 1988

JOACHIM DU BELLAY, 1522–1560

Homesick and feverish he was forced to deal
with money-lenders, touts and creditors
in a sallow city that passed its time
governing a lost empire. Intrigue
slithered among broken columns
where a spy who told the truth
was not believed.
                    Far far away
a whitestone tower slid its finger
into the shadowed moat. Wide fields
turned bronze in Anjou, land of spires,
of chestnut-trees, of sluggish silver rivers.

Rome was a maze of pestilence, each palace
dank like a gaol. A man must fawn

and falsify his tongue,
glancing back over his shoulder before
he dared acknowledge a friend.
                              Chevrons of scarlet
stirred in soft air above the manor-house.
Pigeons that had fed all day on plump
cherries twisted on the spit. The cellars
held good sour wine.
A panelled chapel where his cousin prayed
collected piety, though even here
a poor relation had to watch his step,
say yes or no at intervals
and know his place.
                              Death came
after deafness and a long distaste
for toil, for exile and for life itself.
The soul malingered, lonely, shivering.
He took regret for theme
polishing sonnets until they gleamed
with heartbreak and the endless need
to be elsewhere. He saw
the ironies of time and knew the weight
men place on memories of grandeur.
Each day he walked past ruins till,
returning to his native land, he died
neglected, not yet thirty-eight,
sapped by the years of illness and subservience,
the sting of longing baulked and baulked again,
the foreign frame
that jarred against the painted dreams of home.

POETS IN A LANDSCAPE

Round this wood to the past. Half-shadowed limbs
glimpsed, their smoothness guessed at, yours.
Gorse by the outskirts marks those early
versions of your refusal. But the glades –

raiding such sunstruck reaches of space,
waist-high in gold, breath caught, no watcher near,
fleer at long last willing, wilder flowers.
Hours brought flickering paths again, brambles
hampering the ankle, branches that blocked the way,
grey tangle at the heart we never found.

ET IN ARCADIA EGO

It either means that I
unnamed now bones now dust
inside this box of stone
once like the shepherds who
wondering trace with warm
fingers these carved letters
sauntered through Arcady
sunlit carefree among
the steady harmony
of bees while varying
scents of vine and olive
were braided by the breeze

or else it means that I
I Death I smiling skull
I cold pacer with scythe
and never-failing hour-
glass I the measurer
the cutter-short the one
whose barred shadow will halt
the dance in its movement
the kissing the harvest
the moment the triumph
seems within grasp I Death
am also to be found
stalking through Arcady

ON GOLDEN CAP

Twisted pods on the broom crack like toy gun-fire.
Clouds turn a sea of blue and silver
to blurred end-papers of some musty volume
that might contain the recipe for innocence.

Six hundred feet below, the line of white water
zips itself audibly along the shingle.

I contemplate the rumpled counterpane of England.
On my right, low orange cliffs, a curve of shore,
the flattened triangle of Portland Bill.
To the west, grey uncertain slopes crumbling to the Channel,
Lyme Regis as a little stucco town.
Before me, green forts, green barrows, carved
by the first anonymous sculptors of the earth –
huntsmen, farmers, tribes of the moon and sun.

I came here last as a boy in thirty-nine.
Warfare, a transport ship, V-Ones, mendacious peace
set milestones for my growing up. What lay ahead
was a diary kept in an unknown language
that only those who lived it could transcribe.

This clamber won't, God willing, prefigure another
display of ammunition for whatever cause.
There is enough to spoil the children's world –
a skeleton squatting on each horizon,
nightmares that thrive in the milk and rain,
ambassadors with corrupted breath
to fan the sky.
        For me, inland,
in those precarious years, youth
blossomed clumsily via guilty
encounters that harmed no body.
               Now,
Eros has sprouted bat-wings
and snipes at the naked pair with tainted darts.
Flesh rots on the caressing finger
and from the seed, not sweet
relief, not life. No. Poison gets scattered
in a novel fusillade of love.

If you can't trust the ear of wheat,
the first blind kiss, the dawn, the wind,
the cup of water, what is left?
Who can be called a neighbour?
Where's the future gone?

From a field bordered by blackthorn
cows file obediently into the farm-yard.

September sunlight paints the harvest gold.

Six hundred feet below, the patient tide
zips, unzips the line of shingle.

TWO MINATORY SONNETS

I

The hazel-trees have flickered where you stand
and fuchsia-bells untidily cascade.
The brochure shows a peacock sea, a strand
hazy with summer and a far parade

of youngsters toting drums and blowing brass.
Such triumphs neither you nor I have known.
Our flags lack colour. In the moon-cold glass
who saw what made the other – darkness, bone,

elusive memory, hangnail, fear of witch-
craft – knew whose scalp deserved the wreath. Among
fly fortune-tellers who dared claim the prize?

We hold no acres but the loft is rich
in dreams. The best motets are rarely sung.
Try this imagined sorrow on for size.

2

Allow the gods in passing what they want:
   incense, an earldom, the dream-pantomime
   of sex, gold medal, femur scored by time,
despair – that pagan shadow at the font.

Dead soldiers staring from a photograph
   saw planets easing from the evening one
   by one – love, power, haste, war – and hauled the sun
from barbed wire up to light their epitaph.

Indifferent, unspeaking, garments stained
   by worship, they move by, let thunder trail
or blessing casually from each hand.
         They never flinch at gunfire nor pursue
      the fox-enchanters. All our efforts fail.
         They do not even take what is their due.

Embes
July, 1986

THEN AND NOW

for Witold Gracjan Kawalec

She came to kiss her boy good-night.
The shadowed room still buzzed with day:
'I used the grindstone for my knife –
'there was a stream of sparks. I helped
'pick plums. Oh, the pony threw me –
'it didn't hurt a bit – the grass
'smelt like vanilla. Anyway
'I stuck stamps in my album till –'
She laid a finger on his lips.
'Hush. Listen to your dreams,' she said.

The air still held her scent. He traced
her footsteps as she went downstairs
though somehow now the house had lost
its walls, a talking bird replaced
the weather-vane, the kitchen clock
struck seventeen. His sleigh hissed past
high Christmas trees. The snow was warm
as linen. Laughing postmen turned
their letters into butterflies
that flew away above the hedge.

Now I am old and she is dead.
Remembrances before I sleep
cling to the flesh like cobwebs. Night
slams down a coffin-lid and I
might not wake up to prise it off.
Blood pulsing in my head taps out
its own inept Morse code of sour
regrets and grimmer prophecies.
I've lost the knack of listening for
the dreams she wanted me to hear.

THE SASH

variation on a theme by Valéry

Sky like a blush.

Time, on the point of dying,
frolics gold among roses.

He, mute with rapture,
halts in a garden –
fragrant, darkening –
facing the west where,
barred by one colour,
the shape of a shadow
is soon to be captured –
absorption in nightfall.

High winds
move the clouds
in a slow dance
airily interchanging.

That wayward stripe connects
his silence and the world . . .
which one? the world
of sunset and uncertainty?
or that of buildings,
steps and terraces,
humans with warmth and weight?

Both here and there,
not here but there,
at one with what glows beyond,
yet staying back,
alone and sombre,
unable to share this hour,
the blaze he saw,
so wrapped in evening –
seductive shroud –
where aspirations die
and that hot duty of the flesh.

AFTER MICHAELMAS

> '. . . the dog however was certainly singed.'

Oak-trees rock in the gale.
Last campions star the bank above the ditch.
An archangel stands apart from autumn,
outside the wind,
sword sheathed. One near hill
is brushed by a hurried rain.
Blackberries stain the tongue with a sweet deadness.
Those ramparts had no holly,
no interlacing thorn.

The tribe clutched iron lances.
Banners of yellow cloth licked the wind.

Shading their eyes to peer
over valleys clogged with alder,
the defenders saw watch-fires high on the moor.
The dragon stirred.
They dug a pit, threw shards in
hastily scratched with his picture –
metal tail, metal claws, teeth of flame –
and the top-hatted gentlemen found them
where the ground had rung hollow under their spades.
Barking, the little terrier
scurried into the darkness.

Cadbury Castle, Devon

WILLIAM DYCE: PEGWELL BAY, KENT

A Recollection of October 5th, 1858

for C. M. F.

Cold yellow afternoon. Low tide.
      The jaundiced cliffs
crawl halfway across the canvas.
      Brown wooden spars
of the breakwater separate
      the painter's son
scarved and coated against the chill,
      trailing his spade,
and his womenfolk who in their
      shawls and heavy
skirts stoop, peer, idle, from the few
      stragglers who this
bleak autumn are shrimping, tending
      the three donkeys
or starting to stroll back over
      this desolate

chalk beach with net and catch. The same
        indifferent light
defines, unites and isolates
        them all. Not one
is looking up at the comet.

'BLESSING IN THE AIR'

Lines for Laurie Lee, Cheltenham, October, 1986

That Gloucestershire is gone forever.

Petrol-fumes, the antisocial blare
of transistors, distorted beer-tins,
cartons from Kentucky take-aways,
rainfall that assassinates the woods –
what's called progress trades for cash tasteless
eggs and animals while our neighbours
hide behind a blur of unconcern.

It's wrong to knuckle under to hate.
Your lost locations still surprise us,
here, there, where they are least expected.
The year includes a time for planting,
for hand on grain, for the yellow dance
of wasps in an orchard. Even man
can't quite obliterate the seasons.

You wrote tenderly of motherhood,
taught us not to look sidelong at joy,
gave hints for a randy pastoral,
spelt out sly recipes for summer.
Thanks to you we can perceive each day
the heavy colour of good cider,
the sulphur and the flame of roses.

FLORIDA SUNSETS

Gold sprawls above the Gulf, beyond
the cut-outs of palm-trees and low buildings.
The woman filing her tax-return
has to be reminded of its regular display.
A storm sweeping over the keys might raze
each hasty township to flat sand once more.
Who'll gain the ice-box on the quiz-show smeared
with acid green and orange in the corner?
Cars are threaded along the freeway,
three strings of rear-lights, three of yellow.
The sky burns to cinders. Hours
of purchase do not pause. The test
is to summon the novel out of nothingness.
Markets jostle for custom under neon.

No osprey plunges now into the bay.
The citrus colours in the orchard fade.
Tall cypresses, roots clear of stagnant water,
merge into shadow. Spanish moss droops, ghostly,
by a real-estate office open still for trade.
The red rim of evening is lost behind the bridge
and high stars prick a night crisscrossed by planes.
Each human effort, sparking, shows, goes out.
Ideas lay down a grid on wilderness
and circumvent the swamp, the grass peninsula,
petering out in vacant lots, in dreams
that whisper among waste paper in the dark.

Tampa
Christmas, 1984

A LESSON FOR NARCISSUS

And so in the end you have to make your own admirations.
It was a good idea to dynamite that pond.
Once you've outgrown an adolescent lingering
what lies beneath the surface doesn't count –
full lips wavering whenever there's a breeze,
the look in those unfathomable eyes.
Even when he grabbed you by the shoulders,
wrenched you round
so you saw his face as a dark shape against the sky
you only suffered his bewildered wonder,
the set of sensual tricks you quite enjoyed
before turning back again to the sly water,
back to the rhythm of image and reflection
where safety closes the circle of eye and verb.
A perfect time began once more
free of all interruptions – the luxury of gaze
absorbed in gaze. All that was not
fullface, dim overhanging branch, occasional cloud,
because excluded, became forgotten.
Even cheers from the stadium,
an ambulance siren, the whine of a chained dog
could not distract the watcher from his pool.
Night conveyed peace but never absence –
the prey that was also the hunter in ambush
held on till dawn probed its rose-lights into the water,
showed the face staring where there were no lilies.
When the beard came
and the crow's-feet
the frown that at first was a fracture on ivory
deepened. An echo gave a sigh which even drowned
the surreptitious air of youth.
How could there be such change, that slip from noon,
those smooth gold moments gone for ever?
One tear hit another rising to meet it.
Who needs a proof we can't create?
Mirror, watery mirror between my hands,
don't tell me the truth.

OPUS NUMBER

No other music
summons the night wind
salt spaces roaring
beyond glass

The lightship laying its code
on wreathed wallpaper

The thin curtains trembled

My hand stealing entranced
to the new secrecy of myself

The wireless crackling
as a coil of storm
somewhere along the melody
fell through the dark

The strings command their own
attention yet
that sensual loss –
the first perhaps –
interposes wonder

That torn weather long ago
the thresholds of desire
and the depiction of one face
haunting the same dream

AFTER BOECKLIN

for Emiko

The gods have left this garden.

Overgrown,
paths choked with weeds,
a pool around the silent fountain still and dark,
the area can only stir with shadows.
Finches come and, once, a heron,
inhabiting the air like memories.
But gods no longer stroll here
and worshippers have turned long since
to other groves and slopes where new
indifferent deities set foot and leave again.
Here,
the intruder strays
unchecked by law or guilt,
free, ordinary, scorning wonder,
suddenly coming upon
Aphrodite forgotten among ferns and roses.

Ishikawa-chô
August, 1987

SUMMER LIGHT

for R.

At school we kissed with closed lips,
detected nothing when the earthquake struck
and saw field-darkening wheat
uncomprehendingly.
Haze lay across the distance.
The silent train
sliding in far pastures
was headed for a foreign place called home.

From high brown summits that retain our laughter
those spires,
a line of silver water, world
crisscrossed in green
were indistinct, dismissed –
their treasure to me now
trickling so idly through our sunburned fingers.

Bloom on those years –
our confidence, the way
we flirted with the dark.
The abbey tomb, decaying corpse in marble,
made only the brain shiver. The king
transfixed by arrows on the vault,
coiled dragon, sneering imp
sparked no black glints of terror, being stone,
all stone. In the aisle
bare arms stayed warm. Outside,
the pale hay caught on thorns.

Those hills –
grave sunlight drifting over seven counties
and trespass in an orchard
for purposes of love.
Laburnum dangled
over unripe corn as thick as grass.
The blossom
shredding from the apple-branches robbed
its fragrance from the future.
Our blank eyes missed the hard
metamorphosis into fruit.
It was the near excited then –
tanned cheek, unfocused letter, print of wave.
We coined gold words to squander on each sense
and ate our moments raw.
Plans laid, the calendar
fulfilled so casually – all noons
swung round their guarantee,
the previous day still shone
in three dimensions, tangible.
We met
held hands,

strolled past the old encountered images and knew
the season had no end.

When I return it's the unseen
that's changed.
Horizons yield up mysteries if perhaps
there is less all the time to caress.
Now dead volcanoes answer to their names,
the plough proves tirelessly
the whereabouts of tessera or sword
although a blur of smoke
no longer screens the god in ambush,
blood hammering in the skull.

A light to unify all emblems
held summer in abeyance.
Weather was where you were. My heart
in that breath-taken land
isolated
needed your finger on the catch
before my skin
could recognise the polar wind,
that lying statue flower into threat
or yesterday's triumphs dwindle as they should.
The hours
now woven of barbed wire
set up behind me
a novel frontier I could not re-cross.

We cycled back, brows to the west.
Our secret wandering holiday was done.
Shadows snuffed glass and weather-vane.
Rooks seeking their elms
scrawled ragged alphabets upon the sky.
We sweated while our lungs heaved air,
the range ahead
dissolving as we neared.
There were no maps for starlight.
We had to proceed by guesswork,
go by touch.

Your lust was then unmarred by guilt,
unschooled my eye:

apparent Eden in its way
if not to be aware can ever be
occasion for pride. That pear
grazing the rose–brick wall
swells with its months of light, could well
be rotting at the core.
Does hindsight spoil the joy
with envy or contempt?
And have I exorcised at last
that youth-face glowing, fading in the mirror,
that ghost of happiness?

Time narrowed into dusk.
I'd thought I was familiar
with the value of each contour-line,
the meaning of forbidden words.
What happened baffled proof. Lessons
took place elsewhere. Moonlight
slanted along your pillow. In classrooms,
their windows fastened, we were told
what is experienced has gone.
No tense suspected muscle nor those sweet
irrevocable badges on the thigh
gave any hint of withering. We
smiled on, omens unheeded,
reckless of the dawn.

On a north slope I waited shivering.
You were a spectre gaining density.
Fog beaded on your white sweater,
glittered in your hair.
The quarry we came to smelt of gunpowder.
Gorse and clinging bramble
spilled down cracked rock.
We sat, my arm around your shoulders,
hesitant in the mist.
Bells rang for evensong. Next week
the tides of autumn had receded.
Pools of remembered light brimmed in each glade.
The terms of love
reached nowhere near perfection.
We lay under empty fruit-trees
and our mouths

made promises between each kiss
that melted on the mild and sheltered air.

I left. Years broke
in innocence about us.
Semblance has altered and the past
holds other clearings than the one we knew.
I track alone lost happenings and forget
as you will have forgotten what
dry leaves were crushed beneath us or what birds
shrieked out their warnings.

I think I now
no longer yearn
for journeys taken
to those veiled days,
so eager, gauche,
their purer rapture
tremulously gained
if kept with tears –
yet gaze and gaze
at the swift spring, count
every scattering of petals
with an ache at the wrist –
how can it pass
this nonchalantly, this
unfeelingly, replace
a radiance
you've hardly glimpsed
before it's quenched
forever, gone the way
discarded dreams
are blown unmourned.

THE SORCERER'S SQUARES
or
One Way to Read Paul Klee

This grid of pastel colours could be roofs,
crooked chimney-pots, high factories, pale fields beyond them –
the raw material of bricks and sunlight for a child to organise
into a lyric city set on a tidal river.
The mudflats glisten. Fishermen berth their punts among reeds.
The cry from a tower is sung in an unknown language.
Birds dart from the tiny gardens. At night there are fireworks.
Dry hills rise a little inland where tombs are cut
and when they're sealed the wind brings sand to drift over the
    lintel.
That bluegrey patch low down proves an enigma –
the wrong place for a glimpse of sky or smoke billowing,
not quite the correct sheen for water and anyway
even in a fairy-story ponds don't lie at an angle.
No, it must be an enormous carpet hung out to be beaten.
The prince and his bride will need to walk free of dust.
Flecks within flecks leave scope for differing views,
which is as it should be: find somewhere for hope to inhabit,
where in narrow yards between houses the grass stays clean,
where walls are painted pink or blue or primrose,
kept free of posters, free of slogans, never scrawled on,
where passers-by smile before greeting each other and where
no trace remains of a market after the trading is over.

MAGNIFICAT

In private she absorbed the light
   which grew within her till the dawn
      of rescue reached the stable earth,
         dazzling Simeon before
            he left in peace – light that had danced
               in words the Prophets spoke though mocked
              then, now, next week, by people locked
           in their own darkness. Some, entranced
        by that long glimpse of what is more
      than time, than reason, greet the birth
   of love. The parallel's been drawn.
Death is as temporary as night.

HOUSE OF THE DEAF

No words. The flickering of hands.
No call up stair-well or across
a hallway. Doors slam as in a silent
film. Each room, each hammer-stroke
stays blanketed in cottonwool.

A radio has numbers, lights.
Bells sway, are soundproof.
Friends disappear behind the shoulder,
gone once they're out of touch. Water's
as quiet as ice. Tin saucepans dropped
kiss the tiled floor like feathers.

Beyond the hedge at times
fire-engines, ambulances glide by,
flash intermittent scarlet, twisting blue.
Lightning above opposing roofs
plays with no consequence of thunder.

The world is clearer, submarine.
Blackbirds in the garden part beaks
like tiny crab-claws glimpsed in a still pool.
Enclosed in some November twilight
a firework's stars give a sudden puff of sand,
golden, dispersing, noiseless.

Carol-singers enter the aquarium.
Their mute lips depict the non-existent
jingle of horses bringing the kings,
the unerring sign-language of the sky,
an angel-chorus mouthing joy through glass.

TO DAVID ON HIS ORDINATION

You're now beyond
an unseen bound
which separates
goat-herd from goats –
for who's to tell,
priest, layman, till
those scales appear
on skies of fire,
whether our weight
is short or not?
As minister
or steward there
your hands will move
bread into love
and make a sip
of wine mean hope.
Phrases you speak
roll back the dark
to prove where truth
lives on past death.

After you've blessed,
the bitter crust
marring the soul
is scraped off till,
urged on by spite,
greed, rage and hate,
we all implore
it back once more.
Why is it hard
to be just good?
Why do we first
seek out the worst
and only later
like hasty Peter
fall weeping in
remorse for sin?

Such questions knot
the anxious heart.
As we're alive
the mystery of
our presence here
could bring despair
but lines of praise
untwist the maze
and wrists at prayer
get skilled to steer
each cautious thought
past reefs of doubt
until we find
eternal ground.

Exeter Cathedral
July 1st, 1984

ANNIVERSARY

What can I say
that you will hear
afresh? Love, yes,
that easy word –
too frequent, light,
a syllable
that ends when front
teeth bite the lip
to silence. This,
then, pledged once more –
needing to be
re-justified
in everyday
deeds not sounds, New
Year's prayer uttered
as December
drifts into cold
and hard stars wheel
above hard earth
till from furled root
issue snowdrops,
green barley – trust,
fruition, change,
the bright return
of spring, your mouth
on mine, your hand,
your laughter, your
enchantment, you.

December 28th, 1989

A DAUGHTER'S FIRST TERM AT UNIVERSITY

You've said good-bye. She's standing in the car-park.
You know there are mallards on that pool in the quadrangle.
A Virginia Creeper sprawls crimson by her balcony.
Later a heron will visit those fields beyond suburbs
but now she has no map to decipher tomorrow,
the clock-face is unyielding, the brochure's out of date, she must
invent a city from scratch and fix names on to strangers.
You know all this. The windscreen-wiper doesn't clear your tears.

Phone-calls with costs reversed will assure you that certain
seminars are fun, friends have been found. The fact remains –
the one whom you loved as an everyday presence has been
elected citizen of a world you'll never inhabit.
She's left, rightly so, to gain where others have given,
she's cut the cord, packed her bags, embarked on adulthood,
leaving a shadowy stair-well humming with memories
up which you'll clamber trying to tune in to the past.

When she returns, the week-day thrown open in welcome
will lead again to the stunted monolith, the marsh with its orchids.
From time to time you'll stand together on the same
light bridge, high-arched, under which the long-legged
ibises strut with ludicrous, delicate care.
You'll watch with pride the way her hands brush dirt off strange
and gleaming ores. You'll be given fragmentary
and garbled accounts of patterns made, unwoven,
forged again in distant centuries and ivory rooms.
You'll pay attention but she's gone so far you'll never quite
catch up that unfamiliar figure on the changing fields.

BEETHOVEN, STRING QUARTET IN E FLAT, OPUS 127

He says,
                'This way. Look. There are flowers.
'And look. Over there. Do you see?
'The same flowers.
'Now look back again.'
They've changed.
                        You go
down a stone flight in the garden.
The regular terracotta urns are crowned
with white geraniums or scarlet ones.
You count them dutifully, smile,
there's a step missing, you stumble,
the sky tilts, a conifer
stamps a dark triangle on emptiness.

The air is sweet. A lemon tang
argues against the sweetness. Storm–cumulus
forces sudden drama on the terrace.
Guests flee inside to watch tall windows
stream with rain. The level lawn
sparkles again in sunlight.
The grid of hedges dwindles field by field
until the rhythmic hills
dissolve to cloudscapes,
                        distance,
                                blue.

LOST CONNECTIONS

Paths under town and tarmac
lead no longer to the sacred places

Thin fumes seep through grass-blades
to obliterate all clues

Nowhere is it quiet enough
to catch the whisper of the past

No messengers will betray
the revelation of the copses

When nobody is looking
ripples pass along the ground

That figure lingering in the gateway
will not come out on the film

Deep wells, untasted, covered over,
contain the memory of stars

LEGEND

The great beast cropped the dry gold grass.
Midday.
The farm drowsed shadowless.

A nerve twitched in the curved neck.
A boy was creeping up, his bare feet
dusty with colour from the summer flowers.

The lip curled to whinny but a hand
reached out and smoothed the shining mane.
The soft mouth turned and nuzzled his elbow.

The boy glanced back. No stir
among yards or outbuildings.
He paused, fearful.
     A dam
burst in his heart.
He leaped on,
gripped silver flanks between his thighs
and letting out a shout across the sacred meadow
kicked his heels.

The uncanny wings unfurled.
Four hooves pawed sunlight. Field, thickets,
village with a white snake for river
tilted beneath them as the miraculous
steed started cantering over the breeze.

There are no guide-lines for the first's
the real ride and must be done
alone. Tried by oneself.
What happened elsewhere, in another's life,
cannot apply.
     The wisest way
might be to skim the hedges,
clear a shrine or two, leave sky
for later.
   No.
     The boy
sensed glory, urged a steeper course,
upswept, windstruck, set
for sheer grey ramparts capped with snow
that guarded the home of the gods.

The valley with its mills and olive-groves
swayed into haze.
Turf scrabbling up the mountain lost to scree.
Ahead, cloud seeped round pinnacles of rock
hiding what lay behind.

A probe of lighting and the darkness surged.
Thunder. The winged horse reared. Hooves
slid on a treacherous swirl of hail and the rider
hurled to the hillside
fell, his leg buckled under him.

He was lame for life.
That spurt of freedom though –
veins pumping with defiance,
rush of air in the throat –
that high assault, heading
for their immortal eyrie, buoyant,
the great wings beating . . .

As he limped about the farm,
menial, grubby, often scolded,
his eyes saw more than plough or dunghill
and he sang.

SUPERSTITIONS

Propped ladder,
dropped mirror –
both keep their curse.

Temporary arches
tempt you to try
a world where green means stop,
plus-signs will subtract,
cash-prizes depend on death.

In orchards where the lowest rung
is concealed by grass dotted with windfalls
the top seems lost among friendly shadows.

On the day after, the bits of glass
are only shards of wall or ceiling –
it is the explosion of the image into fragments
that lets the harm through.

Luck is a coin worn smooth
by the fingers of the blind.
Night pounces when the gift's unwrapped.

The midwife tenders
a ticket for the ghost-train: that door
hurtling towards us
may well be paper –
what lies beyond?

Touch oak. Fling salt.
Cross fingers but uncross
quarrelsome blades.
Ensure the flickering spider
stays alive.
          The dark
meteor hisses on past its target.

For now.

Neglect the ritual
and the goddess strikes. Bacteria
drift through the hole punched in the day.
The absent messenger will never re-appear.

THE SACRED GROVE

After Boecklin
          for Keigo

The trees behind the altar glowed.

Three figures in white robes
made their obeisance to a stub of marble
smoking with incense in that windless evening.

What god? What power? What presence hovering
held this hushed glade to draw
that file of worshippers, all faceless, here?

Beyond dark trunks curving with natural grace
the columns of the temple, slender, stood

struck by the last rays of a dying sun.
Towards the right, the day-warmed slopes fell gold
away perhaps to some bright distant sea.

Unless the ceremony takes place at dawn.
The painting swings round and the left's now west,
that right-hand hillside silver-cold with dew.

The atmosphere is quickening, all hours
ahead stretch thorned with tasks, the spirit-goad
waits, anxious for the reverent ones to leave.

Tranquillity seems temporary now.

INSTRUCTIONS TO THE ALCHEMIST

Go down black steps
to a cellar full of echoes.
Work fumbling in the shade
till white light splits the ceiling.
Pass through fire-coloured doors
and watch the cube turn gold –
so bright it hurts the eyes.

Don't glance the other way.
A momentary distraction
traps the gaze among moss and ferns.
Prise open the window.
Crane to see the sky.

The sun's behind the building.

MODERN TIMES

One by one farmers
abandoned their altars.
Propitious gods –
wielders of harvest and the haze of sunlight –
turned ordinary like bread
and blended with ploughed
contours of hills.

The gods of ivy-shadow and the adder's fang
lurked longer.
They needed bribing
when pigs were born
or well-water tasted foul –
presences behind the apple-rack
and at the bedside of the dying child.

TWO INTERPRETATIONS OF A PIECE BY GRIEG

I

Last spring. The one just past.
There were fine days – sun glancing off the fjord –
but snow clung on, reluctant to yield land
to those high flowers.
                    Last spring. It's summer now
and April was the tight, unnoticed bud that grew
to this expansive flaunting, an event
obliterated by its outcome. Scaffolding
gets taken down when the builder's finished
though hedges tend to hide their structure. Hard
weeks of preparation cringe unseen
behind the polished gestures on the stage.
All clumsiness forgotten, temper, fears

get cushioned by the sleek flesh of performance –
fake rant, flung hand, the skill that gains applause.

Last spring. October shrouds
the distances with mist. Leaves fall again.
They've filed away that brief success.
The set has been dismantled.
One notch more can be cut in the door-jamb.
Days that lighten change to nights
that lengthen. Chill sweeps down from the Arctic.
A dark corrals the frost and liquidates
the dormant butterflies, filming the pond
with cold. There was a time for youth, a case
for making plans. Last spring. Not now.

II

The last spring. Last of all.
There'll never be another. Earth
has had its chance. The egg is domed,
unbroken in the dry, abandoned nest.
From the valley-head, the slow
cliff of the glacier grinding nearer
crushes the green room where July
was so successfully rehearsed.
Our leading lady once
recurrent victim of a cardboard suicide
coughs her real lungs out on an iron bed.
No tangle of lighting cables, jars of stale cream,
ripped pages marked in pencil.
The hospital has three dimensions
and the surgeon
knows his lines.

The last spring. The very last
experiment of May. No daffodils
to spurt from softened soil, no thin cascade
skeined by the breeze in gusts of spray
across the rock-face. No crops,
no foliage. Low sun
fixed in the south and fading.
Grass grey and unreplenished. No
swifts to scream in a blue evening.

Long cold. Slow dying. Planet sphered by ice.
Silence. The end of things. Creation over.
The six bright days of Genesis have led
at last to this,
no further spring, no hope, no warmth again.
A white full-stop in space will mark the close.

TEMPLE

The gods broke out
of this marble cage.
An indigo wind
howls through stone bars.

Leaving the ruffled shore
travellers stumble up honey-
coloured steps to a bare
altar where nothing happens.

The dry floor undulates.
We are not here in time.
The roof holds. Whirring birds
have stuck their nests to summer.

LOOKING AHEAD

There is no magic. There is only failure.
No rainfall on the corn-patch to the south of the mesa.
Thunder. And a slanting brushstroke of grey far in the desert.
The old men don clay masks and feathered helmets
but who can ward off the lunge of disaster by chanting?

It may seem worthwhile poling against the current
but on a cold evening when the shadows tangle
welcoming lights of betrayal glow across sodden meadows.
How absurd the plinth looked preened ready for its hero
when he'd watched the argosy set sail and taken to his hammock.
The elders have advised against repairing the farmhouse
or sowing the furrows that have been ravaged by the monster.
Unwrinkled the lake will mirror nothing again tomorrow –
no pale arm brandishing a jewelled scabbard
miraculously dry after its long immersion.

Broken stalks creak in the wind. Their husks are empty.
The learner left the sorcerer's lair without a diploma
to trudge on his own through dark blue landscapes of inaction.
For numbers contain no secrets. The taste of melancholy is addictive.
You can kick against the pricks until your toes start bleeding.
Cancel your subscription to that course on fortune-telling –
if you look up *hope* you'll only find the letter h is missing.

Let the gardener close his eyes when daybreak is threatening
but what will be sold when the golden fruit rots on the branches?
Dust after all has clogged the interstices of the oboe.
The foils in their battered case are rusty and stuck together.
You need pay no heed to the rumble of distant gunfire.

Wars have been won and generals gaoled with no loss of ambition.
The shack you knew before is best though you retch as you enter
because of the smell from those dreams decaying in corners.

THE WEDDING-NIGHT

'She's in there, clothed with shadows, waiting.
The torches have burned low. Midnight is past.
The noise of triumph's fading in the streets.
I have it now, all I achieved unsought.
The throne is mine, the queen is mine,
the ramparts of this city-state

are mine, for I'm the hero, I'm the one
who freed them from the grip of mystery.
Their long disease is over and they've danced
all day and sung and splashed the squares with wine.
No wonder that my bride – so lately widowed –
greets me as the returner of her youth.
She's lovely still. Age does not count although
I linger here and pace the chequered floor
watching the brazier slowly lose its glow.
We both see all too sharply for our birth
divides us – me the poor shepherd-boy from her
of royal blood. But why hang back? I have to prove
that I'm the master now, the one
she owes her life to. So, why be afraid?'

And Oedipus rejoined his wife in bed.

THE ARTIST AT A CERTAIN AGE

The skin curled back. Each muscle turned to smoke.
His writing fingers bared the cubes of bone,
misshapen dice, crude sugar-lumps, hard, grey,
that fell apart and rattled on the table.

The emptiness which used to be a hand
matched the blank page where nothing would be scrawled.
Deep in the skull scraped free of images,
the brutal regent meted out the dark.

THE TRAGEDIAN SPEAKS

No longer do I wield the moth-power,
frail sceptre made of dusk,
authority that flutters its grey wing,
shy eyelid.

There was a time
when I possessed the swiftness of a stone
hurled,
dropping beyond imagined gardens.

No more.

That diamond is blunt
with which I once
scored expectation like a meteor,
hair-line across the summer night.

BALANCE SHEET

gaoled in my fifties
each year an iron bar
I'm told they are still
trading illusions
down by the harbour
creased like a backdrop

masks filched from rivals
bronze clasps and seed-pearls
spilt on the blanket
got pawned for the fleet
that never returned
leaving me bankrupt

before the shipwreck
dancers in blindfold
thronged the sunburnt deck
as lust and heartbreak
seemed worth the duty
customs demanded

though now shattered spars
teeter on the waves
and my medallions
worn smooth by finger
and thumb lie squandered
on the ocean bed

RECONSTRUCTIONS

We have to make our landscapes,
god-shelves
for dark-rooted trees to stand.
A skull is not enough,
a château even –
walls, bones will disappear.
Experts are summoned
with sketch-book, theodolite,
fitting the sections of river together.
Cold scimitar of moon
through branches ragged with scarlet,
frost-scrawl, the haze of June,
arrival of the migrants –
nothing must be left to chance,
no frieze of deer
suspected at the corner of the wood,
not the thumbnail mark
where an outcrop interrupts the horizon,
nor yet the mallow wrapped
in its own arpeggios of light.
How can one tell
how far it is here from anxiety

or gauge the shadow's
weight upon the lawn?
If the plans get mislaid
there can be no improvising –
just so much space has been left
below the flight of the gull,
just so much time may be taken
adjusting the pulse to remorse.
The wilderness is ours
with the burning blade
brandished over the point
of no return. Only elsewhere
can our glances match
the globing of the nectarine,
scurry of wind on wheat.
And no new day has ever
arrived without strings attached.
The dawn wind brings
such unpredicted music
played on a phantom lyre.
Beyond the desert of expectation
may lie, green, unimaginable,
the place where those who have lost their heroes
can feel at home.

UNTITLED

I have lived too long with dragons
stared too often into those lying eyes
as deep as smoke and as
inscrutable as opals
tried too hard
to see what men should never see
the compromise of destiny and hope
have smelt the scorched
metal of their wings and watched
the gold

glint in their talons
heard the dry
scrape and clatter of their coils
never able
to learn their speech
nor clamber on the scaly
neck of one and soar
reeking over the islands
but held by that uncertain gaze
lost compass-sense
and human loyalty
and longed to be
as legendary as they
as far outside the scope
of reason and the laws of time
as burnt with danger and
as undeniable
as they who never were
and are
unfindable

HIGH ORCHIDS

for Lee Harwood

After the solstice, rolling winds brought rain.

The ocean tilts north,
dark under screaming seabirds.

Shadows cast by the escarpment
lengthen now.

From your study, up one floor,
you can see peonies.
Paper is stacked on the table,
with atlas, sextant,
magnifying-glass to hand.

Your books, impeccably arranged,
share space with post-cards
catalogued in boxes.
When the wind's in the south
waves are heard
rasping on shingle.
Here, you braid texts to an intricate
pattern thought up while picking your way
alert along wry
by-paths of learning where the banded
dragonfly hovers near bindweed.
Opening your mahogany
case of instruments
you gauge the exact
dimensions of a trawler
and smile, before turning your mind
to the problem of forests
in the Antipodes.

Storm-gathered, grey, the clouds approached with rain
to drench the offshore islands,
fall on to breakwater, ruffled harbour, wharf,
drum on the upturned hulls dragged above the tide,
run down sandstone cliffs grooved in the Ice Age,
glisten among names cut on the war memorial,
lash the already brimming pools and make
exotic plants waver behind streaming windows.

Beyond the spiral of the stars
waits autumn. Snow. Descent
to zero and a stagnant heart.

June now. Late June.
Below the moor
the crops are still unripe.

From my study –
three counties west of yours –
you see wooded hills
and a cathedral in winter –
also a block
of flats across half the view.

Alone on a level with bird-
flight and swaying branches
we piece words together
into something else.
At nightfall the closed
panes show us ourselves.

Rain sweeps up from the sea and obscures
the tor silhouetted on our right.
Under the spread water, grass and fern
are beaded with silver,
ironed smooth. The torrent,
in between the scrawls of foam,
glints peat-brown,
curving sleek over boulders
we once used as stepping-stones.

A thousand feet below, cars slide to the coast.
Drivers and passengers, dry,
keep in with care the air they have brought with them.
We watch the far silent road through pelting rain.
Then turn, to pass over the brow
where there will be only rock, cattle, wheatears
and heather, ponies standing with their heads down,
bracken, running water, sheep and crows.

For one week-end it's no bad thing
to walk away from wage-earning,
the old literary squabbles,
family-ties –
then leave the land of otter and hawk
to come back, bathed in rain,
take up our usual rôles
and lock away till they are needed
curious specimens of leaf-
formation or feldspar
in the worn cabinet.

The air grows lighter. There are rifts of blue
above the ridge. A raptor hangs on the wind.
We crouch to eat, sheltered by granite.
A ring-ouzel watches us. We swap jokes.
The rain stops altogether.

It's twenty years since our first meeting.
What lies ahead?
Your eyes meet mine in wonder.

Beyond the swollen river
we squeeze the water out of our socks.
I tip half a gill from a boot
that got left behind when the rest of me
leaped for the bank.
A slate–blue heron
flaps lazily across empty grass.
We get out the map. Our route
seems straightforward. Upstream
the turf is wet and steep,
rock–surface slippery.
A gnarled rowan shakes off drops of rain.

At the valley–head the land begins to flatten.
A stone circle
juts on the skyline like a set of thorns.
To the east a patch of bog
is glittering in the sun.
Jumping the brook, you plod ahead.
Then turn and give a shout.

Flickering slightly in the wind,
some red,
some nearly white, some mauve,
orchids lift
fragile above their mottled lizard–leaves.

Would that our desks produced such blooms –
so unexpected, so correct –
as lovely though less perishable.

BARSOOM

the planet Mars in the John Carter novels of Edgar Rice Burroughs

It is a world that has been left to die.
    Cold sun probes thinning air. The last canals
    lead from the ice-caps under ruined walls.
Mere skeletons of farms guard fields gone dry.

In arid light, waves of vermilion moss
    break on abandoned wharves. Tall cities stare
    from vacant windows past worn headlands where
the dead sea-bottoms roll through emptiness.

The planet is alive with echoes. Noons
    possess no shadows. Nights are parched and chill.
        An earthman stands alone, sword bared, far from
        the double towers of threatened Helium
    where Dejah Thoris the incomparable
waits patiently beneath the hurtling moons.

BACKWARD GLANCES

In those days
the boy clutched
a borrowed
bag of dreams
as he paced
the worn park.
Perhaps round
some dusty
evergreen
lurked the wry
angel who
held the key
to manhood.

He went home
before dark
thrilled by slick
photographs
gummed to locked
cinemas.
The slow waves
crashed beyond
iron railings.
Others had
voyaged past
the chalk cape
of remorse.

At evening
in that well–
papered room
the lightship's
pale beam stroked
him as he
stood naked
in the glass.
Postcards stuck
round the frame
proved those he'd
met worthy
of envy.

Parents knew
nothing. Friends
soon forgot
the password.
Poets moved
down dark paths
then vanished.
What secret
did they share?
In which safe
were the bright
diagrams
kept hidden?

The town soon
turned into
a maze. Bus
routes threaded
foreign streets.
Library
books when thumbed
could explode
or hussars
step coldly
from tea-rooms
to arrest
the guilty.

As night was
occupied
territory
a would-be
sleeper had
to crawl through
the red barbed
wire of sun-
set before
he found which
articles
were best for
contraband.

Time would tell
duller lies,
later dawns
let him down
more cruelly.
Each lesson
learned might take
the bitter
taste from hope –
each mystery
solved create
fresh mysteries
to shroud him.

At his back
the same old
presences
with wheedling
voices gave
counsel marred
by prudence
and despair –
yet poised on
that blind brink
who would not
plunge forward
as I did.

SIREN-VOICES

Odysseus heard the song that changed
the waves to meadows, spray to flowers,
rocks to the trunks of spreading trees.

Art is hypocrisy to please –
the salt taste of the passing hours
made palatable, truth re-arranged.

WASTE

One hunk of coal sent out
a horizontal plume
of grey-mauve smoke which caught
a flame and spat and changed
to smoke again – marsh-gas
released to hiss and flare,
a bubble under peat
preserved from that primal
landscape teeming with such
unimaginable
fish, ferns and gastropods
to dissipate in air
x million years too late.

SEEDS OF TIME

Knowing the future is to gauge
        sea-distances. If brief,
too cursory, the glance will miss
        the hard pride, the wonder,
when a mother stands observing
        her pasty-faced boy play
or a painter eyes grey water
        gathering glints of light.
The fifty-year-old, the finished
        oil are as successful
as yesterday's triumph to those
        able to read the world.
These stretches of coastline appear
        to offer mere riddles
of ugliness. The child has scraped
        an agonising note
from his fiddle. The eye and ear
        of love alone find truth.

THE ENGLISHMAN ABROAD

Clumps of asphodel
grow by the fallen pillars.

The manuscript is stacked
face down. A vase with an athlete
tying his sandal
holds pencils and rulers.

One window looks down the long
slope to the harbour.

A lizard scuttles over a stone hand.

The hard sky makes vertical shadows.
In dry soil the cypress-roots
probe among bones of heroes and shepherds.

The last myth falling overboard
was drowned between that island and the cape.

Another window shows farms and mountains.
Perhaps the goat-footed playboy
is still up there, waiting.

He pours a cup of heavy wine.
As he drinks, his reflection
is draped over lemon-trees and a white
outcrop free of flowers –
bright, ghostlike, alien.

TRANS-SIBERIAN

a belated footnote to Blaise Cendrars

At the midnight border, between tall
yellow derricks, they jack up the train.
Wider chassis trundling dutifully
get fixed in a clanging shed garish with neon.
Outside, long lines of under-carriages –
horizontal skeletons in the moonlight –
sustain the phantoms of former journeys.
The returning couple in my compartment
have all their Bratwurst confiscated.
The customs-woman grins. The wife's in tears.

At dawn, birch-forests flicker. Knapweed,
ragwort, willow-herb, toadflax. Huge crows.
Near each level-crossing an attendant stands
to attention, baton raised. Full employment.
Minsk station. One citizen in two
was killed resisting Germans. Hitler,
Bonaparte – both, taking on the Sixth of the World,
beaten by endless steppes, the endless versts,
the iron will of a beleaguered people.

No advertisements (except for Aeroflot)
but vast posters with giant doves.
Here, too, in this unbelieving land,
Grant Us Thy Peace. In crammed cemeteries,
a red star crowns the graves. St. Basil's
has dwindled to a museum. Gone
the gruff chanting, blue-grey puffs of incense.
No sputtering candle-light on gold. Frescoes
but no ikons decorate this lofty labyrinth
under its candy-coloured domes. Opposite,
the white toad-face of Lenin keeps the eyes shut
inside his private Madame Tussaud's. Brides
in fluttering muslin lay red nosegays
for the Unknown Soldier, then file reverently past
the metal busts of Stalin and other
plebeian satraps. What must they think
of jeans and taxis, chewing-gum,
transistors spewing pop-cacophony,

ideals so little different from 'The West'?
No green hair – yet. The Metro is spotless
beneath preposterous chandeliers.
Walls are unscrawled with aerosol, pavements
free of trash. GOM is a cross between the Crystal
Palace and a gaol by Piranesi.

Yaroslavski Station. The Trans-Siberian
leaves punctually at 15:05. Each carriage
has a samovar and a tap for drinking-water.
The attendant vacuums your compartment.
There are four classes. I am in the fourth.
The other trains you pass have wooden seats,
hammocks get slung across the corridor,
but these are not for foreigners. Like the shops.
Youths stand outside furtively hoping
the visitor will procure them vodka, amber, fur hats.
Hard currency. Hard for them to acquire. Hard too
to be a supplicant for your own produce
in your own land.

Immense rivers
flow towards the Arctic. One passenger
lives in an air-base on the permafrost.
They never see the sun six months of the year.
We chat over cabbage-soup as I eye with envy
the empty roads. The coalyards, factories
belong in the England of my childhood –
mysterious chutes and stacks, rusty wheels.
They have dip-pens in the Post Office. I send
some splattered postcards many thousand miles.

The further east you go, more uniforms,
more tanks. Tartar faces frequent.
Reaching to the steep pink banks of Lake Baikal
the white *taiga* of birches haunted by butterflies,
the black *taiga* of conifers where legends require
shamans and hunters who are part-snake, part-wolf.

The modern art is timorous and prim.
Why should puritanism and the revolutionary
spirit go hand in hand? Cromwell . . . Mao . . .
Kruschchev . . . Maybe they never really wanted

to cure society, just make it easier for us
to be controlled. Reform. Conform.

At Chita there's a train going to Pyongyang.
Beyond those mountains lies Mongolia.
Wizened peasant-women in black sell carrots.
You are not supposed to photograph bridges or stations –
not even Skovorodino like a cake with green icing,
not even the long mechanical span over the Amur
gilded by evening light with a thunderstorm over Manchuria.
Ice-cream by the river-beach, the men in bathing-caps.
A wonderful museum with stuffed tigers,
slabs of red marble, Palaeolithic figurines.

The last lap runs along the Chinese border, the one
station in common ablaze with searchlights,
empty, a maze of concrete and metal barricades,
a kind of Checkpoint Fyodor or Chang.
I keep one illegal rouble as a souvenir
and clamber aboard the *Felix Dzerjinsky* –
he was a Hero of the Revolution and his portrait,
trench-coat slung dramatically over his shoulders,
frowns on those about to dine on caviare.

Three weeks ago I docked at the Hook of Holland.
Now the Pacific stretches to Japan.
I'm still at large and travelling hopefully.

Nakhodka, Summer 1987

STUDIES OF THE MALE NUDE

(taken at Taormina by Baron Wilhelm von Gloeden in 1899)

Boy of sepia
crowned with roses
shows light shed on
parts of human
nature which had
not been handled
till the baron
brought his camera.

He revealed much
hidden talent
as the locals
keen to help in
these researches
lent his lenses
what before they'd
held in secret.

Dying mourned by
seven children
one had never
been ashamed of
that far summer
when he'd posed such
bashful charms in
shades of sepia.

But a grandson
rips up prints which
soil his blood and
flings at the feet
of stunned tourists
confetti made
of sepia skin
and blurred roses.

MOVING SNAPSHOTS

The wave's flung edge of foam reaches
    so far, draws back. Again,
a further cast, white hiss of lace,
    thrown slanting on the beach,
pauses, slides, darkens the hot sand.
    Approaching, curled over,
toppling, spilt, the same slope-rhythm
    repeated gains its ground.

The boy's arm in the aftermath
    of light hurled the ball straight
up to the zenith. Second floor
    windows revealed the chilled
rose and tarnished gilt of mirrors.
    Spinning, each hemisphere
looked stable, fixed shine, fixed shadow.
    Reaching the high limit
it plummeted, stinging the palms.
    He launched it again, one
more exploration of brightness.
    Flowers shrank into twilight.
The tabby cat skirted the lawn
    grown cold under dewfall.

BREAK-UP

A long pink house
crowning the slope
and meant for summer
now in the stark
light of January
lies unprepared

Chipped gryphons
guard the gravel
drive drab with weeds

She sat at the keyboard
while wide french windows
let in the sun

Guests underlined
the sense of permanence
as tea was served
in fragile cups
and tall vases brimmed
with dying flowers

Doors banged all day
and arrows thudded
into legitimate
targets across
the tended lawn

One room alone
is furnished now
the others shuttered
are ruled by cold dust

Drawing the curtains
he spotted a toad
squatting on the terrace

Flakes of plaster
in the mossy kitchen

fall on to crates
of empty bottles

There were other signs
in sky and foliage
handwriting on letters
and eyes that refused
to meet his own

Distant scarecrows
flapped tattered sleeves
and unexplained headlights
stabbed the bedroom
wall in the small hours

Smoke from a grudging
log-fire billows back
over the stone desk
where he sits pen in hand
coughs and drinks
then scribbles again

Each winter poem
couched as a plea
for her to return
forgets the midnight
promise of August
comma'd by knives

OUT OF FAVOUR

The gates have been closed to me.
I scrabble against unyielding iron.
Once, via the password or a bribe,
I roamed at will inside the town.
Not now. At nightfall, hungry,
I creep back to the settlement,
get scolded for my absence, sip
thin soup near a grudging fire.
Traders at times stop by, their boasts
stir phantoms in the smoky room,
but when they go, only a straw
mattress takes the weight of my dreams.

GIVING UP

The sky is cobwebbed and a stream
of dust flows between grey banks.
Men and women wearing rags
cower by pools of ash.
Days, if you can call them days,
come, go. The stagnant air
gets dark, grows pale.
In the charred light one figure goes
missing from the accustomed place,
but soon another, hunched, waits there,
silent, for the final summons.

INCREASING PERSPECTIVE

The tide has scrawled no answer on the fading shore.

Nothing but darkness now to press upon the bone.
No imagery beyond the poisonous hedge of berries.

Those peaks in the Antarctic, jet, sheer, jagged with snow,
form a barrier, dreams one side, death the other.
I want fate to hand me the right cards out of a cloud.

Moonlight striding punctually through the ballroom
let invisible dancers sway in time to the quiet.
An approaching ridge of high pressure is forecast
which may affect the ice-sapphires in your rings.

A brass telescope lay gathering dust by the window.
I heard the rasp of brooms in the yard this morning
as they swept up a sky of broken crystal.
The astronomer felt unable to compute the fleeing triremes.
Your eyes bruised me with their indifference.

Despite barrage-balloons and flashes below the horizon
the landscape stays obedient to earlier laws.
The furrows are still in place, the geese have to be fed.
Those bursts of martial music from the blackened wireless
die before they reach the thin rat edging round the dairy.
The noon communiqué had warned of meteor showers.

Behind curtains we have watched sour mouths biting on the past.
Those cubes of glass left by the angel are cold to the touch.
The films have all gone rancid in the camera.
Ancestors were forced at gunpoint through the gates of the
    citadel.
Words in an unknown language have just come up on the cobalt
    screen.
It's time to re-arrange the northern furniture.
I cannot remember the name of those low blue flowers.

PANES

variation on a theme by René Char

      Through you I see
pale rain, approaching friends

      Outsiders glimpse
a vase, log-fire, book-ends

      Yet you glass back
      my anxious eyes
      and passers-by
      turning to look
      towards the east
      are dazzled by
      the setting sun

IN THE YARD

Grey evening after sunlit day.
A thin breeze frets the conifers.
One chaffinch balances on wire,
lifts off with a scornful noise.

Clouds thicken over the hill.
The air gets colder, darker.
Ghosts grow bolder. The huge bay-tree
turns sombre, hides its centre.

Night is a denial of shape.
Squares of gold alone
remain of the houses.
A planet melts to shine and shadow.

Grey cancels April and threats of change
warn the optimist off. The first
raindrops have a glib sadness.
Invisible, the earth patters.

ANTIGONE ENTOMBED

Farewell to white.

The cavern door
clangs to and night
presses my poor
and guiltless eyes
gaoled in dark stone.

The enterprise
of death alone
remains. What voice
can intercede
now? I've no choice
trapped here. No deed
of saintliness
is offered me.

To acquiesce
my destiny
at last – to wait
in silence till
the claws of fate
close on their kill –
unless I can
anticipate
my ending, plan
to twist my hate
against my own
existence, hang
myself, atone
for wrong with wrong.

I loved the dawn . . .
the lamb's-wool-cloud
of summer drawn
across the proud
blue of a day . . .
my ivory dice . . .
snow . . . birch-trees . . . spray . . .
linen . . . milk . . . ice . . .

Farewell to white
for death is near.

I worked in light,
free, without fear,
believed that first
decree we're bound
to keep and cursed
the royal command
that meant we could
not mourn our own
dead brother's blood . . .
They left each bone
for crows.
   So black
is welcome.
    I
would not go back
to light but die
by my own hand.

Farewell to white.

I understand
now.
  Black is right.

SONG OF THE MADMAN

From the corners of my new home
lawns slant to overhanging
shrubbery. There is no longer
the screaming of a radio in my ears.
But I am not alone. My needs
such as they are get attended to.
I wake and wash and have
breakfast by the open window.
I can feed the finches through the bars.
Those skies, though, noon-clouded,
rain-shivering . . . they tease me.
I work at my painting and play
chess with myself every evening.
It's peaceful here. If it weren't for that
corpse laid out in the next bedroom.

IMPOSTOR

'Il est bon de cacher ce qu'on a dans le coeur.'
— LE MISANTHROPE

I laugh and pray and lend an ear.
The mask must take some in.
Fixed joy above a bitter heart.
Head bowed to hide a sneer.

I am the giver who'll begrudge each gift,
the soft admirer ill inside with hate.
Neat palisades surround a slum-yard
crammed with coiled weeds and corrugated iron.

The hero's sympathy is done so well.
What elegance! What discipline! Offstage,
lumps of greasy cottonwool
litter the floorboards.

Alceste was right. Let's bare the mind,
traffic in bile and vengeance, spare
no feelings till the smarting truth is out.
Start restaurants inside the abattoir.
Unearth the hatchet. Keep the breaches raw.

Alceste was wrong. Smoke-screens
conceal the line of bayonets but also drift
before grey willows mirrored in a stream.

THE RECRUIT

Spreads the cornfield
ripe with summer
and the elms,
their heavy load of leaves,

yes, the elms,
tell of the elms

Sprawls the reaper
sleeping, brownthroated,
sickle beside him
also the cider jug,
yes, the cider,
mention the cider,
moon cold on orchard,
kiss under apples

Drumfall crosses the heat
letting the air
fall into line
tensing, insistent

March the redcoats
threading the hedgerows
lifting the white dust,
yes, the dust,
stress the white dust

Dreams the reaper
abandoned in shadow
(trees were included,
but their shadow?)
Blocks of unharvested
corn flecked with poppies
drowsy, wavering,
bright spots of blood
to sprinkle the summer

Drumming gets nearer,
wind sways the barley,
stirs now the reaper,
sun dropped to westward,
air a touch cooler,
last of the reaping
to finish tomorrow,
soon, in the future,
yes, the future,
who used the word?

A DREAM OF AUTUMN

She came through the yellow forest
     bringing gifts – old coins
that changed to beech-leaves at my touch,
thin, dry. Her hair was bonfire-smoke
grey, altering, like the distance
in her eyes. My pale hoard had been
squandered on so many others
it seemed my store was drained empty.
The river in spate was pouring
its steely blur over rocks long
exposed to the winds, stained golden
with lichen. The mockery told.
Though what I'd had to offer stayed
as a brief pledge of union,
concern, even love, far too soon
dissolving to indifference.
Her palms showed towards me, bracken
flickered tawny around her thighs,
the holly, rowan, on the slope
beyond her, lent their glossy fruit
for her lips, and, craven, I turned
     back along the soft
path to the stonework of the bridge.

ENDGAME

The sea has withdrawn from these shores,
and reddening skies
unfold low fields that have been harvested
too often, without thought.
Dust fills the wind. Time
writhes among the branches,
dies. There can be calm,
a sterile calm, when all is done,
when all is said.

APOLOGIA PRO VITA SUA

Neither from mountain
nor the Sybil's chair
comes the casual
brochure a scholar
may use or discard –
no fierce shine tumbling
in the mouth up-cupped,
nor, head bent over
that crack in the cave-
floor, a dubious smoke
sucked in. Second-hand
trances are tedious
and self-respecting
adults should shrug off
cheap epiphanies.

Like an old-fashioned
pilgrim exploring
what was once called truth
he sets out across
an arid heathland
with no horizon.
His route hugs the same
contour-line between
height without shadow
and eddies of fog
where sense is dethroned.

Proud, unambitious,
neither a would-be
demigod nor earl
of hell, he'd rather
skip the lent guide-book,
see things for himself
and if he's able
stay on the level.

Owing no obols,
convinced that he'll be
awarded no dark

wreath, no accolade,
he moves without help
one step at a time,
while adders slither
and the crow flaps home.

A battered knapsack
stuffed with messages
in a disused script
hangs on his shoulder.
Trudging in silence
he's left well-charted
lands far behind him
and dreams against hope
this unmarked trek will
lead in a circle
so in the end he'll
manage to win back
whatever was lost.

Noise settles elsewhere –
down in the valley
where backs get slapped, palms
smeared with grease – or up
well publicised crags
where slyer clamberers
ape the archangels
beating the hot air
from ill-fitting wings.

He bears no envy,
no grudge against fate.
The path he's chosen
looks unexciting.
Attention clusters
round the ambitious –
those who claim they've culled
light bouncing off rock
or chewed telltale leaves.

25th

for Lynn

There have been silver rivers, silver seas.
Birches grow silver bark. A silver fox
tracks prey on snow. The silver pheasant flaunts
its tail across a Chinese manuscript.
Rain has made roads and roofs run silver. Mist
can blanket any world in silver. Now
the grass we tread is silver, silver bricks
sustain all buildings, oak and beech and elm
show silver leaves and silver ravens caw
from their bright branches. Roses are silver.
Peonies, larkspurs, dandelions are silver.
Proud stags with silver shadows browse through tufts
of silver bracken. In a silver sky
the gulls ride gusts of air on silver wings.
The wind's gone silver. You have silver eyes
and what you watch turns silver. Bread though cut
today from silver loaves tastes just the same.
Cheddar stands silver by the silver ingots
of butter and the burgundy splashes
in heavy drops like mercury but smells
and slips across the tongue as southern wine.
Silver your lips, your knowing hands. Today
we walk as queen and king of silver on
a silver carpet threaded by the years
of silver we have lived together here
or formerly, alone, with children, now
alone once more – patterns of joy or hardship,
the differences shared and understood,
the warmth, the laughter, wonder, travel, all
the love that has made up our silver age.

December 28th, 1988

RETROSPECTIVE

I don't re-read my published work.
What's done is done
and better left alone.
Who knows what sour surprise may lurk?

This morning on my way
to Early Service – autumn day,
mist swirling in the valley, dew
to soak each shoe –
I paused, peered down
at some plump mushrooms, white-capped, flecked with brown.

Across the grass when I looked back
my footprints made a temporary track.

So Far
(1998)

To Lynn, again and always

WALES RE-VISITED

yr hen wlad fy nhadau

At home I have had to live as an alien.

The suspension-bridge, grey
rainbow spanning mud and tide,
landed me among the elms of autumn.

I was born on an October cliff
overlooking docks and islands.
Drizzle issued soft from the empty west.
My pram brushed thick hedges of fuchsia.

They took me young to learn a different language
far from those slopes red with bracken
where clearer water slides down levels of slate.

I remembered cairns where saints stood studying heaven,
dark galleries veined with gold and anthracite,
a saffron coastline littered with cowries and crab-shells,
those silhouetted castles, their high halls floored with grass.

Ships moor near a tower where lads play chess.
Shadows of heroes fight by the ruffled tarn.
A harper gives his message to the clouds.
I do not understand the words he sings.
I can no longer tell where I belong.

Not there where the legends have taken root,
not in my clanging birthplace, nor my adopted home,
not where I'm staying, nor where I want to be,
not where I travel to, nor the lands I've left,
not even there at last –
that green and windswept graveyard
where my forebears lie.

TREE-RINGS

Grey beeches line this upward-curving lane.
One stump juts raw
among bilberries scattered with sawdust.
The rings revealed to daylight vary –
some thinner, some darker.
Running my fingernail from heart to bark
I graze a hundred years.
                        Memories
lie on the outer half – my first school
where I had to make a map of Africa out of dough;
bombs dropping and the teacher
making shadow-foxes on the shelter wall.

Here is the summer we fell in love.
Here our daughter was born.
And here our son.
                        These circles though
pushed outwards before we came to life.
Pale yellow succeeded brown
as cures were found, books got written,
zeppelins took the air and kings mislaid their thrones.
But here, below the moor, they only recorded
the history of the wind –
flourish of leaves,
fall of leaves,
snow, stars wheeling, hawk's shrill cry.

FROM THE CHALKLANDS

Not foraminifera now it seems –
   this at least is the latest fashion
   for science stays a wayward thing, swayed
   by pride, pig-headedness and the need
   to make one's mark. It can never claim
   impartiality. Any find
   gets filtered via human weakness.
   One eye peering down a microscope
   detects the swarming half and discounts
   inconvenient truth not in focus.

   This week the known cosmos will contract
   to a small ball then explode again.
   Yesterday infinite expansion
   filled the theme given out as gospel.
   Pundits prate deaf to future laughter –
   at school one master instructed us
   nobody could ever reach the moon.
   What so-called facts are being taught now?

   A hot wind blows over the bare down.
   Thunderclouds pile in creamy masses.
   Cowslips dangle pallor at our feet.
   Thin grass on the slope to the hill-fort
   shows flints here and there. Yellowhammers
   perched on wires repeat their rasping tune.

   To gum labels on larks or to know
   vertical air-currents are hoisting
   lumps of ice at sixty miles an hour
   should not obliterate the wonder.

   Nor can words alas catch and convey
summer . . . intriguing sky . . . smell of elder.

THE LIE OF THE LAND

Dead summer's bracken, crust
of an old scab, stained the hillside

    Getting out of the car
    the wayfarer
    pats his pockets to make sure
    of map and compass.

Gnarled hawthorn-trees,
leafless, unstirred by the wind,
have lacquered their berries

    The problem is the same – to match
    faint grids and wavy lines
    with what is actually there.

A beech-hedge, tawny,
(though coined still with green)
led to the open moor

    Heather spreads smooth to the outcrop.
    Reaching the brink, however, he'll discover
    an iron-grey torrent, rowdy, intervenes.

        *

Bear left. But now that jutting church-
tower's disappeared.
Consult the map once more. If I am on
that orange 4 I ought to see
a fir-plantation. And then
where are those pylons?
                Certainty
disintegrates. The contours
ripple in my hand.
It's cold.

        *

What was foreseen is rarely there. One must
beware the thinnest powdering of snow.
A plan does nothing but conceal
its outcome. Surveyors rely far
too much on the individual. No herd of deer
will ever flow as gracefully
upon that field again. The sun
has slipped behind another cloud.
Can we in all humility relate
the strata that have gone before
to this reliant surface, this sense
of being nowhere? It would seem
from shark's teeth on a mountain-top
even geology deceives.

FIN DE SAISON

Red grapes glued together
lure the wasps

Time to bring down the leather trunks
dust them off

Chrysanthemums droop listless
in the sullen park
An abandoned hoop
leans on the fountain-rim

The commissionaire yawns at his post

Half the dining-room
has been closed behind screens

The slant-eyed boy in his sailor suit
no longer kicks his heels
by those dingy palm-trees

The lake is pressed flat by September

At ten precisely
the dowager with the Pomeranian
still goes for her glass of the sulphurous waters
passing the deserted bandstand

The gravel is moist
and littered with pale leaves

At dawn we saw the first
powdering of snow on the mountains

WINTER HOLIDAY

for Lee Harwood

The mountains towered into driving grey.
Nine a.m. twilight. Pewter glint
of water coiling that broke into
the whitest spray. Goldfinches
fluttered in the occasional hawthorn,
leafless, with withered berries, boughs
furred in turquoise lichen.
                    Higher,
whipped by mist, we heard
invisible torrents falling
past boulder, bare rowan.
The bright grass patched with flattened
bracken gone rusty with January
gave way to a litter of rock
glazed with ice.
                    Later,
on snow, pawmark and bootprint
presupposed dog and hiker
yet we met no-one. The compass
drew us from blankness into blankness
punctuated by honks of a raven.

The weather cleared. Chilled sunlight hurled
my silhouette on rolling cloud.
The world we'd lost then reappeared in green,
shelving past tarn and outcrop to the shore.

But can a day's biography do more
than point to detail after detail, squeeze
those hours unnoticed on my watch to joy
in retrospect? Words go too fast and skim
those intervals where truth is taken in.

The climb with its attendant marvels,
telescoped, veers into falsehood –
dries out – loses the sap – the gleam –
the tremor of inaccuracy –
the life.
            I opened a book
in my uncle's library
and found a cyclamen, purple, scentless,
spreadeagled between the pages.
Each day I pass on the stairs
a sulphur butterfly some clergyman
gassed in the last century and mounted
on cottonwool behind a slice of glass.

What can I say?
We left the world for winter,
struggling with the wind –
yet, nearer sea level, there were catkins –
a primrose – and one
rhododendron flowering in a formal garden.

Gwynedd, 1993

KERNOW

Thrift and vetch. A peacock sea
loses blue in spume against
kittiwake-frequented cliffs.
Seals offshore resemble pink
ants'-eggs floating. On the wind
swarms of Painted Ladies try
latching on to petals. I,
sniffing brine and blossom, glimpse
skimming on their millstones saints
known in Cornwall only – Teath,
Breward, Mabyn, Tudy. Doom
hums along the rigging on
Tristram's amorous embassy.
Bells start tolling undersea
proving Lyonesse was lost
for, were waves transparent, towers
wreathed in weed would show at each
window-slit drowned eyes that gaze
over puzzling fields where grey
fish swoop down instead of gulls
and the contours waver. Here,
history and myth combine,
spindrift blurs the edge of land
and a sunset green with salt
ushers in the hiss of night.

Tresungers Point, Autumn 1996

THE LION OF VENICE IN THE BRITISH MUSEUM

Last seen in winter mist
high on his pillar
as if just alighted
out of the shifting
greys of history

Paws grabbing the outspread book,
makeshift wings still unfurled,
comic ears warily
assessing cold influence
of water on marble

Patched, ageless, vulnerable,
trapped in this entrance-hall,
inspected and glowering
though blank eyes past contempt
give nothing away

    Waiting indifferently
    to stare out again
    at fog or at sunlight
    till the stump of his column
    stands in the sea

FERRARA

for Peter Russell

I   *Palazzo Schifanoia*

The fact these frescoes
are flaked and peeling
should inhibit most
interpretations
but bright chariots
and garlands can still
be discerned –joyous
mysteries pagan
in costume, festive
in their intention.

The motive at least
is clear: to banish
boredom from the court –

a praiseworthy aim
shared by the poet
writing with relish
of a hero gone
mad and warrior
maidens deflected
by sly enchantments.

Light of heart he may
well have been although
living as he did
at the cardinal's
beck and call he must
have attended Mass –
confirming each day
how faith was vital
to his characters
and also himself.

II *Duomo*

Among the shadows the sacristan,
fanning a huge grey sheet of cardboard,
surely unfairly
quenched the votive candles
before slamming the west door to.

A man drove up in rather
a smart car to collect
the gypsy and her child
who had spent the morning
begging in a desultory way
by the rubbed marble lion.
It was time, it seemed, for lunch.

Over our own prosciutto and wine,
it had been, we decided soberly,
no ghost there in the side-chapel
but a remarkably thin nun
darting behind the altar
to replenish the vases.

III   *Via Mirasole*

No roses now. No jasmine.
A jazz-trumpet comes
from someone's radio.
Two silver-furred cats
scurry beneath the laurel
and a dry leaf falls
in Ariosto's garden.

A DAY WITHOUT SUITCASES

Five hours unrolled in the train.
Obedient olive-groves. Dry sky.
White villages with goats scuttling.
Sudden plunge over the jagged brow
of a chasm. Stretch of field with soil dark
red like the flank of a cow.
Unpack in another hotel.
Investigate time with no travel.

Strolling at leisure to a distant world
whose intricate arches have forgotten
the cruelty practised and simply
catch the slow daylight in curled
grooves of yellowed marble
while latticed reflections take over
the long pool maculate with carp.

Beyond jasmine gardens high cypress
have lofted immobile black
flames of demarcation. Thus far
from one's pitch. No further. Back
to echoing platforms with clocks, leaving
the winter oranges to shrivel in the gutter.

On this occasion at least I shall not see
that snow-cloaked shoulder of the Sierra
recede to ochre nor hear again this palm-tree
scrape its fronds except in memory
consulting secrets locked now in the camera.

I sip wine by a fountain in the expanding sunlight
reluctant, reconciled, aware that opportune
researchers after the event advise
the eye to linger on an afternoon.

This southern glare distributes beauty in harsher
cubes of shadow and limewash. No compromise
lets in the half-tones. No blur. No merging.

History worked with a knife. It's a land
without dreams. The soul's irrelevant.

I feel the brightness glancing off my hand.

Granada, April 1993

ASKLEPION

Here, sir, you are allowed
to die. You, madam, may
give birth. The further side
of that stone marker such
processes in and out
of what we call living
are strictly forbidden.

Why? you ask. There is no
why, no question, no gift
of knowledge other than
acceptance. Once inside
the sacred precinct you
will perhaps understand.

I say 'perhaps' for few
apart perhaps (*snicker*)
from your humble servant
can follow the founder
to all those dark regions.

Snakes will slither over
your prostrate bodies meant
as reminders of hours
you would sooner forget.

Remorse, fear and longing
for what might have been make
the skin shrink at their touch.

Are you still sure you wish
to partake of the cure?

I'm here to welcome you.

Epidauros, Autumn 1993

TROEZEN

for Peter Jay

A ruined church –
stone rafters, fluted pillars
tumbled in confusion –
straddles the flattened
temple. On this dry
rise of ground above
the former stadium
they worshipped the sly
goddess.
       The queen,
parched with longing,
peered between columns
to spy on her stepson

naked with javelins
in barren light.

Lemon-groves spread
where an indigo gulf
lapped the shore-road.
Hearing the curse
Poseidon obedient
maddened the stallions.
Tangled in reins
the slandered prince
was dragged over boulders,
through thorns, to die mangled –
wrenched from his beauty,
identified only
by brightness of hair.

Olive-trees, sporadic,
rustling, silvery,
replace the palace
where Phaedra faced
with disfiguring truth
poisoned herself.
Earthquake over,
sea-monster back in its lair,
the widower-king mourned the torn
corpse of his son
promised to Artemis.
Wailing of women
foretokened his future –
to fall like his father
to death in the sea.

With brutal logic
the sunbaked legend
set out to prove
these mortal two
irreconcilable –
warring of chastity
(one kind of single-
mindedness) with lust
(another kind) –
rôles composed
for a dedicated boy

and a would-be dissolute
stepmother.
          Bystanders also
got clawed by revenge –
tragedy rarely
focuses only
on the guilty,
on the victim.

Beliefs become built
where some were razed –
earth-father, sky-mother,
vice versa. She with dark
animal blood, he with the moon-
cold in his veins
how could, this side
of doom, these blend?

Hard soil. Spiked plant. One butterfly.
Black crags sheer to the west.
Chirr of a grasshopper.

Then silence.

A hot wind sweeps across the vanished town.

EGYPTOLOGY: WORKING TITLE

for Lynn

I

Consider these doorways in the barren
hillscape of the dead.
No blade of grass, no thorn-bush, just
dust, rock, sand and
an unforgiving sky.

Towards the dawnside though, across
the green area of cultivation –
date-palms and irrigation-channels with egrets waiting –
beyond the swift blue-changing river lies
the perfect city.
                    Incense-trees
stud the orchard. Cats have pride of place.
Artisans squat before their shops
adjusting tiny scales to measure gold.
                    The temenos itself –
swish of stiff linen past impassive
statues, maze of shadows cast
by a grove of pillars daubed with cinnabar,
offering-tables heaped with jars of wheat,
honey, amulets and lotus-flowers.

Banners keep stirring in a listless breeze.
The sacred geese are led fussing to the shore.

The sun at noon above the Nile
divides the living from the dead.

At evening from the eastern desert
cobras of darkness slither between buildings
blotting out the light. Night-terrors
scrape against granite and brickwork.

Stars in the square lake sparkle one by one.

II

Two lions guard the vermilion
disc on the tomb wall.
Permanent here, unflaking, see
immaculate plumage of the ibis,
mauve lustre on this bunch of grapes.
Also the dusky profile of a jackal
waiting to pounce.

Intent on their unchanging labour
husband and wife together
plough furrows behind a dappled cow.
For the three seasons,
stratified in flood and earth and fruit,

explain the truth of seed and reaping
as successive stages held in the divine eye.
And no transition. No development.

Time here became snared in paint.
On the stone-ceiling the gaunt
sky-goddess is devouring, meting out
the ten red suns that mark each day.
Although that tense is wrong. She *is*.
They *are*. But nothing is happening
and no distinction's made
between a ritual and the event.

Far below, each night,
slow oars are plied, rhythmic in black water.
Mummified hearing catches a faint
splash echoed as the sun-god
upright, unspeaking, on the boat of death
gets rowed once more back to his starting-place.

Daybreak spills gold over the skyline.
Light raps on each unopened door.
Although the phenomenon recurs
it is the emblem we remember
shown underground with such meticulous care.

Luxor, January 1996

INTO AFRICA

for Paul Hyland

To risk it past the cape of no return.
To cross a non-existent line
that separates the unknown from the known.
Steer on under a sky unpricked
by our familiar stars
and pressing southward keep
on our port side the gold and green

fringing that immense enigma till
we come at last to latitudes of fire
where noon may churn the ocean into flame
and shrivel up the planks beneath our feet
charring us all to wraiths of soot.

A cemetery at the river's mouth
admonishes the mariner.
Give up all hope of proof –
that map inked in with lakes and silver-mines
named after monarchs, other travellers –
mere tags to tame the moon
and give identity to pumice.
Forget the logs of ebony, the tusks, the hides,
the chests of precious stones, the slaves, the plunder.
Head back leaving the canopy intact
and guard the imagined image free from harm.

Upstream there's a marker-stone
incised with warnings none today can read.
A dry branch hung with human skulls
protects a sudden turning in the path.
Range upon range of misted hills
conceal the enormous sameness –
a sea-bound mind
can't navigate such towering waves,
red, ochre, rock–capped, sheer, tree'd, ribbed with sand.

Success is to return alive.
The arrow aimed at the suspected heart
becomes a weapon forged from smoke
that points the way, wavers,
misleads and leaves no trace
of heroism, honourable wound
or knowledge filched from darkness.
What was supposed to have been achieved is lost
and one forever with a torrid air
that quivers over distance and deceives.

Miles out to sea again
the flow of chocolate–coloured silt
yields finally to blue.

VISIT TO AN UNKNOWN SUBURB

Ten when I got in. At the dead
hour. Commuters have hurried through this space
now angled with dusty sunlight,
echoing. No shoppers scurry yet.
At the metal barrier, half manned,
arrival's not distinguished from departure –
used tickets get yielded to the same
coin-greyed hand clipping a new one.

Time to spare. A café is open
across the station-yard.
Waitress already yawning, tabby sprawled by the window,
view of tramlines, peeling posters,
pyramids of coal.

To check the necessary documents:
application-forms, visa,
two photographs (unsmiling, black
and white, head
and shoulders only, verified on the back as me
by bona fide ministers of religion
and men of law), age, sex, height, weight, each
grandmother's maiden name (in full), known scars,
amount of teeth (with fillings noted),
justification for existence,
number of unborn children,
date of death.

Click the scratched briefcase to and pay.
Small tip plonked on the glass-topped
table with blue bamboo legs. Smiling,
sidle towards the door and leave,
setting the OPEN placard swinging.
Sky autumn-hard. Grubby trees
stuck in asphalt shed parchment leaves.

Dingy blocks of flats. Washing strung
along concrete balconies to catch a dwindling warmth.

Slaughterhouse. Hosed cobblestones.
A glimpse of swaying girders
dangled from cranes. Gasometer.
Some tufted quite unplanned
allotments. Makeshift sheds.

The streets press closer – chemist's,
confectioner's have glass fronts.
Boxes of earth-stained turnips merely
propped at an angle on the pavement.

Enquiry. Passers-by seem not to know.
Some indicate a far-off cooling-tower,
others point to a church.
The trouble is that this is not a town.
You'd know you'd left it but would find
it hard to pinpoint where the frontier was.

At last a glittering police-station. Time's
running short. I see. First left,
right at the memorial to the fallen,
across the square to the far corner,
down the tree-lined avenue then take
the second bridge over the canal.
No optimist could miss it.
Thankyou.
            Panting,
I thread quieter streets,
all windows closed, gardens trim
behind groomed yellow hedges or fences of upright
planks protected with faded creosote.

Reach finally the place. Check in.
Fill out a brown form. Not late
although of course I have to wait beyond
my appointed time. Summoned.
Complete another form (pink this time).
Hang about once more.
Beneath the worn wooden floor
dry basements must be crammed

from top to bottom containing
dossiers in triplicate describing
in unnecessary detail all
who queued for hours to be identified
and went away like me (I hope)
never to return.

The permit is essential,
allows one (as the name implies)
to breathe and eat and sleep and even dream.
Of paramount importance now
next October it will matter less
than the plane-leaf trodden earlier in the gutter.

I quit the office, clasping the stiff card in triumph,
welcome to walk these alien boulevards unchallenged –
but not to vote, get married,
purchase property, become
a member of the armed forces,
own a car, join a political
party, work in a lawyer's
chambers or take photographs
of ports or railway-bridges.
All liberty is circumscribed.
Make do with what you can.

Laugh, drink, work, benefit
from what this country has to offer –
look around.
        But do not beg,
deface a public building, disobey
police instructions,
attend seditious meetings or attempt
to smuggle gingham, breadfruit, aspirin, zinc or lighter-fuel.
Oh, and you may not read
books penned by totally
misguided authors.
          Otherwise
you are completely free.

PAST CREDENCE

It's never really been tried
deployment of faith
trusting in power to shift Everest

Always a little hanging-back
reliance on the safety-clause
reservation skulking in the words

'I command you to move!'
(uttered brazenly)
then looking round shamefaced
'See? It hasn't budged.'
(the tone one of relief)

But
    if you could believe
wholeheartedly
and feel conviction
rooting down from the soles of the feet . . .

What chasms shown!
What heavenly avalanches!

STABLE

On a planet dragged through
emptiness by the sun
a pregnant woman sought
shelter at the wrong time
of the year in a far

corner of a clumsy
empire and was given
grudgingly an outhouse

She brought into a world
sordid and unprepared
a baby as victim
for humankind cannot
afford the luxury
of innocence liking
uncertainty and speed
more than the risk of faith
kneeling by a newborn
child on the stable ground

TRIUMPHAL ENTRY

for Joan Bakewell

Palm-fronds and garments flung beneath the hooves,
clamour of welcome for a conqueror,
inauguration of an age chain-free . . .

Despite all earlier hints
the outcome seemed to let the shouters down.
This was to be an empire of submission:
instead of protest, service –
instead of insurrection, peace.

At the other end of the week, God said,
'Let there be blood.' And there was blood.
His palms that cured the blind and mad
got hammered to the crossbar.
The makeshift tree became stained this time
with the red knowledge of obedience.

No friends stood by their king who hung there scorned –
a felon, a failure, a mere laughing-stock
who pleaded to the dark unanswering sky.

We're meant to clasp that starless paradox.
That apparent loss of God contains our hope –
all that we dread unshirked and undergone
by one who dared the worst the world could do.

An empty tomb at daybreak shone with proof.
One wounded hand unlocked the gate of death
to show the proper end of frailty and pain
is that quiet passing into paradise –
no dust, no yelling, no mistaken dream;
admission to a place where we belong.

THE CLEANSING

for Jack Emery

A pallid spring sun shone on the forecourt.
Inside the building it was dim and stuffy
and people came and went about their business.

Suddenly we saw light gather to itself.
A human shape, fused from another April,
entered our temple like a shaft of fire.

The shadows burned away. Stark radiance
pushing from floor to rafters
dazzled the traders.
                    The man made all of light
hurled trestles down so the money rolled glittering,
smashed wicker cages so the captive doves
flew whirring through blue clouds of incense.

He swept like a meteor with scourge and flame
condemning us who'd turned the place for prayer
into a space for robbery and bargaining.

He left, and it was as though the day had been withdrawn.
We stared at the wreckage in this new noon dusk –
the shattered furniture, the litter of tarnished coins.

Someone said, 'Who was that?'
There was a frightened pause.
Another answered. 'He's called the Prince of Peace.'

CORONATION OF THE VIRGIN

The tragedy is past. She wears the crown
her Son alive again placed there. The Cross,
plus-sign of knowledge, has dethroned the tree.

When the primeval mother snapped the stalk
of that alluring fruit, to wonder why
cost Eden. Mary though kept no supply
of question-marks to flick at what had been
pronounced. The guardian thrust the flaming sword
back in its scabbard. Eve's descendants may
reclaim that forfeited inheritance
and live at one with all that has been made –
provided we accept that freedom means
aligning action with instruction as
we try to hear the rustle of such wings
as beat that day in Nazareth when fore-
armed with bewilderment the messenger
confuted likelihood and brought the bruised
blueprint of paradise through into time.

She saw at once: the way to be is found
by turning human standards upside down,
the debt of hatred can't be paid in kind
and Number One must never be oneself –
laws obvious as the dawn, as nourishing
as bread, as necessary as the air,
as gladdening as wine.
                                       And yet we still
prefer to slink along the foliage
and grope in shadows for a tainted peach.
We'd rather leer through a distorting glass
than let the light of heaven assist our gaze.

There is no cure but prayer. There is no path
except the pilgrimage that Mary took
from that bare room illuminated by
an angel to a rented stable, up
worn temple-steps, through miles of dunes rock-strewn
to Egypt, back to grace a wedding-feast
(events she came to see that stood for birth,
acceptance, rescue, miracle) and then
past triumph, trial and heartbreak on to death.
She held His lifeless body as she'd held
the living Child and all the world went dark.

Past mourning then lay daybreak. Wounded feet
stole with no trace across the silent garden.
At night, alone, her resurrected Son
came to assuage her grief and prove that death
is never now conclusion. Therefore, when,
years later, in another quiet room,
she knew her end was close, surrounded by
those she held dear, she felt no sense of loss.
The crown was poised above her dying head.
The life she'd lived had shown how she had loved
beyond obedience and how love repaired
the rift in expectation time had made.

ST. JOHN, BROADCLYST

Stare at the cross
then shut my eyes –
a plain design
stamped dark on red
fades slowly till
I raise again
reluctant lids
and guilty by
default behold
once more the stark
brass unadorned.

The symbol bears
nailed to it through
eternity
no compromise
but waits till all
who pray in time
keep two bars fixed
across the sight
so as to give
the mortal will
unerring aim.

DEMONIC WINE

> *One of the fathers, in great Severity, called Poesie,*
> Vinum Daemonum, *because it filleth the Imagination,*
> *and yet it is, but with the shadow of a* lie.
> — BACON

Images twist in a stone cup
brimming with scarlet liquid.
The truth is not what it seems.
Alteration clings to the task.

No grape was ever this shade.
Lacking, the bead of rain, curved gloss
skins hold on moonless nights,
ooze that drew in the wasps.

Lost autumns reborn, transfigured
in scent and savour, own the same
quality dreams have on waking,
gone though clear. Could such

fermentation just be achieved
in hell? No whiff of sulphur
flickers around this cork. No scaly
wings rasp by the sipper.

Earthly tendons sawed birch-stakes,
tugged wires taut, hooped casks – though
wielded no sway over ochre
soil, vicissitudes of June.

Ideals that dazzled the mind
in sowing at last gain substance
even if hue and tang however
beguiling never precisely match

expectation making the upshot
part of the charm, like tones on some jug
fired in the kiln; for magic's involved –
only a touch of the murkier

arts not total exposure
to flames of the fallen,
simply that tincture of pride
present in all we try.

We put our name to the alchemy
(fruit-heap distilled to liquor,
random musing to typescript)
to claim the handiwork

since labelling château and change
we brazen out the lie, intending
next time at least to do better,
sharp practice that peels imperfection.

THE WIDOW'S GARDEN

The widow's garden
this grey December
day displays fallen
apples dull yellow
on the ochre ground.
Stripped branches offer
a brief vantage-point
for raucous starlings,
their iridescent
plumage lending them
a prehistoric
skin. Indeed the gulls
black on the sky could
be pterodactyls
as they float squabbling.

At weekends he dug
reluctantly, more
than willing to break
off for a gossip.
Translucent leaves drift
from the raspberry-canes
on to the metal
wheelbarrow lying
on its side. The spent
hydrangeas dangle
their mauve globes. Bean-poles
lift a high series
of overlapping
triangles. Time here
seems halted. The paths
untenanted make
an ordered maze round
stiff cabbages, dry
stalks, a last cold rose.

No frost. No wind. Night
dogging night has left
so far no imprint,
dark stamp of winter
rimmed with white. The beds
in abeyance give
no hint of April
nor do empty shrubs
promise a summer
shadow.
        She watches
the bare afternoon
through the peeling grid
of a window. Death
and the worker hand
in hand inspected
the layout before
turning the tanned soil
over in a sly
anticipation
of what would be. Whorled
fossil, possible
arrowhead, clay pipe,
blurred florin fingered
in twilight are not
weighed in the balance
against grief. The bush
planted when they first
came here will bear next
autumn fruit tainted
with memory. Too
many echoes criss-
cross the area
unpredictably
like the greenfinches.
She walks there rarely.
His spade, hoe and fork
lean stained in the shed.

He went and she will
go but whoever
arrives to disturb
what they planned – the tiled

borders, the wires nailed
to the low brick wall –
will only alter
what he had taken
on from another
assisting the green
each year to uncoil
from unpromising
rectangles of earth.

CONSIDERATIONS

Afterglow. That sheen –
phantom of triumph
under the skyline.
All reminiscence
now – misshapen sun
laughably mirrored
on slate running mauve
from rain. Aftermath.

Down blind curves of world
a saffron expanse
of light scythed. Dry stalks,
low, lightened of grain,
proclaim shone stubble
to the clouds. To be
burned, ploughed deep, summer
memory undone.

Firelight. Far darkness
encroaching with sparks
like stars kept at bay.
Philosophies hugged
near the heart in youth –
mere replies losing
heat to spin through space
as blank stones. Twilight.

Doubt. Soot on the grate.
Zeal slipping noiseless
away among ripped
pages of scarlet
air. Cold proof of time.
The moulding hand seems
powerless. Witness
what is. Going out.

Moonset. Last pallor
robbing woods and slopes
washed in colourless
blue. Linger unseen,
ears pricked for the horn–
call. In wonder when
it might come. Never,
stranger. Or else soon.

Snowfall. Forgetful
of aims (hard–edged three
hours ago but blurred
in descent of flakes)
we've just shadowy
tools to make the whole
thing out and the right
word may still be no.

Ink spilling smothers
the bright copybook,
each maxim coiled one
way. Easy to shirk
all sense of sunrise,
trusting your viceroy
to stay four feet for
ever from the brink.

Dawn struck. A silent
fanfare, yesterday's
banners, their symbols
charred. Dark procession –
hearse and garlands pass
the field of conflict
where sprawl the slaughtered
horses of the sun.

IRON WAY

falling far across bright fields
high white rain
gets bent by the wind
with my Sunday train
via unfamiliar hills
fleeing from an immense rainbow

westering sun
slips over paperbacks
crosswords and plastic cups of drink
mimicking other journeys
taken alone to the brink
of known daylight

a valid return ticket
made out to nightfall
stays safe in my pocket
as time lingers
in the lit coils of a river
and ruffled crows pick at grass

among elms on the skyline
the stump of a rainbow
juts an otherworldly glow
magic or menace
touchdown of a spaceship
or the spilt palette of childhood

the speed never varies
as stations are offered
like hopes then withdrawn
as lamps come on in the scudding houses
and travellers concede the fare is
inclusive of anxiety

eyes twitch from the page
check bags and briefcases
though the detour has meant
unsure hour of arrival
and darkness hides the way
the afternoon's been spent

HAWTHORNDEN CASTLE, NOVEMBER 1993

for Peter Josyph and Anthony Rudolf

Watching the wild
dry leaves fly up
in a sudden
gust and the rooks
knocked sideways, braced
awkwardly, then
recovering
direction I
recall the white
valley a week
ago criss-crossed
with daintiest
deer-tracks and stamped
with their forked runes
by slow-pacing
pheasants. Autumn
littering grass
and paths appears
to have replaced
winter. Perhaps
the calendar
reversed will now
offer summer
for Christmas, ripe
fruit shrinking give
way to blossom
and daffodils
dwindling to tight
bulbs make Shelley's
line about spring
seem no longer
applicable.

FRIENDLY FIRE

In a semi-circle watching, well fed,
the Yule log flare and crumble,
they talk of the year. Tinsel
glitters on fir and photo-frame.
Familiar scenes crowd mantelpiece and windowsill –
stagecoach approaching a frost-white inn,
Dutch skaters beneath a leaden sky,
carol-singers stamping their boots, perky
robins perched by a snowbank, candles,
holly-wreaths, even The Christ-Child on hay
with starstruck shepherds, ethnic kings.

In heat of warfare some kink in progress
may mean an ally slays
unwittingly an ally. The aim
perhaps a fraction out. And so no bugle. No
citation. A telegram papers over any
loss that can't be blamed on the enemy.

After each armistice
grieving neighbours exchange
absence and heartbreak.
                   Knowledge
victim and killer wore the same
uniform gives an added
twist to the bayonet.

Kindling lit, a misplaced rifle-shot,
some quirk in destiny, red sparks crawling on soot,
grenade released too soon – so many
images for the one match.
                 We have been known
to poke a fire with blackened swords –
fuel for ashes, mourning in the hearth.

THE ROOMS

Mirror returning
Adam to heroine
window to lightswitch
framed map to vase
swings when he sidesteps
shifting the angles
bookshelf past sofa
him back to himself

He glimpses fingers
unknotting his tie
via invisible
strata of reference
object to object
in straitening segments
whereby each moment
dazzlingly handled
can be treasured forever
in glass fabrications
those welcoming patterns
Pythagoras planned

Between self and images
not just the dust-motes
the cold slice of crystal
but dwindling sunflash
to rim any vertical
layer of twilight
as corner's sent glancing
to corner and back

Over his shoulder
though neither is stirring
she sees how her self
and temporary lover
race in and out of
reflex and eyeball
as secondary vision
catches deflected
watcher to watcher
watcher to watched

Turning to gaze at her
not in the mirror
he offers his throat bared

She closes her eyes

Neither can tell now
what might be reflected
recalling the bishop's
legitimate puzzle
whether in absence
reality's held

Quitting the room they
willingly jettison
old-fangled methods
of gauging desire
bequeathing the scene
a barely translucent
system of archives
locked in the lost cell
invented by time

In granting the dusklight
freedom to juggle
with acts of the past
they're nude now together
and far from the clockface
replay in a vacuum
what may have occurred

PORTRAIT

Few things appeal
in her November:
gilt on a Sienese madonna,
twilight, fire crumbling,
smell of potpourri.

Even stiffened fingers
vision greying over
allow lacework,
bottling damsons,
Gibbon's pessimistic prose.

Thick albums of photographs
remain unopened.
The rare remembered joys
stay skilfully evoked
on sleepless nights.

She greets old friends
barring the threshold.
Her telephone
rings dutifully for a time,
gives up.

She hums no tune
weeding the walled half-acre,
rubs her locked back
then rests on the sunlit bench
watching the winds pour overhead –
not interested in letters,
nor a morning paper,
nor the death of those she knew.

PRISONER OF TIME

Tower room by starlight.
Hunched at the table.
Nail-studded door.
Spiral stairway.
Smell of mould.
Pitch-dark. Glimmer
of night sky. Pitch-
dark once more.

Down the uneven
steps. Arrow-slits
gaining in pallor.
Under the arch
at the foot broad
daylight. Spring
flowers. Child
on each hand.
Prattle. Warm breeze.
Only so far. Half-
way across bright
grass the moment
tugs at the leash.
That time long gone
vanishes. Plans
at the start.
Drawbridge down.
Highway dwindling
beyond blue moat.
Fatherhood.
The distance. No. Jerked
back up the staircase
knuckles barked
shins scraped.
Jolting against
granite edges
curved wall.
Door slammed to.
Bolt shot. Key twisted
in lock. Back
in their place
pain age
impotence.
Tower room.
Barred window.
Small hours.

REVERIE

For I was once the lord of autumn, stood
till darkness crystallised against my fingertips.
Abandoned sceptres on that wicker bench
admonished me. Once a monarch always one
even if the realm has slid beneath the sea.
The bailiff, scrolls of sunlight in his hand,
was making an inventory of the northern furniture.
All that's been said has to be said again.
Be wary, though – one mustn't tilt the skull
brimming with remorse. With animals, their dreams
and memories remain identical.
In exile, on the shores of hell,
our past selves slither by and murmur to each other.
Humans are all the time attempting to evade
the silent burglars of the heart.

Nothing but twilight pressed against the bone.
The mind's a marble forecourt. Chipped naïads
glower from each corner. The diagonal flight of steps
leads up to where the castle used to be.
Returning with a cardboard box of glass eggs
I knew anticipation by the voice alone.
Echo spoke first, dismayed me. It's the angel
cowering behind each moment we can count on
who sets the unbearable alarm-clock. What's left
is imagery beyond the poison-barrier.
When I was frisked they found that pocket-book
with a photograph of the dark. It was used
in evidence. The convalescent heroines
devoured transparent loaves. I lacked,
it seemed, even that nourishment.

LIFE STUDIES

How many dream of becoming their statues
cocooned securely in the time to come
though dust may clog those sightless eyeballs
and droppings from unhatched pigeons
stain metal hair

What pleasures what triumphs to be recorded
three dimensions folded cold
to trap forever any event that runs
flashing down the hours
breasts the tape amid the irony of cheers
and proceeds like a phoenix
to the athlete's pyre

The deliberator's bronze hands
clutch bronze chair-arms
while the diarist stands
pensive in the hallway
clay pen poised above spread book

If one of them is naked
a monument to love
fig-leaf clamped askew over stone genitals
a different occasion gets saved from warfare
a mineral uniform
an equally useless sword
a sculptured plume
medals of alabaster

Fixed in fame and walkable around
each plinth dominates a tatty square
looms at the top of a flight of white steps
or closes the vista in some worn parkland

Each of the many rôles defined at last
no hesitancy any more
no need for promises
recriminations
or gestures sketched on the dusk

These statues stud our lives

Once cast or carven they recede from us
a sloughed-off viper's skin
the husk of a shed chrysalis
for we in fact will have gone on
have slithered to further meeting-points
hard crossroads
or else been showing off sticky wings
to new indifferent admirers

Still
the forms

In shaping them in wax or marble
with such care
betraying such devotion
we had nobody but ourselves in view

NIGHT TEARS

Peace after weeping. And the world,
withdrawn to stillness,
uncovers a stunned quiet. The ear detects
an eddying silence never heard before.
She sleeps again, the nightmare understood –
fear of rejection, mother lost, a darkened noon
lurking with unmet terror.
                              Slips into dream –
wet cheek now drying, heart at a gentler pace –
the land around her reassembling
where all she loves belongs, the animals,
the pictures, puzzles, tufted lawn, in place,
predictable, secure and reconciled.

BLACKTHORN WINTER

for Nicholas

Spring by the calendar but up the slope
white flakes get scattered by a cutting wind.
The hinds graze on their own or step or lie
indifferent to the skittering lambs, low crow
or higher circling buzzard. Soon my son
will quit his training for the real thing
while I veer from the column, hunker down
by cuckoo-pint and bramble to record
moonrise, return of swifts and bryony
turned red. Fake winter froth is stiff along
a line of trees gone creamy in the sun –
a fragrant snowdrift for the breeze to shred
in petals on fresh turf. I've seen him act

in tragedy and farce, doublet or clogs,
always with wonder at his supple way
with riddling, pratfalls, sudden menace, song –
correct appurtenances of play for that
is what it all most seriously is:
light making patterns of the deer's quick legs,
the downsweep of a never fatal sword,
verses that glint with tidings of a world
well past the usual skyline. Haze today
prohibits distance where the grey-etched ships
are gliding on their charts to harbour. Gaze
is narrowed to this land-locked heath where all
we dare tell of the future is that first
hesitant Brimstone flickering by the stream.
My former blossom blackening at the edge,
I watch with prayers behind my lips as he,
my son I love, puts forth his tentative
green buds and may they thicken in success.
Somewhere, deep in the shadows of a combe,
the stags stand with new antlers. This cold spring
must still be startled into summer. Flowers
cast lavishly from leafless blackthorn can
delude us with a January scene
until they curl and fade, char at the rim,
get trampled, turn at last to humus which
will lay the groundwork for another year.

The Quantocks, April 1991

WHITE LANE

To take dawn by surprise. Go
on finding no fork to force
sudden choice, no side-turning
with sight of a bright orchard,
no itch to hack through the green
barriers hemming the roadway.
Place no trust in quivering
compass-needles. What occurs
crosses the preconception
of dreams. The literal proves
hostile to assessment. Time
and again magnetism
robs the path of a vista.
Stars and hearsay can distract
due attention paid to one's
whereabouts at moments when
the epiphany hoped for
takes forever to attain.

Grey June summoned hawthorn heaped
in blank clouds along the banks
with milky drifts of daisies,
tall, drooping after the shower,
lining the ditches. The lane
kept turning this way and that,
its surface scuffed here and there
revealing the chalk so that
what green there was appeared quite
outdone by white. The ever-
curving hedgerows, the arching
sycamores that met above
our heads held back perspective
to their flowers and leaves till they
all at once opening out
displayed sunlit and prancing
the lean form of a white horse
carved in the flank of a hill.

LIRIODENDRON TULIPIFERA 'FASTIGIATUM'

for Michael Hamburger

On Delos once, the hero saw
a sapling growing near the stone
altar of Apollo and, struck
spellbound by its loveliness, stood
lost in veneration. This damp
autumnal morning sauntering
through The Botanical Gardens
(variegated leaves on the grass
and scattered among cold asters –
less colourful than usual
under these low grey clouds) I share,
here, far, for a startled moment,
the wonder of Odysseus. Tall,
unlike any tree I've ever
seen, slender, its grace on this chilled
Sabbath (quiet now the church-bells have
swung their summons) seems to require
a broad air from Handel to pay
a pagan tribute. No-one else
is about. My footsteps have stopped
crunching gravel. I hear mallards
busy on the unseen river.
Nor can my lips, parted in awe,
release the right music to match
the miracle of its secret
growth from one insignificant
seed to this green silhouette cut
out against an alien sky.
Next year a drooping oriflamme
of foliage to the left might form
a disappointing symmetry.
The Greek seafarer never put
time to the test by going back
to the island. Earthquake, disease,
drought, lightning-flash – anything could
have riven or withered the fresh
beauty he brought to mind catching
sight of the supple princess, hair
loose in the salt wind as she sped

playing along the shore that bright
legendary day after the storm.

Oxford, October 1990

A CIGARETTE GHOST

Sometimes, during the small
hours in our dark bedroom (faint
gleam through red curtains, fleck
of light on wardrobe-mirror) I'll,
snapping to full consciousness, detect
across my nostrils, unmistakably,
an acrid drift of cigarette-smoke.

There's no-one there. The familiar
décor of glints and shadows stays
empty as earlier. I sniff.
The reek's still there but owns
no smouldering as origin. No presence
makes itself felt or dreamt.
Nothing in the night is jolted
out of the ordinary – just
this tang of smoke that tends to hang
invisibly in space
then fades.
              Who could it be? Why should
a lingering habit stain the air?

Reflective phantom, while you stroll
in some adjacent zone, you seem
supremely unconcerned about
the current tenants of this place.
I am intrigued however by
your intermittent presence here
and wonder if one night maybe
the glow as you inhale might show

one fleeting glimpse of mouth and brow
to give if not acquaintance then
beginnings of identity.

ATHLETE TYING A SANDAL

I

Dark corridor

Late autumn

Gravel beyond a window
in yellow shadow from the vine

This small bas-relief
palely incised
hangs over a bookcase
musty with novels
left here by tourists
long in their graves

Downslope from the balustrade
the last afternoon rays
touch olive-trees into puffs of silver

Roots grope in the same
ochre soil where once this plaque
lay buried with blue-scurfed coins
among fragments of earthenware

II

His self-absorption ought
to deflect one's gaze
for nothing matters
but the race he'll win
though it was never run

Dry spikes of grass
remain untrodden in one
unidentified stadium

Time stopped before the test
consigned garlands
to their shrivelled seed-pod
but spared him wounding
shouts for another
as well as an unwanted
statue half-shrouded
in the possible
tatters of success

III

Cracked now and framed
in rosewood his supple attitude
the carver froze for some
admirer who dictated
important details
of thigh and profile
matches in miniature
what I am led with little
reluctance to recall

Private years shared
make me less a voyeur
than a gauger of images

Thought slides under word

His outdated grace
luminous still in the gloom
retains an enviable

outline unblurred
by the steam that clouded
one school changing-room

IV

I find my own lost history here
reduced in size and barely two-
dimensional for memory
fashions its own smooth replicas
ready for stacking
against the bone
walls of regret

Alone in the gathering dusk
I put out a finger
running it along his cold
hip till I come to the hard
silly acorn of sex

Fiesole, November 1991

OBITUARY

The school magazine
included your name
in the dark list
among so many
older and younger

I mourn
the loss of you
from imagining –
that occasional dream-exit
for ever closed.

It was all so long ago.
What do I dare remember?
You have been moved
beyond the reach
of fingers glued to history.

The living
have impertinent memories.
You must be spared that jerky
playback of caresses,
re-editing of black and moonlight,
whispers attributed again and again
to lips that have forgotten their lines.

Humbled, alive, I realise
you have withdrawn my right
to stray in certain areas
long taken for granted
in the freehold of the past.

EASTER IN MONTREAL

Above the city
as at rush-hour dipped
headlights queue then lurch
onward through the dusk
alone by a high
window I allow
the mind's gaze to stray
from present twilight
and see long before
neon, Chevrolets
or the silhouette
of glass skyscrapers
one crouching savage
by a frozen swamp
waiting for the kill.

Thin panes can banish
the dark Arctic air
from this centrally
heated room where flights
of time and fancy
can be indulged in –
guiltily if truth
is in fact the sole
ingredient verse
should never omit
though its property –
unvarnished or else
multi-faceted –
was you remember
jestingly questioned
by the Roman judge
who despite his wife's
untimely message
(which in retrospect
shows such unnerving

prescience) could not
accept the measure
of her dream which held
veritas flaming.

For though that moment
like any other
framed the eternal
he was ill-equipped
to gauge 'the beyond
in our midst' – nor could
he, pagan, urbane,
having his own hands
free, grasp how the ropes
wound tight round those wrists
would fail to hamper
the unconvicted
man brought before him.

His guards kept yawning,
rubbed their unshaven
jawline, blinked gritty
eyelids. It was too
early in the day –
that fresh light stirring
the nearby cocks to
raucous wakefulness
lent an off-putting
clarity to what
went on. Not within
dying memory
had another dawn
like this one come up
to pencil lengthy
shadows in over
the mosaic floor
of the judgement-hall
stretching out across
that time-furrowed land
of apprehension
until they vanished
beyond the broken
horizon.
      Pilate,

bored, quizzical, still
followed the letter
of the law.
                    Dazzling
silence encountered
his enquiry – a
transparent language
coming in dumbshow
from elsewhere. He joked,
looked baffled, sighed, frowned,
groped for the right key.
None of his well-thumbed
lexicons could help
de-code these tacit
guidelines for how could
first and *last* become
interchangeable?
slave equal *master*?
yield get redefined
as *conquer*? the black
cul-de-sac of death
be metamorphosed
into a gateway?

No-one perhaps is
able to picture
salvation save as
a means of escape
from tendrils of doubt
lashing our ankles.
Should Pilate be blamed
for trying to free
a non-criminal?
He was weak but since
all Jerusalem
stood at boiling-point
(this was of course two
thousand years ago)
he sought to maintain
a political
peace at any cost
though none to himself.
The roots of motive

tangled so deeply
in soil and manure
can nourish heroes
toppled off their plinth
by changing fashion
as well as crafty
killers rewarded
with bland cenotaphs
by plotters who need
to re-label thugs
as freedom-fighters.

It is too easy
to loll in judgement
condemning the past.
When the bully-boys
throng round to denounce
guileless neighbours who'll
spring to their defence?
How many of us
will stand in the road,
palms raised, to challenge
the oncoming tanks
of history? Most
will greet the status
quo with open arms
for makers of dams,
deflectors of tides,
canal-architects –
those who pause for thought
before stumbling on
past the red signposts
are few in number.

Stiff reeds. The grey pools
rough with ice. He peers,
hunched, his copper skin
protected these months
of low sun by furs
from lynx and beaver.
Scarlet plumes adorn
his black hair. He aims
with luck to bring down

a brace of glossy
waterfowl, a white
hare or better still
a young buck.
                    Rowing
against the rolling
meltwater pale-faced
explorers wearing
queer metal helmets
will drive such hunters
from the unmapped grid
of this imagined
city as their shrewd
successors fell trees
to furnish the slopes
with ferro-concrete.

No wolves today. No
moose or caribou
closer than cold lakes
farther to the north.
Hawks though can still be
glimpsed rending their prey
on the leafless boughs
of a high park where
tracksuited joggers
pass the slow Sunday
families – a 'Mount
Royal' named after
a monarch living
on the other side
of a sea thousands
of miles to the east.

Hindsight frequently
claims to have rescued
victims from vicious
treadmills of error.
Any self-taught crank
with half a conscience
or whole newsprint can
explain a bloodstained
chessboard of empire

as war between teams
equally guilty –
or vice versa.

We need to be sure
what barbarism
entails before we
weigh advantages
of law and comfort
against ignorance
and mutilation.
After all, those who
organise train-loads
of atomic waste
or make films that praise
violence and drug-
addiction cannot
bleat from the witness-
box about progress.
Well-wishers drool on
and on about 'rights'
but to encourage
focus on self is
misguided. Putting
your plight in the place
of another gives
compassion its true
command: only by
imagining hurt
can the will to harm
be stifled at start.
Real barbarism
is no more than this –
utter indifference
to the suffering
of others.
        To get
this across should be
the absolute aim
of the civilised.
Fashionable pens
have been dipping for
far too long in lies

expressly distilled
to mislead the young.
Unwelcome notions –
service without thirst
for payment, respect
for privacy, self–
suppression – become
crucified minute
by minute for truth
did not just get nailed
to a synthetic
tree one Good Weekday
long ago – even
if few nowadays
seem to feel the need
to commemorate
the event in grief
crossed with gratitude.

Taking a calm look
round New World and Old
we might be tempted
to think no-one has
ever really tried
to listen to what
remained unspoken
at that makeshift trial –
those voiceless questions
clamouring for our
response, the dew still
on them, glittering
and clean.
                    The moment
isn't right. Not now.
Not yet at any
rate. Some other time
perhaps – when we're not
too busy.
                    And we
smile just a little
ruefully and shake
our heads in modest
refusal before

turning back once more
to those comforting
shadows we have grown
so accustomed to.

BIOGRAPHY

all he remembered
lying in the gloom
during those last hours

    the rustling of leaves
in a sycamore
      long since felled

    the cold purl
of a stream

    that high farm
where buzzards
screeched floating

      her hand
across
his brow
though she
had been
dead some
    years

      the
quiet
the
dark
the
thin
dreams
the

PAST ORAL

for Tony Lopez

Idyllic landscape where
beyond speech a laundered
calendar lays down gloss
on laurel leaves or lends
unending time for youths sunbronzed
rivals in song-contests
never mind the clean sheep

A written tradition
brought the age down of gold.
Somewhere along the lines
began a serious
consideration of the tomb
as increase of shadow
cancelled Arcadia.

THE HUMBLE ADMINISTRATOR'S GARDEN

for Tasha

A Chinese scroll on the neutral
colour of this museum wall depicts
a minute figure all on his own
low down in the righthand corner.

Hastening over a high-arched
bridge, he's apparently heading
for that pavilion open to the moon
where he will sit, sip wine and ply
his ink-brush to compose four thoughtful lines.

First, though, he'll have to thread
a gloomy maze that seems to bar his way.
Above this rather sinister
tangle of shadows and foliage,

a broad lake stretches, placidly silver,
its distant shore rimming a range of lofty mountains.

The eye, having travelled with interest
from foreground river up to that jagged skyline,
drops back in disbelief again to ensure
the title has been deciphered correctly.
For this vast landscape containing (in monochrome)
crags, torrents, dense forest, soaring peaks
seems, frankly, far too lavish a setting –
given our civil servant's vaunted lack of pretension.

But, after a hard day at someone else's
beck and call, copying out
so many decrees and documents
heaped on a table of scarlet lacquer,
it must give such oblique –
such elegant – delight and satisfaction
to come home to this imagined scene.

In fact, one stepping-stone helps the weary
bureaucrat over a trickle of water.
Then he must brush past one scrawny
frostbitten azalea before squeezing
inside his flimsy garden-hut
(four foot by three).
                    Squatting
to chafe his ink-blacked hands, he'll smoke
one pinch of cheap tobacco
and gaze unthinking at the night.

Next to the afore-mentioned
shrub the brook
drips
grudgingly into a tiny
pond
flanked by a miniature
rock
        or
            two.

Seattle, May 1994

434

COMMISSION

The oaks burned on towards winter.

Steam from the ferryman's voice.
Our horses stamping wet boards.

Sloping desks in the library,
fresh parchment ready –
white vellum, lustrous –
and the pigments they promised:
gold unalloyed with copper,
lapis lazuli.

Quills.
     Blade.
          Thin brushes.
We'll labour, holding our breath
(those rolls of leaf so thin, so light)
and watch eternity take shape
before our daylong eyes.

DUTCH STILL-LIFE

I

An hour glass. Manuscript. Palette.
    Cut rose. Cup on its side. Cow's skull.
Peeled lemon. Lute. Such milestones set
    for vanity. Still life is dull
without the toys of art. Although
    this painting is a paradigm
there's still life here – glow, tint – to show
    how objects can be caught in time.

Frail, doomed or voided things still prove
that what has been put down with love
stays grasped in amber and defies
a puritan wish to disprize
attempts with strings or brush or quill
to seize delight and keep life still
as tang of citrus, hiss of sand,
      fragrance from flower and gloss on bone
or porcelain betray the hand
      intending only to disown.

EIGHTEENTH-CENTURY BLOCKS

for Lynn

I

A billet-doux. The scent of pinewoods.
Gilt pin (to keep a message secret)
pricking the thumb, draws blood.
The garden's so badly lit. Who's gone with whom?

Horns are called on to counterpoint
betrayal that was not betrayal
yet it was.

II

The folly, bent on showing an English
autumn what a Greek temple should be like,
traps the moonlight between its pillars
and shimmers the wrong way up
in a formal lake authentic with ducks.

III

The squire, his foot on a tapestried stool,
drinks green tea and scans the pamphlet. Above,
rococo curlicues of fruit, pods,
ears of corn hang chiselled in limewood.
Perhaps (la, sir) some creditor
is lurking behind that Indian screen.
Milady's fixing patches on
but there's surely time for at least one
hand of cards before the masquerade.

It's good sometimes to feign to be
what we aren't –
a highwayman, an abigail,
a shepherdess, a fop.

IV

The shadowy queue of lovers,
garlanded, frivolous,
chatter bitter nothings
paying scant attention
to that distant island
wrapped in its haze of gold.

Maybe they don't believe in such a place.
At any rate they are far too many
to be embarking on that fragile craft.

A VERY ENGLISH ART

for Michael and Melissa

Wet sky over the village or
watery sunlight on a rounded slope
where sheep graze untended or
overseen by one boy in a red cap

(sole touch of bright colour) or
foliage casting an unfinished jigsaw
of pale shadow on a paler abbey wall

The painter, with his umbrella,
easel, brass-bound box of pigments,
has gone home now and left the scenes
to flying light, to intermittent rain.
Tucked safe in his portfolio
the green and grey of weather,
drift of smoke, an ochre aqueduct,
a winding path, meticulous
crossbars of a cottage window,
sunset beginning in a lake
dotted with indications of waterfowl,
a park at evening, groomed and opulent,
where a stag's long shadow falls on yellow grass.

Some trips abroad allowed the brush
to wrap crags in a thunderstorm,
shed midday brilliance on marble,
lift minarets above a sand-dune,
construct a vertical drama
crumpled with glaciers –
all very well but alien
when observation can begin
with what is near as well as far,
a low bridge across standing water,
blue field beyond –
a rain-washed steeple against massed cloud –
curved street with glinting cobbles –
kitchen garden with silver
dew-points among the currant-bushes.

Art is the here and is the there,
the seen, the dreamed, the known, the longed for,
a winding path, meticulous
crossbars of a cottage window,
sunset beginning in a lake . . .

1819: AUTUMN IN WINCHESTER

Mist-shrouded weeks. A handkerchief mauve-stained
with blackberry-juice foreshadowed the final one
pressed to his mouth to staunch the blood. He walked and found
the clustered orchards yellowing. Life on the turn.

Frail insects whined along the river-side
willow-silvered. Darkened barns held the tang and drip
of crushed apples. By a cropped field, sunset-dyed,
one poppy drooped, translucent.
                                    Time seemed ripe
without renewal – merely lingering
before the end. Watching, he wondered idly why
the restless migrants wing back here each spring.
He would see one more autumn and then die.

CHARLES HAMILTON SORLEY, 1895–1915

'It is easy to be dead' – C.H.S.

The signpost points four ways. A grassy slope
        Leads to a shallow river under trees
Hung with rooks' nests. Southward, fields show broad hope
        Of harvest and along this lane drugged bees

Work on mauve clover. Opposite, a third
        Track peters out near ramparts overrun
Two hundred decades back – but you preferred
        An emptier land beneath the dropping sun,

Bleak, unexplored and uninviting, yet
    Its very featurelessness lured you, drew
        Enquiry far beyond horizons where
    You wished for winter and for rain. You knew
The risks involved but shunned without regret
        Paths aimed at safety, ripeness or despair.

NAXOS

Electric sunset. Makeshift isle.
Passion awaited or recalled.
In greasepaint the bewildered god
cries out and skims the unseen waves.

Two grasp at a mistaken joy.
Imagined death entwines would-be
seductiveness. The outcome gets
transliteration into stars.

They kiss sprawled on the cardboard rocks
and sing a love they do not feel.
She keeps an ear cocked for the beat
but nothing stirs between his thighs.

Performance is a lie that tells
far more than this about the truth.
All music overrides the need
to be believed in or seen through.

Illusion must co-operate
with wish-fulfilment if the sound
can play a variant on our nerves
that echoes once the curtain's down.

DUFY'S FLAGS

for Bob and Paddy

Abstract, inaccurate, they serve
as grids slung anyhow, assigned
to clash with that amazing blue –
wide offing triangled with yachts,
sky brushed behind an esplanade.
(The scrawled crowds dawdle, stroll, get hot,

twirl canes, push prams, flirt, pass, intent
on summer.) Flaunted from the dome
of the casino, strung across
a straight grey roadway, marking out
water for a regatta – frieze
or on their own, they patch the air
with gaiety – translucent, brash,
festive, askew and lacking all
offensive claim to reverence.

Each gives a space of reference
transferred from the palette to call
attention with a sudden splash
of red or hint at emblems where
a skeletal lion rides the breeze,
maned, nonchalant in gold. Without
their usual pomp, this azure cross,
that grassgreen shield make polychrome
cacophony. Each banner's meant
for an anarchic gala – not
to deck some chauvinist parade.
This time the artist calls the shots.
The innocence implied rings true.
By scorning caution he's defined
an endless day we don't deserve.

BEN NICHOLSON

I

Six rectangles beside
half a dozen circles
placed freehand give a blank
symmetry of scraped lines
on textures of pallor
slyly belied because
the frame makes a seventh

II

No distinction gets offered
between an interior
and the outside world
                                since quay
with figures
                and windowsill
displaying bowl and jam-jar
stand juxtaposed on the same
plane
            as brown fishing-boats bob
by the deal armchair
                                while sky
and rug are both vertical

OWL SONG COMMA

In Memoriam Basil Bunting

> *for Ric Caddel*

Buff envelopes shroud these archives.
My hands, living, intrusive,
leaf with a frisson of reverence
through his black notebook
half-filled, purchased for privacy.

Insights, drafts, discarded experiments
have all survived him.
Each phrase jotted with tentative
confidence fills in more of our picture:
language searching to confirm.

Nothing was for other eyes.
Any poet gropes to a final
version. None perhaps should stumble
along this posthumous track
hitting or missing.

The last page with writing though –
a lovely fragment pondering
moonlight slanted on the metal
indicator of a sundial –
five lines concluding with this title

Durham, March 1993

IN MEMORIAM

Christopher Headington 1930–1996

Today I saw the first
Brimstone fluttering high
in the still leafless trees –
as Lepidopterist
Extraordinary you claimed
last June, I remember,
that our word 'butterfly'
derives from the vivid
yellow of its wings.
        Ah,
why did you have to die
on that snow-covered slope,
dear friend of nearly four
decades? I walk in grief
along the paths we trod
so often together
recalling old jokes (none
of which ever grew stale)
and all those long-vanished
love-affairs shared to our
mingled delight and woe –
these too, no matter how
often we rehearsed each
sensuous detail, lost
none of their bloom.
           You've left
behind mercifully

a legacy on disc
of intricate music
composed and played. I see
you curved over the keys
bringing – it seemed with no
effort – a work of yours
into sound from some scrawled
page propped in front of you.

You performed Debussy
and Chopin with special
magic though loved perhaps
more the immaculate
structures of Ravel – so
lucid and civilised
when contrasted with, say,
the turgid and clumsy
'music' in inverted
commas of Harrison
Birtwistle – you always
with a mischievous smile
said the name was made up.

Latterly though a slave
to some complex diet
or other you'd somehow
down any favourite dish
having (at length) explained
it was technically banned –
the way in the old days
when you'd pledged not to smoke
until noon you would take
a puff from anyone's
cigarette you could find
from breakfast-time on since
that didn't count.
          You loved
your red Porsche and let
me drive it once without
betraying any hint
of nervousness. We toured
Italy in your green
Sunbeam one sweet summer

long ago when our hearts
were younger and gayer –
not that you ever seemed
in enthusiasm
for art or zest for life
to age.
            But now you're gone.
We've seen the coffin through
our tears and had to hear
those undeniable
words of consolation.
We miss you more than can
be said – just hope you are
surrounded by a choir
of boy-angels with wings
brighter than a Brimstone's
who'll sing for you and all
the company of heaven
those canticles of joy
you'll carry on writing
throughout eternity.

Versions
(1999)

These translations are dedicated in gratitude to those responsible for my interest in language and literature: Ronald Gray, Ray Kelly, Roland Le Grand, Wilfrid Noyce, Douglas Parmée and Jack Rambridge.

WHAT? GIVE ME LEAVE TO LOVE ANOTHER?...

What? Give me leave to love another? Go
    And stub my fire out in the first I meet?
    Stray like a vagabond up any street?
Unbridled run as my whim takes me? No,

That isn't love. No, the erotic dart
    Has only grazed you superficially.
    If you'd been injured to the quick like me
There'd still be sulphur smouldering in your heart.

You would suspect your shadow and invoke
    Me everywhere, each hour, in deed, in thought,
        Aflame with fear and jealousy and greed.

        Love takes you ambling not at breakneck speed –
    Your feelings fit some dalliance at Court
Where there is little fire and lots of smoke.

RONSARD: *Sonnets pour Hélène*, I.xx

'BEFORE THEIR TIME YOUR TEMPLES WILL TURN GREY . . .'

'Before their time your temples will turn grey,
Few years will pass until your race is run,
Your day will fade before the setting sun
While lured by hope your mind mislays its way.

Your verse will wither without winning me,
My destiny will engineer your fall,
My love ungranted cause your death and all
Your sighs get jeered at by posterity.

You'll be a laughing stock for all the world,
Have built on the uncertainty of sand
And tried in vain to decorate the sky.'

Thus spoke the nymph whose charms I can't withstand
Just as the heavens to seal her words unfurled
A bolt of lightning as my augury.

RONSARD: *Les Amours de 1552*, xix

LONG WINTER NIGHTS . . .

Long winter nights. The moon is slow to wear
    dark time along its dilatory way.
    The cock belatedly announces day.
Night lasts a year to one who's grey with care.

I'm saved from anguish – your illusory
    form comes to slake my love with its feigned charms
    and lying nightlong naked in my arms
decoys me sweetly if deceptively.

Virgin in life, proud of your cruelty:
unreal, you're enjoyed in privacy.
    Next to your double I find sleep and rest.
        Nothing's refused me. Slumber in disguise
        fools my threadbare desire with its lies.
    To fool oneself in love is second-best.

RONSARD: *Sonnets pour Hélène*, II.xlii

WHEN YOU ARE OLD – AT DUSK . . .

When you are old – at dusk – by candle-flame –
Sitting beside the fire with yarn and spool
You'll muse in wonder while your hands fall still,
'When I was lovely, Ronsard gave me fame.'

Your servant then, hearing that murmured claim,
Already half asleep, tired from her work,
At my name – the mere sound – will start awake
To shower immortal praises on your name.

My boneless ghost, once I'm beneath the earth,
Will rest within the shadowed laurel grove.
You will be old and chilled, hunched by the hearth,
Regretting both your pride and my scorned love.

Don't count the blossoms on some future spray
But gather living roses day by day.

RONSARD: *Sonnets pour Hélène*, II.xliii

THE VERY MOMENT I BEGIN TO TAKE . . .

The very moment I begin to take
    In my soft bed the rest I'm longing for
My saddened self, abandoning heart-ache,
    Makes its unhampered way to you once more.

It seems then I hold safe within my breast
    The joy to which my hopes have vainly sped –
For, judging you forever unpossessed,
    I thought I'd split apart from tears unshed.

Sweet sleep, sweet darkness pleasuring my mind,
  Lovely repose, dear calm, all fears away –
    Continue my enchantment every night;

If my poor heart in love must never find
  True satisfaction in the light of day,
    At least allow a lie to give delight.

LOUISE LABÉ: *Sonnet IX*

THE DISINHERITED

for Peter Jay

I am the dark one – widowed – unconsoled –
The Prince of Aquitaine whose tower is riven;
My spangled lute, now my one star is cold,
Bears Melancholy's sun gone black in heaven.

Night gripped the tomb. Through you I was consoled –
Bring back the Italian sea, those cliffs, that cavern,
The flower that pleased my bleak heart and the fold
Of vine on trellis where the rose is woven.

Am I Love? Sun-God? Lusignan? Biron?
The kiss the queen gave makes my brow still burn.
I've dreamed in grottoes where the siren swims.

And twice as victor I've crossed Acheron,
Learning on Orpheus' lyre to play in turn
Her saintly sighing and the fairy's screams.

NERVAL: *El Desdichado*

CATS

Both ardent lovers and stern scientists
Wish in the ripeness of their time to mould
A home-life around cats which, egotists
Like them, like comfort and dislike the cold.

Approving reverie and sensuousness
They seek the quiet and horror of the dark.
Dis would have made them steeds to draw his hearse
If they could bend their pride to wear a yoke.

They take on, musing, noble attitudes
Like sphinxes sprawled in their far solitudes
Seeming to slumber in some endless dream.

Their fur is sparked with electricity
And points of gold, like magic sand-grains, gleam
Mysteriously starred in either eye.

BAUDELAIRE: *Les Chats*

CONTEMPLATION

for Christopher Hampton

No need, my sorrow, now to fret. Calm down.
You wished for evening to fall. It's there.
A darker atmosphere enfolds the town,
To some bringing repose, to others care.

While Pleasure's henchmen use the lash to force
The pitiable throng of mortals on
To slavish fairgrounds where they'll pluck remorse,
Come, sorrow, now, give me your hand – they've gone

Away – we'll watch the dead years in their creased
Outdated dresses lean on heaven's rail,
Regret rise smiling from the river-bed,

Beneath an arch the dying sunlight fail,
And, like a long shroud dragging in the east,
Hear, dear one, hear night's soft approaching tread.

BAUDELAIRE: *Recueillement*

BENEATH THE TREES

All through the wild and radiant woods,
    Reciting lines none asked to hear,
    In purple robes, with jewelled gear,
Go players – monarchs – demigods.

King Herod brandishes his blade.
    Flaunting each gem, each peacock's eye,
    Flowered Cleopatra minces by
In tinselled finery arrayed.

Then, swaggering, their wolfskins on,
    Tanned Theseus and Adonis pass,
      Each carrying a golden bow.

Pierrot lugs the demijohn.
      Then, last of all, come, muted, slow,
    The dreaming Poet and his Ass.

THÉODORE DE BANVILLE: *Sous Bois*

IN TRIUMPH FLED . . .

for Peter Redgrove

In triumph fled, a handsome suicide,
Log red with glory, foam of blood, gold, storm –
Plus laughter if beyond there's still a spread
Of purple ready for my absent tomb.

But now from all that splendour not a shred
Remains, it's midnight, in our shadowed feast –
Except what's poured from one proud gleam of head,
A torchless nonchalance that I've caressed –

Yours, always there, such beauty, yours; I'll call
The sole retention from a vanished sky
A little childish grandeur you've put on –

A brightness like, on cushions where you lie,
The warrior's helmet of some youthful queen,
From which, to image you, roses would fall.

MALLARMÉ: *'Victorieusement fui . . .'*

SPRUNG FROM THE NARROW SHOULDERS . . .

for John Flower

Sprung from the narrow shoulders spun
in transitory glass to cheat
soured dusk of bloom by holding none
this unused neck looks incomplete.

Two mouths can never, it would seem,
have (not my mother nor her love)
drunk at the same elusive dream –
the sylph spoke moulded cold above!

The empty vase unsullied by
a long drawn out viduity
though dying will not acquiesce

(bland kiss with flavours of the tomb!)
in letting lying breath express
a rose inside this darkening room.

MALLARMÉ: *'Surgi de la croupe . . .'*

MY GYPSY DAYS

Off I'd go, fists in pockets ripped at seams,
My coat, too, getting like the ghost of one –
I was the Muse's liege beneath the sun
And had, you see, such great romantic dreams!

My only trousers had a monstrous hole.
Tom Thumb a-dream I'd scatter on the way
Some rhymes. The Plough's the inn where I would stay.
My stars would rustle softly round the Pole.

I'd listen, sitting by the road on fine
September evenings – feel the drops of dew
Form on my brow like any heady wine;

Then, rhyming in wild shadows, I would start
To pluck the laces of each wounded shoe
Like lyre-strings, one foot against my heart!

RIMBAUD: *Ma Bohème*

VOWELS

for Lawrence Sail

A black, E white, I red, U green, O blue:
One day I'll tell each vowel what it does:
A, black fur shroud of glistening bugs that buzz
And cluster round some putrid residue,

Shadow-gulfs; E, blank candour – mists and tents,
Proud glacier's spears, white kings, trembling flower-sprays;
I, purple, blood spat, laugh from lips which blaze
In anger or a drunken penitence;

U, gyres, divine vibrations of green seas,
Peace of leas flecked with flocks, creased brows that ease
When alchemists believe they've reached the prize;

O, supreme strident trumpet, silence crossed
By wheeling worlds and angels: – O, the lost
Last letter, Omega, mauve ray . . . Whose Eyes . . .

RIMBAUD: *Voyelles*

HELEN

I come at last from caves of death to greet
    blue sky. Waves echo on the harbour steps.
    Dawn after dawn I've seen the shadowed ships
        catch light along the edge of golden oars.

My lonely fingers call the kings who let
    my pure hands stroke their beards, salt-flecked for, young,
    I used to weep. High in the stern they sang
        their murky triumphs, those receding shores.

I hear the conches and the bugles blare
   a stricter rhythm to the dipping blades;
the oarsmen's singing disciplines the roar
   and, lofty in each prow, the figured gods –
     their strange, archaic smiles mocked by the sea –
     hold out their tolerant, carved arms to me.

VALÉRY: *Hélène*

I'VE REALISED AT LAST . . .

for Anthony Rudolf

I've realised at last that nothing's mine
not even this fine gold of rotting leaves
still less those flying yesterdays that gain
with great wing-strokes such bright alternatives.

She was with them, that withered emigrant,
frail loveliness with secrets that deter,
muffled in mist. By now she'll have been sent
elsewhere, through woods of rainfall. As before,

I'm on the brink of an unlikely winter –
the finch persists in singing out one call
which will not cease, like ivy. Who can state

its meaning, though? My health begins to fail
as those brief flames against the fog encounter
a glacial wind, flare, sink . . . It's getting late.

PHILIPPE JACCOTTET: from *L'Effraie*

AN EARLY APOLLO

As often, through the still unfoliaged boughs,
a morning penetrates that's wholly spring –
so in the head of this Apollo
is nothing to prevent the lustre

of all poetry from almost striking us
stone dead: for in his gaze there's still no shadow,
his temples still too cool for laurel-wreaths,
and only later will his brows begin

to form a garden of tall roses
from which the petals, one by one released,
will drift down to the trembling of a mouth

that's silent still unused and glittering –
now only sipping something with its smile
as if his songs were being instilled in him.

RILKE: *Früher Apollo*

BLUE HYDRANGEA

Just like the green left in a paintbox are
these flattened leaves, dry, blunt and featureless
behind the umbels which do not possess
their blue but hold one mirrored from afar –

blue mirrored after tears and inexact
as if the whole shrub willed that hue away
again, and as in old blue letters packed
in lofts there's yellow in it, mauve and grey –

blue washed too often like some child's smock which,
no longer worn now, nothing happens to
now childhood's gone as though it had not been.

Then suddenly the blue seems to renew
itself and gains before your eyes a rich
sheen complementing joyously the green.

RILKE: *Blaue Hortensie*

BEFORE RAINFALL IN SUMMER

Outside and all at once from all the green
something, you can't tell what, gets drawn away;
the park seems to steal near the window-bay
in silence – just, insistent and unseen,

a plover calls a warning from the wood
as if some hermit urged his message, for
that note of loneliness – so pressing – could
be voicing a request which the downpour

will satisfy. The drawing-room's walls, hung
with portraits, have already moved away
as though reluctant to hear what we say.

Each carpet mirrors with its faded tones
a treacherous gleam in certain afternoons
which made us so afraid when we were young.

RILKE: *Vor dem Sommerregen*

EARLY MORNING, VENICE

Like royalty these pampered windows see
each day what condescends to make us sigh:
the city, every time a gleam of sky
finds a response in water, comes to be

at no especial hour. Each morning shows
once more the opals which she wore the day
before and draws from the canal those rows
of mirror-images for redisplay,
reminding her of other suns that rose.
And only then does she concede, the way

a nymph Zeus touched might think back drugged with joy.
The jewelled ear-ring trembles at her ear;
but she allows one dome to reappear
and smiling idly eyes her pretty toy.

RILKE: *Venezianischer Morgen*

LATE AUTUMN: VENICE

I.M. Bob Brooks

The town behaves no longer like a lure
catching the days as they break surface.
The palaces of glass ring now
more brittle at your glance. From gardens droops

the summer like a heap of marionettes,
pell-mell, exhausted, slain.
Yet from the bones of buried forests
intention rises: as though overnight

the admiral were planning to increase
the galleys in his clanging arsenal
and tar to-morrow's air with a flotilla –

one that would throng, all oars swift-beating,
its flags assembled sheer as dawn,
to take the wind, resplendent, dangerous.

RILKE: *Spätherbst in Venedig*

THE CICADA AND THE ANT

Cicada having sung in tune
     Since June
Found that her store of food was low
When winter winds began to blow –
No morsel left of worm or fly
To keep an insect blithe and spry.
She called on Neighbour Ant to say
Starvation was not far away
Imploring her to lend some grain
To keep her going till the spring
Brought warmer weather once again.
'And cross my heart,' she said, 'I'll bring
'You back by August all you've lent
'With interest at five per cent.'
Now Ant's no lender – it's the first
Of all her faults though not the worst.
She asked this borrower what she'd done
During those months of summer sun.
'Both night and day I lost no chance
'Of singing to all passers-by.'
'You sang? How nice to hear that! I
'Suggest it's time you learnt to dance.'

LA FONTAINE: *La Cigale et la Fourmi*

462

THE DEPARTURE OF THE PRODIGAL SON

To go away from everything confused
that's ours and yet does not belong to us,
but, like the water in old wells,
mirrors us quivering and destroys what's shown;
to leave what fastens to us still like thorns –
to look then all at once at this, at that,
things one no longer saw,
so usual were they in their daily rôle –
to see them gently and forgivingly,
as if at a beginning and close to;
and dimly realising there had been –
impersonally, everywhere – a pain
which childhood had been full of to the brim:
and still to go away, hand leaving hand
as though a freshly healed scab were ripped off,
and go away – but where? To the unknown,
far off to warmer and dissimilar lands
that will be merely décor for each action,
indifferent, just wall or garden;
and go away – though why? Through impulse, cunning,
impatience, an obscure anticipation,
not understanding yet misunderstood.
To take all this on one – perhaps
dropping in vain what had been grasped,
dying alone, not knowing why –

is this the threshold of a newer life?

RILKE: *Der Auszug des verlorenen Sohnes*

THE PANTHER

in the Jardin des Plantes, Paris

His gaze has grown so weary as it passed
the bars it can hold nothing any more.
He seems to see a thousand bars and past
those thousand bars no world more than before.

The soundless pacing of his supple stride
turns in the smallest circle like a dance
of power round one axis where inside
the cage his will keeps its dazed vigilance.

Just now and then the curtain of the eye
lifts hushed to let one image in to start
along the tension of the limbs and lie
extinct at last inside the heart.

RILKE: *Der Panther*

THE SUNDIAL

for Michael Hamburger

Seldom does a hint of damp decay
stray from the garden shadows where drops hear
other water dripping and the call
of one wild bird – till some dank scents drift near
the sundial set among marjoram and thyme
to mark the minutes of a summer's day.

Just sometimes, when the owner in her bright
straw hat (a servant with her) lets her shadow fall
across the rim, the figures losing light
go secretive and will not tell the time.

Or should some sudden summer shower
come darkening the air to douse
the tossing trees, the dial will not show

(just for an interval) the current hour
since time has taken refuge in the glow
of flower-paintings in the white-washed summer-house.

RILKE: *Die Sonnenuhr*

MANY NATURALLY . . .

Many naturally die below
where heavy oars scrape in the dark.
Others aloft near where the helm is fixed
know bird-flight and the countries of the stars.

Many will always lie and heavy-limbed
where complex roots of life must intertwine.
For others though the chairs are placed
by fortune-tellers or by queens
and there they sit as though at home
so light of brow, so light of gesture.

And yet a shadow slanting from the former
falls to those other lives
for the lightly alive are bound to the heavy
as both are tied to air and to the earth.

Nor can I rid my eyelids of fatigue
pressed there by countless races lost in time,
nor keep from the appalled mind's eye
the silent fall of all those distant stars.

So many fates are woven near my own.
Existence goes on playing among them all.
My share as well is more than this one life's
so slender flame, so narrow lyre.

HUGO VON HOFMANNSTHAL: *'Manche freilich . . .'*

IN THE MANNER OF PAUL VERLAINE

for Martin Sorrell

It is the moonlight's fault that I have won
    the right to this nocturnal mask I've worn
    for Saturn turns forlorn the urn he's borne
when my wan moods like moons wane one by one.

Songs without words written without request
    and offering new discordant chords to play
    on purpose rubbed soft hearts up the wrong way –
the zest, most manifest, that they possessed!

It isn't that you weren't with a good grace
    forgiving one for giving you offence:
    I pardon now my boyhood innocence
returning lacquered if not lacking grace.

I pardon too that old convenient lie
    in fact in favour of insipid pleasure
    which funnily enough when stung by leisure
I've been a little bit infected by.

VERLAINE: *A la Manière de Paul Verlaine*

RONDEAU

It's dark now, child. The sparks you stole are cold.
There is no longer night, no longer day.
Sleep . . . till those girls come by who as they strolled
Would say, No, never! or would say, Yes, stay!

You hear their steps? Not heavy on their way . . .
Such light feet . . . Love should let its wings unfold.
It's dark now, child. The sparks you stole are cold.

The days pass and the weeks pass all in vain
        Neither time past
     Nor love returns again
Beneath the Pont Mirabeau flows the Seine

      Let the hour chime night arrive
      Days go by I stay alive

APOLLINAIRE: *Le Pont Mirabeau*

MARIE

      You danced there when you were quite small
      Will you still dance there when you're old
      They prance and caper at the ball
      One day the bells will all have tolled
      Marie won't you come back at all

      The masks we wear are so discreet
      The music seems as far away
      As where the sky and skyline meet
Ah yes I'll love you but in a half-hearted way
      And what is wrong with me is sweet

      The flocks set off into the snow
      Those flakes of silver flecks of wool
      Some soldiers pass why can't I show
      A heart I own not one that's cool
      Then warm and yet what do I know

      Do I know why your hair will fade
      That curls now like an angry sea
      Do I know why your hair will fade
      Like leaves along the autumn we
      Have littered with the vows we made

I used to walk along the Seine
An old book underneath my arm
The river is so like my pain
It flows unquenchable and calm
And won't the week-end come again

APOLLINAIRE: *Marie*

RICHARD II YEAR FORTY

My country is a craft adrift
Abandoned by her coward crew
And I am like that monarch who
Unfortunate in every gift
Remained the king of all he'd rue

Living is now a stratagem
No wind can dry tears that accrue
All that I love I must condemn
Give them what used to be my due
I stay the king of all I rue

Hearts may stop without meaning to
And blood flow with no heat in store
Since four's no longer two plus two
Lets beggar those who live next door
I'll stay the king of all I rue

Let sun set or day break again
The sky has forfeited its hue
Farewell the Paris that I knew
Those tender Aprils by the Seine
I stay the king of all I rue

Leave pools to mirror woods once green
Birds should not make such a to-do
Songs have been put in quarantine

The fowler's entered right on cue
I'll stay the king of all I rue

There is an hour arranged for pain
When Joan of Arc urged her campaign
Ah cut my homeland into two
The day dawned with no hint of blue
I stay the king of all I rue

ARAGON: *Richard II Quarante*

THOUGHTS ON THE DURATION OF EXILE

I

Don't drive a nail in the wall –
you can chuck your coat over a chair.
Why so much care for four days?
Tomorrow you'll be back home.

Leave the little sapling without water –
why plant yet another tree?
Before it's as high as that little step there
you'll be laughing far away.

Pull your cap over your face when folk go by!
Why thumb through a foreign grammar?
The message to call you home again
will be couched in a language you know.

The way plaster falls from the ceiling
(Do nothing about that either!)
those iron railings will crumble away
set up at the frontier
by force against justice.

II

Now look at the nail you've driven in the wall:
when do you think you'll be back home?
Would you like to know what you really think?

Day after day
you work for liberation
sitting in your room and writing away.
Would you like to know what you think about your work?
How about the way you've kept watering
the little chestnut-tree in the corner of the yard!

BRECHT: *Gedanken über die Dauer des Exils*

THE LION IN A CHINESE TEA-CUP

The bad are afraid of your claws
The good delight in your grace –
I'd like to hear that sort of thing said
About my verse

BRECHT: *Auf einen chinesischen Teewurzellöwen*

HOLLYWOOD

Each morning to earn my bread
I go to the market where lies are bought
taking my place full of hope
among the vendors.

BRECHT: *Hollywood*

CHANGING THE WHEEL

I sit by the side of the road
while the driver changes the wheel.
I'm not keen on the place I'm coming from.
I'm not keen on the place I'm going to.
So why do I watch the wheel being changed
with such impatience?

BRECHT: *Der Radwechsel*

SMOKE

A small house among trees by the lake
and smoke rising from the chimney.
Without it
how comfortless they'd be
the house, the trees, the lake.

BRECHT: *Der Rauch*

YOUR BLOOD: SOME SORT OF EPIC

My legend lacks, poor darling, just
      a bit of depth, a bit of sky.
All my grand verbs have turned to dust.
      That epidemic thinned them. Try
not to lose heart. I won't require
      your blood, spine, naked breasts. They live

without that power to inspire
        my fame they used to have. Forgive
my rancour. Mirrors won't go on
        tattooing me. My song is sour.
These hands of mine, now that they've gone
        as bloodthirsty as wolves, devour
their own invention. I'm someone
        who thrives on decadence. A leech
destroys my phrases one by one
        as you scrap pages that would reach
nowhere – like branches when you do not dare
even to finger the last fruit they bear.

ALAIN BOSQUET: *Ton Sang: Une Epopée*

IN PRAISE OF SHADOW

There where at its utmost
the landscape unfolds
Ravenna lies laden –
orphan of salt and wind.

But if past the plain
other life is shadowed,
draws comfort,
it's the modest word to be looked for here
not the bombastic phrase
where blankness gets denser.

DANIELE SERAFINI: *Elogio dell'Ombra*

MARGINAL LIGHT

You brought me an old-fashioned March
freed from the inactivities of winter
fixed inside the chattering wood,
custodian of brilliant afflictions.
You gave me the tranquillity of noon,
an easy feat that fades and then refrains –
and marginal light, suspended
between the merit of being born
and the anxiety of dying.

DANIELE SERAFINI: *Luce di Confine*

EXETER

I do not know if it is lull or absence of wind
that stirs me in this sleepless August,
a hostage here to parapets and spires,
far from the sea-coast where,
like light stretched loud among the rocks,
one face emerges clear among the shadows.

Here summer is not born
but dying blurs with autumn –
perhaps it is the lull in the wind that I am seeking,
a hoarse silence which conveys
not voices, not memories,
but deadened light, reflection of another life.

DANIELE SERAFINI: *Exeter*

A TRACE OF YOU, FATHER

I went round searching for a trace of you,
your dream that got dispersed along
a history scrawled above Seville
marring the sky of thirty-six.

That dream in those days bred a creed
breaking the ties that bound us.
I followed different routes, other horizons.

The town to-day no longer contains
that rank odour of death –
only the charm of orange-trees in flower,
the memory of you carried on the breeze.

Time alters accents, burns the distances up.
And now I find the trace I sought
no longer hostile, no more my enemy.

DANIELE SERAFINI: *Di te, padre*

FOR HARRY GUEST

Look now can't you see the way
the light too seems a captive
of this October – all that's left
from the anxieties of summer;
light kept so lightly hidden, altering
under a sky that fades to mother-of-pearl
towards the beechwood, beyond the downs.

The speckled autumn starts to drift,
distils the shapes and colours of your song –
the light too lingers, droops fatigued
on walls of ochre, on your roses.

DANIELE SERAFINI: *Per Harry Guest*

478

From the Japanese

They're . . . There . . . Their
blossoms. On the hill there.
'They're cherry-trees.'
                              There!
That's all I can say!

TEISHITSU

Crow settling
on the dead branch.
Autumn dusk.

BASHÔ

When drinking all alone
no moon –
no flowers.

BASHÔ

Plum-branch on the mirror's back –
a spring no-one has seen.

BASHÔ

Purple hibiscus by the road –
but my horse
cropped it.

BASHÔ

I hate crows as a rule
    but somehow
    this morning
    on the snow . . .

BASHÔ

Sea raging
          while above
the island slanting spreads
The Milky Way

BASHÔ

This road
and no-one on it –
autumn nightfall.

BASHÔ

At Takadate

Where once
those bright warriors . . .
Where their dreams . . .
. . . the summer grass now waves

BASHÔ

Last Poem

Falling ill on a journey –
still,
dreams go on wandering
over the dry fields

BASHÔ

The Anniversary of Bashô's Death

Wandering dreams –
the sound of the wind
over burned stubble

ONITSURA

Red hint of dawn –
cockcrow
among peach-flowers

KIKAKU

. . . the sound made
by a scarecrow
                falling
                all by itself

BONCHÔ

Morning-glory's captured my well-bucket
so it means
borrowing water

CHIYO

I leave, you stay —
two autumns

BUSON

The blossom's fallen —
now once again it's become
a temple through trees.

BUSON

Widower

The scar hurt again
when I trod on her comb
just now in our
bedroom

BUSON

This is the world:
three days pass, you look up,
the blossom's out or fallen.

RYÔTA

Tarnished alas
the gold has gone . . .
. . . old times recalled
among spring leaves

CHORA

On the Death of His Child

Life is as drops of dew
ah yes
as drops of dew
ah yet

ISSA

Stepmother

This was my birthplace, I
draw near,
make contact, no —
a flower with thorns.

ISSA

The Next-to-Last Poem

Man's body moves
from that first washing to the last —
the interim
mere gibberish.

ISSA

Biting the bright fruit
I hear the temple-bell boom.
Tartness on my tongue.

SHIKI

A winter seagull
in life no home
in death no grave

KATÔ SHÛSON

Komoro Castle

Near the old castle
a traveller grieves among white clouds.
Green chickweed hasn't sprung yet.
There's no young grass.
On the nearby hills a covering of silver:
the light snow is dissolving in the daylight.

Warmer brightness.
No scents float from the fields.
A slight mist hangs over March.
A sparse hint of colour shows new wheat.
Groups of wayfarers
scurry along the lane between the farms.

It is too dark to see the volcano.
A sad tune is played on a flute.
Reaching an inn by the river
I hear its waves creep by.
Drinking a glass of wine,
opaque, making the mind opaque,
I console myself for a while
as I make my way.

SHIMAZAKI TÔSON

Uncollected Poems

AN ANNIVERSARY POEM

Were I one winter's morning to describe
that rose-branch with eleven drops
suspended after the shower,
would you, I wonder –

A curved stick set with thorns
dark in the sheen of rain . . .

Half-spheres of bright water
though not translucent, almost blue,
clearer than the pools elsewhere,
hanging there,
like –

    no,
like nothing else, like
beads of moisture clinging
to the underside of a rose-twig,
which is flowerless,
its leaves brown in the gleam of rainfall,
one December,
before noon.

Do I at last understand?

You smile,
give nothing away

Neither does my love for you
accept comparisons

THE DRAMA'S THE OBJECT

for Christopher Fry

Words fail the tribute-bringer
for here on the shelf are stored
such images that keep their fire
igniting chancel, studio or stage

A lad dazzled by prophecy
hauled his mother over the green
domes of the downs. Alien,
uneasy farmers witnessed
the advent of the thunder-cloud
cancelled by seraphs.

They moved on a land in flux
where leaf becoming rock
turns into flame – where man
breaks from his brittle
case of ordinariness
to surprise us with the brilliance of his wings.

One performer
eyeing the love-star in an ageing sky
savours the paradox of time
where the heart finds humour in its end-stopped cage
and voyagers walk the plank of their desires
blindfold, smiling.

For laughter saved
the lithe witch from the pyre
as wryness rescued
a countess from her loneliness.

Four captives shared a dream
and the dream became words
ringing among us.

Images evade the tribute-bringer.
The bones
of gratitude alone
remain.

CAMBRIDGE, DECEMBER 13th, 1950

for D.

You've left my dreams now though I'd never meant
   Our chance encounter to be exorcised.
   The mirror hurls me back a face surprised
By age. Those lips you kissed stay reticent.

Did we until that eye-flash think we might
   Trade snow for firelight, smirk, then turn the key?
   Our hands confused time with discovery.
We came to squander what was ours by right.

Sky clear and starry. White world underfoot.
   We spoke. Some misted words hung on the air
Then, mingling, dissipated as we put

     Caution behind us. Wryly, I recall
   The way you'd looked before we climbed that stair –
     Dark, far, not smiling, unapproachable.

Exeter 13/12/1990

EXHIBITION

for Cory

The apples lie soft domes where they have tumbled
and last red butterflies pause and try their wings.
Carved wood, carved stone hold an October shine,
harvested, honeyed, after plan and hammering.

Each finished work no longer is the maker's.
It travels to other areas of resonance or neglect.
Dry seeds are purchased for bowls in foreign apartments
where the eventual tendrils cast their private shadows.

You may specify time, the identity of the actors,
which coppice, which stratum, how many southern stars.
And sanity is active within certain flexible laws
thus ruling out the lamasery or the elephant-seal.

The setting can be this wide, the pigments weigh so much.
Each of the court-cards gets given a third dimension.
An amateur might well have overlooked the bluegreen
streak of a lightning-conductor down that obelisk.

What I committed to cold ink springs into line,
turns sensuous, grows humane 'the phrase made flesh' –
this supple woman, these tense lovers: they
are not what I intended and much more.

HORACE TO LIGURINUS

Each time you leave
it's just as though
the sun has been
gauzed over while
the cosmos flips
gaudiness to
monochrome. All
brilliance, you see,
trails at your heels.
Each pace taken
on your bare feet
from this bed we've
rumpled measures
the distance of
your legacy
as ease gets crossed
by doubt to haunt
my flying dreams
for how can I –
lying here drained,

grateful – believe
I'll ever be
granted again
such spurts of joy
despite these white
and drying stains –
the only proof
departing youth
amazingly
accords to age.

THE DARK BETWEEN THE SETTLEMENTS

The space between the settlements
owl-flown.
No wind.
A church-tower spells the quarter.
Whitened expanse squared off by hedgerows.
In one bare field a crippled oak.
Imagined camera
glides over quickset, following
a line of tiny paw-prints
only as far as the flurry.
Beyond those blood-specks
uninterrupted snow.
A pause. To test the equipment.
Ghostly microphone straining
fails to pick up
the beat of feathers winging to the barn.

The scene between the settlements
matt to the lens.
Beads of moonlight
drip here and there through cloud,
glint on the grey-filmed stream,
draw momentary colour from a boulder,
dried holly-berries, contorted beech-leaves.

Dormant. In extended winter.
Thus avoiding sunrise hold the cold.
Weekdays
shrouded in arctic dusk fearing no
upsurge of time. The tape
tries to catch only silence,
runs on with the merest hiss.
Corpse in chains
hangs anonymous at the crossroads.
No creak of wagon.
Brittle laburnum
dangles nothing but ice.
Deserted lanes. Signpost
obliterated. Ruts
crisscrossing undisturbed.
The crust of white stays hard
on milestone, wall and gallows.

The fear between the settlements
unabated.
All that's planned
quivers round the edges of the treaty.
Lamplight
managing an aperture in the curtains
gets propped at an angle on the frost.
Selects a bent cabbage-stalk,
scatter of breadcrumbs,
blue rubber bone.
Let the apparatus nonetheless
squint through the slit.
Oil-painting ruddy with fireglow
depicts an empty
snow-gripped landscape.
It is as though
the absent victims left their stain.
Unaltered ritual
of need and innocence. Two lines
of red footmarks cross the lower
right corner but the dog
occupying much of the woven rug
on the brick floor in front of the fireplace
is not a retriever
nor a bloodhound. The crime
may simply have invented

their being there. The carmine
icicles in the flickering winter picture
betray no trace of fraud. A rifle,
leant casually in a corner of the hall,
is loaded.

ZONE SYSTEMS

for Tasha

Start with grey.
                    Say, that cloud
as reflex in the ice-scuffed pond.

One way shifting towards
an egret's breast-feather. Back
via grey to soot,
obsidian or ebony.

Gradations. Even so,
there is no such thing as black.
(Or white.) Crime possibly
justified. Saintly doubt.
Matt, yes. (As metaphor.)
Lustrous, too. Ink spilt.
Gloss lent.
                    Not colour.

Tones only. Grey wine. Grey fruit.
Grey foliage. And dark to darker.
Taking as emblem a cube of dice.
The raccoon's mask. Page torn
from some cheap prayer-book.

A prism from frost to vulcanite.
How many shades of grey?

Assessment of the Kodak.
Shadow's pallor on stone.

FLYING THROUGH RAIN

A lone seagull
grey against grey
ceiling of low
cloud – as drizzle
increases grease
on pavements, vans
(reluctantly)
skid to a halt
before zebra
crossings and in
winter-empty
front gardens tin
dustbins their lids
askew glisten –
flaps sharpened wings
in unconcerned
rhythm above
plodders like me
who've left home this
a.m. (headlines
branding the mind
re air-strikes on
the faraway
and defenceless)
disinclined to
be cumbered with
an umbrella.

THE BOYHOOD OF RALEIGH

He would have seen smaller fields,
more coppices, fewer houses.
No pylons – red mud for tarmac –
scythers parallel in rhythm
rather than that tractor circling.

        The selfsame
scoop of pewter-coloured sea –
April's drift of flagging bluebells –
that buzzard's forebear flinching
from a similar trio of rooks.

        Green ridge
of distant gorseland.
Cloud-smudged West Country sky.
Sandstone church on its knoll.

From the family pew at the front
he'd have seen the altar closer,
rood-screen gone then as now.
Perhaps, cooling a finger on this pillar,
he'd have gazed up during Divine
Service at those bosses –
some boyish inattentiveness not yet
deflected by the dark philosophy
which would intrigue him for a while.
Still, near the end, his verses prove
he had crept back to holiness,
threat of the axe-blade
scraping at his nape.

East Budleigh, 1997

GAME

Dusk taking over a court among conifers
though still discernible in thickening shadows
the ghostly tennis-ball and two boys in white flannels
whose dogged exchanges continuing voiceless
let the bored parents pacing back hand in hand
over the sweet-smelling layer of pine-needles
smile in collusion at that stubborn intention
to have done with the set before succumbing to darkness

All four are dead now. War. Then sorrow. The net
sags as a frontier between tufts of ragweed.
Gossamer drifts where victor and loser
stood preparing to serve. Well below earshot
welcoming gunfire waited over the water
where the bone huntsman got ready to barter
a wad of black telegrams for broken athletes.

Upstairs in the shrine put up during mourning
tasselled caps hang fading by a vixen's paw
dust-greyed now gummed to its wooden shield.
In blurred team-photographs beardless features
recede year by year from their side of the glass.
No-one flicks cobwebs from the prongs of antlers.
On one varnished oar nailed dry to the wall
a roll-call formed a triumphant ladder of gold.
The date has faded. Each bright initial is tarnished.

SUSPICION

His reputation precedes him setting
a bone in the teeth of some grey ship seen
on the sound steaming doubtless at the rate
of knots though seeming to the naked eye
not to be moving like the metaphor

One's told his gait holds something of the pitch
and sway linked in the mind of landlubbers
with the whiff of toddy and salt whistling
in the shrouds of craft that will always pay
scant heed to the cold blare of a foghorn

A wooden foot tapping closer along
the companionway evokes in fact far
less a life hell-bent on piracy than
half-hearted bouts with naturalism
for all who've parsed his smile know how he stole

Few have dared to lift the patch concealing
the bluer maybe more malevolent
iris yet there are other trick snapshots
placed at random in that child's pop-up book
which could offer slyer revelations

The lamp above binnacle and logbook
compensates for intrusion of starlight
while leagues to starboard across an inked sea
a glimmer of foam catches where a reef
thorned in ambush scrapes the roll of a wave

Slow-passing longitudes invisible
and liquescent though they are undergo
transformation into chimes while the slung
hammocks down below rock dreamers peopling
the night-void with those once loved or still loved

The mariner no-one on land has met
knowing he will be greeted first of all
by the harbour-master who will require
some method of identification
wastes no time stashing his secret cargo

The crew have specific orders and can
be relied on to back up whatever
tale he intends to supply to excuse
crates six foot by six smelling of camphor
and brown unwieldy sacks which chink if moved

Hearsay trickling rife along the quayside
brings with it a desire to be deceived
for should the explanation once turn out
to be so homespun as to lack spangles
the disappointment might be hard to bear

Fantasy has been dangling from unseen
sun-darkened earlobes the gaudiest rings
a clamorous port palm-girt and organised
in tropical cubes of grubby bluewash
and corrugated iron can provide

Mention of a skeleton crew projects
another image so barnacled spars
weed-cloaked in ghostly lattice-work move manned
by bones across the moon and all orders
get understood from an unspeaking skull

Even so precariously balanced
on the few remaining struts of the keel
some brass-bound chests their lids askew betray
a hint of faceted rubies glinting
like a blood-crust over the stacked ingots

Jungles have been ripped open and cliffs hacked
into to trap on brooches the hot gloom
of foliage lurking in emeralds
also the winking citrus quality
topazes have when forced into the light

Those anxious in the lofty casino
above the wharf are too new to the game
to think that what occurs will masquerade
as destiny equipped with wands to prod
a nest of basilisks with poisoned eyes

Under those unlit chandeliers talk fails
and urbane glances interchanged lose poise
and warmth as each detects the peeling-off
of habit with something raw and novel
gaping now behind serge and furbelows

Suppose the rescue all have counted on
leaves it to chance no conduct guaranteed
to greener isles rather perhaps shipwreck
or mutiny when their slim wrists shackled
they'll go down gurgling to oblivion

If all along the grinning privateer
has diagnosed disaster in scarlet
aces and towers splintered by lightning
no need to feign amazement if a plank
is tied in horizontal readiness

No help can be expected inland now
the hills are in hostile hands while greasy
smoke eddies from abandoned mansions where
childhood memories are having to be
re-defined in acid for absentees

Who hang about in vain and under siege
perusing brochures that dishonestly
describe to-morrow and learning at last
to place their trust below that skyline where
a camouflaged destroyer climbs the waves

So cunningly disguised no glass they have
will discern a disparity between
metalwork and sea-surface till the guns
opening up seemingly from nowhere
pound the town to mirrored heaps of rubble

A SEQUENCE OF PAINTINGS

Each time beyond a cool
blue sea the untrodden
contour of an island
treeless concealing much
of the skyline shrewdly
disdains all detail so
no dream can gain foothold

This side of the calm strait
the shore is always snarled
in cactus or iron thorn
with one small boat upturned
to prove the keel intact
and seaworthy although
no oars are seen lying
nearby on the dry sand

The last canvas done when
he knew he was dying
depicts just one wrecked craft
beached sideways on to make
its skeleton of spars
black like charred latticework
dominate the foreground

The water this time spreads
to a bare horizon

No landfall lifts above
this sea to daunt or lure

BROKEN ANKLE

After three months
to walk again
if with a limp
propped on an old
man's cherrywood
stick with a grey
rubber ferrule.

Summer gardens
too long unseen
veer their cool skies
to September
and I hobble
contentedly
past dishevelled
borders.
            Purple
dahlias stare
idly – bronze ones,
red, yellow, all
droop, too bulky
to stir whereas
when leaves skim by,
dry, gold, they cheat
the eye briefly
into seeing
them as scudding
butterflies.
            Rooks
hang, flapping wings,
but make little
headway in these
fresh gusts which fetch
hints of decay.
Mushrooms cluster
in dampened grass
where Japanese
maples scarlet-
tinged line the path.

When trapped the whole
day in one room,
leg wrapped in green
fibreglass, I'd
view through the panes
unfragrant flowers
as I listened
to hard quartets
by Dutilleux
or Elliott
Carter, relished
Chaplin's antics
on video,
re-read *La Peau
de chagrin*, *Men
and Women*, *Two
on a Tower*
(interspersed of
course with well-thumbed
mystery stories)
or leafed through some
thick catalogues
glimpsing again
more wistfully
watercolours –
lakes glassing woods
and pink-bricked farms
built before cars
were invented.

This day, the near
air flickering
with autumn scents,
skyline of clouds
above the far
curve of moorland,
feels like rebirth –
a lame Adam
sent out to take
stock even though
Eden in this
latter-day case
has its meaning

reversed:
       reaching
the stile, I look
struck with longing
up the rough slope
of ragweed, dock
and thistledown
to where worn Iron
Age ramparts coil
screened by a clump
of trees.
       Gazing
though, I can't go
further. To roam
unsteadily
the well–groomed lawns
of this fading
garden must be
alone allowed
to–day.
       Withered,
the wilderness
beyond has been
re–defined on
the map as no–
man's–land.
       Ah well,
another time
perhaps.
       Warned off
by the angel's
stern frown and white-
hot sword–blade I
turn round with one
reluctant sigh
and set about
retracing my
unequal steps.

A PADLOCKED CRUCIFIX

to Tasha who photographed it in New Mexico

No-one can leave
this dry ornate
mission church (put
up by Spaniards
on an alien
desert to shut
the high brilliant
air out) clutching
this purloined sign
of pain and hope
in case the theft
should hint we're free –
a paradox
an angel might
appreciate
though not a saint
who'd struggle to
unfix the chain
to prove one should
trust all comers –
nor you and I
who think we're fit
to slink past those
crumbling cement
watch-towers into
the open jail
of Purgatory –
but should you peer
more nearly you'll
see a dark slit
in the upright
(latten not wood)
to drop maybe
a dime in – so,
behind the pierced
hands the gash in
the side the brow
that's sticky still
with blood, the chink

of fake silver
tells that the cross
is an alms box
with a double
function – to urge
sacrifice as
well as holding
it out in three
dimensions for
us to ponder

Thanksgiving, November, 2001
Philadelphia

THE JESTERS

for Witold

Six figures of gold and khaki
each caught in mid-flicker
like the three-dimensional
photograph of a flame

Since face and gaping mask are one
a secret laughter never heard
could echo in moonlight as glee or scorn
viewed through one window of the studio

Six companions and a monarch
chafe over there in blocks of wood or stone

As soon as the future chisel allows
the anarchic twelve
will slyly disobey their king
who'll smile aloof pretending not to mind

Such grace, such enigma
form magnets for forgiveness

FOR

to Lynn

There are perhaps no stopping-off
points save to ask forgiveness for
what may be inexcusable
should you faltering on the stoop
forget the vow said at sunrise
for those horses once untethered
will forge ahead along unknown
thoroughfares where what used to be
seldom undoes what is where what
was not intended to occur
in fact enthrals for rain that fell
turned to mist and hooves plodding lift
sparkles from the mire for who'd urge
the team forward having wrongly
forfeited those daily glances
at the unexpected or hatched
sullen schemes to hack a detour
round what was divulged long ago
in a dream even when that scar
burned into grass by the left-hand
strut of the rainbow hides no cracked
container of invalid coins

ACKNOWLEDGEMENTS

The collection *So Far* was published by Stride. *Versions*, published by Odyssey, has been expanded to include the fable by La Fontaine (p. 462) as well as the poems from the Japanese (p. 479 ff.), some of which appeared in *The Elek Book of Oriental Verse* (1979), edited by Keith Bosley.

'Towards a Pindaric Ode' (p. 37) was set to music by Christopher Headington and first performed at Morley College on 29 January 1965 by Laura Sarti and Clare Walmesley accompanied by Paul Hamburger.

'The Inheritance' (p. 141) was first broadcast on BBC Radio 3 on 15 June 1973 with the following cast:

SON	Gary Watson
SISTER	Frances Horovitz
YOUNG MAN	Peter Craze
NARRATOR	Hugh Dickson

The producer was George MacBeth.

'Triumphal Entry' (p. 395) and 'The Cleansing' (p. 396) were commissioned by The Drama House to be televised on BBC 2 on Palm Sunday, 1995, and printed in *Words from Jerusalem* by BBC Education.

'The Drama's the Object' (p. 490) was written for the Silver Jubilee Celebration on 5 May 1990 of Christopher Fry's Presidency of the West Country Writers' Association.

'Suspicion' (p. 499) was included in *Birthday Boy*, a Festschrift for Lee Harwood's 60th birthday published by Ship of Fools in June 1999.

Acknowledgement is due to the editors of *Acumen*, *Ambit*, *Fire*, *Oasis*, *The North*, *Poetry Kantô* and *Voices for Kosovo* in which some of the uncollected poems have appeared.

INDEX OF TITLES

TRANSLATED BY HARRY GUEST

VICTOR HUGO
The Distance, The Shadows
SELECTED POEMS

As in France ('Victor Hugo, hélas!' answered Gide famously, when asked who was the greatest French poet of the 19th century), Hugo the poet has long been undervalued in England – partly because of the enormous range and variety of his poetry, and partly because of the lack of good translations. On its appearance in 1981, Harry Guest's was the first comprehensive selection of Hugo's poems to appear in English during the 20th century. In this new edition, published to mark the bicentenary of the poet's birth, Hugo's finest qualities are on display through his translator's empathetic skill: his passion for social justice, his simple humanity, and an imaginative breadth of vision which few poets have equalled.

'These translations are uncanny; the voice and style are perfectly modern, yet the poems and the personality are purely or almost purely Victor Hugo.' – PETER LEVI

Some new and recent poetry from Anvil

GAVIN BANTOCK
Just Think of It

OLIVER BERNARD
Verse &c.

NINA BOGIN
The Winter Orchards

PETER DALE
Under the Breath

DICK DAVIS
Belonging

MICHAEL HAMBURGER
From a Diary of Non-Events

JAMES HARPUR
Oracle Bones

PHILIP HOLMES
Lighting the Steps

MARIUS KOCIEJOWSKI
Music's Bride

GABRIEL LEVIN
Ostraca

E A MARKHAM
A Rough Climate

DENNIS O'DRISCOLL
Exemplary Damages

SALLY PURCELL
Collected Poems

GRETA STODDART
At Home in the Dark

JULIAN TURNER
Crossing the Outskirts

DANIEL WEISSBORT
Letters to Ted

Some poetry in translation from Anvil

JOSEP CARNER: *Nabí*
Translated by J L Gili

DANTE: *The Divine Comedy*
Translated by Peter Dale

NIKOS GATSOS: *Amorgos*
Translated by Sally Purcell

GOETHE: *Roman Elegies* and other poems
Translated by Michael Hamburger

NIKOLAY GUMILYOV: *The Pillar of Fire*
Translated by Richard McKane

YEHUDA HALEVI: *Poems from the Diwan*
Translated by Gabriel Levin

NÂZIM HİKMET: *Beyond the Walls*
Translated by Ruth Christie and Richard McKane

POEMS OF JULES LAFORGUE
POEMS OF FRANÇOIS VILLON
Translated by Peter Dale

IVAN V. LALIĆ: *Fading Contact*
Translated by Francis R Jones

FEDERICO GARCÍA LORCA: *A Season in Granada*
Edited and translated by Christopher Maurer

FRIEDRICH NIETZSCHE: *Dithyrambs of Dionysus*
Translated by R J Hollingdale

PO CHÜ-I: *The Selected Poems of Po Chü-i*
Translated by David Hinton

VASKO POPA: *Collected Poems*
Translated by Anne Pennington and Francis R Jones

RAINER MARIA RILKE: *Turning-Point*
Translated by Michael Hamburger

RABINDRANATH TAGORE: *Song Offerings*
(Gitanjali)
Translated by Joe Winter